Framing Equality

Framing Equality

The Politics of Gay Marriage Wars

Omar G. Encarnación

OXFORD
UNIVERSITY PRESS

Oxford University Press is a department of the University of Oxford.
It furthers the University's objective of excellence in research, scholarship,
and education by publishing worldwide. Oxford is a registered trademark of
Oxford University Press in the UK and in certain other countries.

Published in the United States of America by Oxford University Press
198 Madison Avenue, New York, NY 10016, United States of America.

© Oxford University Press 2025

The moral rights of the author have been asserted.

All rights reserved. No part of this publication may be reproduced, stored in a retrieval system, transmitted, used for text and data mining, or used for training artificial intelligence, in any form or by any means, without the prior permission in writing of Oxford University Press, or as expressly permitted by law, by license or under terms agreed with the appropriate reprographics rights organization. Inquiries concerning reproduction outside the scope of the above should be sent to the Rights Department, Oxford University Press, at the address above.

You must not circulate this work in any other form
and you must impose this same condition on any acquirer.

CIP data is on file at the Library of Congress

ISBN 9780190880309

DOI: 10.1093/9780190880330.001.0001

Printed by Marquis, Canada

Contents

Acknowledgments   vi

Introduction   1

1. On Gay Marriage Wars   19
2. Spain: A Moral Framing   49
3. The United States: A Legal Framing   89
4. Brazil: A Political Framing   129
5. Comparative Discussion and Takeaways   169

Index   196

Acknowledgments

Bringing this book about the struggle for same-sex marriage in the United States, Spain, and Brazil to fruition was a struggle in its own right. I quickly discovered how daunting it would be to get a handle on the politics of gay marriage in three countries located on three continents with very distinct gay marriage trajectories. And it did not help that archival materials and journalistic sources were spread over four languages: English, Spanish, Catalan, and Portuguese. As if all of this was not enough of a challenge, midway through the writing of the book, in the spring of 2020, the world was hit with the coronavirus pandemic. Because of the mandatory lockdown, even the most mundane research activities, like going to the library, were out of the question, to say nothing of catching a plane to Los Angeles or Madrid to conduct fieldwork.

Coping with the pandemic proved to be unnerving. I experienced the onset of the pandemic by myself in my apartment in New York City, one of the first global hotspots of coronavirus disease. Panic was everywhere, a sentiment intensified by the unrelenting sound of sirens, the result of a level of emergency calls not seen in the city since the terrorist attacks of September 11, 2001. As was the case with many academics, I was thrown seemingly overnight into remote teaching with the assistance of technologies I had never heard of before and much less used, like Zoom and Google Meet. In retrospect, the pandemic's impact on the book was, on balance, positive. Prolonging the writing of the book was a blessing in disguise. Mostly isolated from the world, I had more time to explore the history of the marriage equality movement and to reflect on the arguments I wanted to make. Ironically, the pandemic made it easier to interview gay marriage activists and others involved in the struggle for same-sex marriage. Like me, they were confined to their homes and eager to connect with others.

A book this ambitious and complex could not have been possible without the help of many people, starting with my teachers in the Department of Politics at Princeton University, where I was trained in comparative politics some thirty years ago. Because of the classic comparative structure of this book, I was compelled to revisit much of what I learned in graduate school about comparative political analysis—from how to frame provocative comparative questions to what makes for a good case study and a compelling argument. In particular, I want to thank Professors Nancy Bermeo and Kathleen Thelen. They taught me comparative politics and research methods, respectively. They also influenced my interest in political comparisons between Western Europe and South America. But, just as important, if not more, is that I have continued to find inspiration in their scholarly work. They also remain a source of professional support to this day. Few students can think of themselves as lucky as I am with their academic mentors.

I am also grateful for having had the opportunity to talk to many of the activists who led the struggle for gay marriage worldwide and the historians, journalists, and archivists who traced these struggles in real-time. In Spain, I was fortunate to speak to some of the most critical players in the Spanish marriage equality movement, including Miquel A. Fernández, Jesús Generelo, Beatriz Gimeno, and Antoni Ruiz. In Brazil, I had very fruitful exchanges with Gustavo Bernardes, Bruno Bimbi, Rita Colaço, Paulo Iotti, Luiz Mott, Toni Reis, João Silvério Trevisan, Carlos Tufvesson, and Jean Wyllys. In the United States, I am grateful for the assistance provided by Molly Ball, Elizabeth Birch, Charles Francis, Charles Kaiser, Amy Mello, Holly Pruitt, Jonathan Rauch, Patrick Sammon, Jeff Trammell, and Evan Wolfson, who is credited as the architect of the American gay marriage campaign. He graciously granted me several in-person interviews. More importantly, he was very kind and generous with me, even when we disagreed on many aspects of the American campaign, especially its messaging and legacy.

Academic peers helped in small and big ways—from a short e-mail reacting to something I wrote or said publicly to a careful, in-depth review of one or several of the book's chapters. I am thankful to Richard Aldous, Sheri Berman, Flávia Millena Biroli Tokarski, Kerman Calvo, Javier Corrales, Jeannette Estruth, June Erlick, Montserrat Feixas Vihé, Robert Fishman, Geoffroy Huard, Mneesha Gellman, James Green, Peter Klein, Diego Muro, Jorge Schwartz, Ari Shaw, Michael Staunton, Karen Sullivan, Celia Valiente, and Deborah Yashar. I am also thankful to the anonymous reviewers from Oxford University Press and the participants in the workshop on "The Comparative Politics of Backlash." Organized by Karen Alter and Michael Zürn, the workshop met in Berlin in 2017 and Northwestern University in 2018. The workshop's many discussions about backlash provided an early and fruitful venue to explore the ideas and arguments that animate this book.

I am also very fortunate that this book inspired many essays published before or simultaneously with the book. These essays provided a rare opportunity to get feedback from editors, peer reviewers, and even ordinary readers. They include "The Global Backlash against Gay Rights: How Homophobia Became a Political Tool," published in *Foreign Affairs* in 2017; "A Latin Puzzle:

viii Acknowledgments

Gay Rights Landscapes in Argentina and Brazil," published in *Human Rights Quarterly* in 2018; "The Gay Rights Backlash: Contrasting Views from the United States and Latin America," published in *The British Journal of Politics and International Relations*, in 2020; "How Spain Became an LGBTQ Rights Pioneer," forthcoming in *Current History*; and "LGBTQ Rights in Backsliding Democracies: Bolsonaro's Brazil with Reflections on the United States," forthcoming in *Latin American Research Review*. In June 2024, I published an opinion essay in *The New York Times*, "America Got Gay Marriage, but it Came at a Cost," that drew directly from this book. My editor at the paper, Tim Schneider, offered a wealth of advice that is reflected across the book, but especially in the analysis of the United States.

Angela Chnapko, my long-time editor at Oxford University Press, was a constant source of support, as was Bard College, my academic home since 1998. As in the past, Bard provided a stimulating intellectual environment and much-needed financial support through the Bard Research Council and the Bard politics program. Over the years, several former and present Bard students, including Isabel Camas, Maya Kelly, Pin-Shan Lai, and Gabriel Sub, served as research assistants for this book. I am very grateful for their labor.

Numerous archives, libraries, and investigation centers provided critical research assistance. They include the LGBTQ+ Collection at the New York Public Library; the Mattachine Society of Washington, D.C.; the Frank Kameny Collection at the Library of Congress; the Freedom to Marry archives at the Sterling Library of Yale University; the Human Rights Campaign Collection at the Kroch Library of Cornell University; the National Library of Spain; the Center for the Study of the Spanish Civil War in Salamanca; the Pedro Zerolo Foundation in Madrid; and Lawyers for Sexual and Gender Diversity in São Paulo.

Finally, I want to acknowledge my husband, John Edward Kinney, for his love, cheerfulness, and generosity.

Introduction

Happiness for political scientists, it has been said, comes when a bunch of countries are hit simultaneously by the same phenomenon, like the Great Depression or the COVID-19 pandemic.[1] Such extraordinary happenings afford a rare opportunity for countries to reveal aspects of their politics that under normal circumstances may go undetected: a hidden strength, a surprising vulnerability, or an unexpected resilience. They also pose the challenge of explaining why countries might respond differently to a similar event. Bearing all of this in mind, it would be fair to conclude that the marriage equality movement, which toppled the centuries-old view of marriage as the exclusive union of one man and one woman in dozens of nations around the world at roughly the same time, brought plenty of cheer to the political science community.

Beginning in the late 1990s, the marriage equality movement triggered the so-called war over gay marriage, one of the most controversial and consequential of the many culture wars that erupted in the twilight of the twentieth century across much of the West, alongside wars over guns, abortion, and affirmative action.[2] A culture war is no ordinary conflict over a difference of opinion or attitudes. According to James Davison Hunter, the sociologist credited with coining the term, "A culture war emerges over fundamentally different conceptions of moral authority, over different ideas and beliefs about truth, the good, obligation to one another, the nature of community, and so on. It is, therefore, a cultural conflict at its deepest level."[3]

The war over gay marriage entailed a head-on collision between emboldened gay rights activists and powerful interest groups and institutions, many of them religious. Each side of the conflict spoke in a language that made compromise seem impossible. Gay marriage activists borrowed the rhetoric of

---

[1] On the origins of this popular aphorism, see Kathleen Thelen, "Historical Institutionalism in Comparative Politics," *American Review of Political Science* 2 (1999), 398.

[2] My use of the phrase "gay marriage" in this book rather than the more politically correct term "same-sex marriage" is a matter of personal preference. This preference also reflects a desire to link this book to the significant scholarship cited in this book that uses the term "gay marriage" and related terms, such as "gay rights," "gay activists," and "gay community."

[3] James Davison Hunter, *Culture Wars: The Struggle to Define America* (New York: Basic Books, 1991), 49.

Framing Equality. Omar G. Encarnación, Oxford University Press. © Oxford University Press (2025).
DOI: 10.1093/9780190880330.003.0001

2 Framing Equality

earlier campaigns for equality by African Americans and women by declaring gay marriage "a basic human right,"[4] "the civil rights issue of our times,"[5] and the "final frontier in the emancipation of gays and lesbians."[6] Religious leaders issued apocalyptic jeremiads about the consequences of what they derisively called "redefining marriage." Pope Benedict XVI, known around the world as "God's Rottweiler" for his tenacious defense of ultra-conservative Catholic doctrine, compared gay marriage to the Antichrist and warned that it was "a threat to human dignity and the future of humanity itself."[7] In the United States, evangelical Pastor Robert Jeffress called gay marriage "the greatest sign of the End Times," while Mike Huckabee, a former governor of Arkansas and an ordained Southern Baptist pastor, predicted that because of gay marriage "Christianity will soon be outlawed to make room for gay rights."[8]

Many politicians were caught in the crossfire. Their commitment to equality and inclusion was seriously tested by the early wave of public opposition that greeted the marriage equality movement. Some, like Barack Obama, sought common ground by opposing gay marriage because of religious reasons while supporting same-sex civil unions that offered the benefits, privileges, and rights of marriage—but without labeling them "marriage." In a 2004 interview, Obama noted that "marriage is between a man and a woman. . . . But what I also believe is that we have an obligation to make sure that gays and lesbians have the rights of citizenship that afford them visitation to hospitals, that allow them to transfer property to each other, to make sure that they are not discriminated against on the job."[9] Eventually, most politicians were forced to take a side in the gay marriage struggle. In 2012, amid his reelection campaign, Obama became the first sitting American president to endorse gay marriage.

The war over gay marriage also resulted in unprecedented victories for the gay rights movement. Since it was first legalized in the Netherlands in 2001, gay marriage has become the law of the land in some forty countries

---

[4] "Gay Marriage as a Basic Human Right," *The New York Times*, May 3, 1996.

[5] Michael K. Lavers, "NAACP President: Marriage Is 'Civil Rights Issue of Our Times,'" *The Washington Blade*, May 21, 2012. Available at https://www.washingtonblade.com/2012/05/21/naacp-president-marriage-is-civil-rights-issue-of-our-times/.

[6] Mary Bernstein, Brenna Harvey, and Nancy A. Naples, "Marriage, the Final Frontier? Same-Sex Marriage and the Future of the Lesbian and Gay Movement," *Sociological Forum* 33, no. 1 (March 2018), 30–52.

[7] Gian Guido Vecchi, "Ratzinger: Nozze gay e aborto segni del potere dell'Anticristo," *Corriere Della Sera*, May 3, 2020. Available at https://www.corriere.it/cronache/20_maggio_03/ratzinger-nozze-gay-aborto-segni-potere-dell-anticristo-5071d4d6-8d23-11ea-876b-8ec8c59e51b8.shtml.

[8] Brian Tashman, "Wars and Terrorists and Floods, Oh My: The Right's Five Worst Predictions about Marriage Equality," Right Wing Watch, April 28, 2015. Available at www.rightwingwatch.org/post/war-and-terrorists-and-floods-oh-my-the-rights-five-worst-predictions-about-marriage-equality.

[9] Katy Steinmetz, "See Obama's 20 Year Evolution on LGBTQ Rights," *Time*, April 10, 2015. Available at https://time.com/3816952/obama-gay-lesbian-transgender-lgbt-rights/.

in virtually every region of the world. More surprising, perhaps, is the rapid speed at which the marriage equality revolution was achieved, especially when contrasted to other social revolutions—such as the struggle for equality by women, African Americans, and Indigenous peoples. Remarking on the success of the marriage equality movement, the *Los Angeles Times* noted in 2012 that "gays may have the fastest of all civil rights movements."[10] The paper added: "If, as the Rev. Martin Luther King Jr. once said, the arc of the moral universe is long but bends toward justice, then it's arguably moving faster and bending quicker in the direction of gay rights than any civil rights movement before."

Similarities notwithstanding, the war over gay marriage did not make for a shared political experience across national borders. As seen in this book, from the institutional arenas in which the struggle was fought to the severity of the conservative backlash to the legacy left behind for LGBTQ equality, gay marriage wars have made for a wildly diverse set of political experiences. In some countries, such as Spain, Argentina, Uruguay, Germany, and France, the fight over gay marriage turned into political warfare, as the major political parties duked it out in the national legislature. However, despite driving a wedge between liberals and conservatives, the fault lines in the political fight about gay marriage did not fall neatly along the left-right ideological divide in every country. In the majority of countries that legislated gay marriage, it was a left-wing party that signed gay marriage into law, usually in the face of stiff opposition from conservative parties. But in some countries, including the United Kingdom and Chile, it was a conservative political party that enacted gay marriage legislation.

In other countries, such as the United States, Brazil, Colombia, and Mexico, gay marriage became an epic legal fight. Litigating gay marriage brought a lot of anxiety and confusion for gay marriage activists as well as for ordinary gay and lesbian couples seeking the right to marry. Because of the complexity of the issue of gay marriage and the way it intersects with individual rights, family law, and religion (to say nothing of how excruciatingly slow most legal systems move), in most countries, it took years, if not decades, for the courts to settle the fight once and for all. And in almost every case, court rulings favoring gay marriage unleashed a political firestorm, with conservatives charging that judges were legislating from the bench and putting their judgment ahead of the people's will. In 2010, three justices from Iowa's Supreme Court were recalled after being part of a unanimous decision that legalized gay marriage

[10] Mark Z. Barabak, "Gays May Have the Fastest of All Civil Rights Movements," *The Los Angeles Times*, May 20, 2012. Available at https://www.latimes.com/style/la-xpm-2012-may-20-la-na-gay-rights-movement-20120521-story.html.

4 Framing Equality

in that state. The unprecedented vote "was celebrated by conservatives as a popular rebuke of judicial overreach, even as it alarmed proponents of an independent judiciary."[11]

Yet other countries turned the struggle for gay marriage into a public spectacle by putting the issue up for a popular vote in the form of a national referendum. Such ballot measures on gay marriage were usually justified with the argument that marriage is too important an institution to leave it to politicians and judges to decide. "Let the people decide," the argument went. Gay rights activists and their allies tried to undermine this argument by contending that gay marriage referendums are unbecoming of a democratic society because they put the rights of a minority at the whims of the majority. The United States pioneered the practice of putting gay rights to a popular vote in the 1970s as a means to marshal the public's disapproval of homosexuality to derail an ascendant gay rights movement. But it was Ireland, in 2015, that held the world's first national gay marriage referendum. It resulted in a decisive win for the pro-gay marriage side and a stunning defeat for the historically powerful Irish Catholic Church.

Differences in the severity of the conservative backlash to gay marriage are just as compelling. In some countries, this backlash was muted and barely noticeable. To appease social conservatives and increase the number of legislators in favor of legalizing gay marriage, the gay marriage laws enacted in the Netherlands and Belgium, which also happen to be the oldest ones in the world, restricted the ability of gay couples to adopt. In the Netherlands, "gay adoptions" were allowed as long as they did not involve foreign children, while in Belgium, they were prohibited altogether. These adoption restrictions, which were eventually lifted, effectively created different categories of marriage for homosexual and heterosexual couples.

But in other countries, the conservative backlash mushroomed into an all-out assault on the gay community. Across the United States, dozens of states enacted gay marriage bans by defining marriage as the exclusive union of one man and one woman. Publicity campaigns in support of these bans featured demonizing and dehumanizing attacks that trafficked in homophobic tropes about homosexuals preying on children. In Brazil, evangelical leaders blocked all attempts by the national legislature to legalize same-sex civil unions and gay marriage. They claimed that any official recognition of homosexual unions would hinder their ability to preach against homosexuality. Catholic bishops in France mobilized millions of

---

[11] A. G. Sulzberger, "Ouster of Iowa Judges Sends Signal to Bench," *The New York Times*, November 3, 2010. Available at https://www.nytimes.com/2010/11/04/us/politics/04judges.html.

people against gay marriage, a show of force intended to intimidate gay marriage activists and the politicians who supported them. Their Mexican peers threatened to excommunicate any politician who supported gay marriage.

As for the legacy for LGBTQ equality, in some countries, the post-gay marriage years have been marked by the dawn of a new era of LGBTQ affirmation and rights. In Spain, for example, following the passage of the gay marriage law, the government officially expressed its remorse to the gay community for the pain and suffering caused by homophobic laws. It also issued reparations intended to compensate those who lost wages and pensions due to discriminatory actions undertaken by the government against LGBTQ people, enacted laws intended to facilitate those undergoing a gender transition, and made assisted reproductive technologies available to same-sex couples. In the United States, by contrast, the war over gay marriage opened the door to new forms of anti-LGBTQ discrimination and exclusion, such as bans on the teaching of homosexuality in schools, drag performances, and gender-affirming medical care.

Prompted by the rich diversity of the political experiences afforded by gay marriage wars, this book pays attention to a small set of questions that emerge when the conflict over gay marriage is seen through broad comparative lenses. What political forces shaped the culture war over gay marriage? Why were some marriage equality movements more successful than others at mitigating backlash from conservative political forces? And how do we make sense of the different political legacies that the war over gay marriage left behind for LGBTQ equality? As seen previously, while in some countries the legalization of gay marriage ushered in a new era of LGBTQ equality and inclusion, in others it created an opening for new forms of anti-gay discrimination and exclusion.

A Summary of the Arguments

Barely noticed, if noticed at all, about how the politics of gay marriage wars have diverged around the world is the framing of gay marriage by those fronting the struggle. While all gay marriage campaigns have framed their activism as a struggle for "marriage equality," the precise nature of the claims for equality that these campaigns have made has varied a great deal. Across countries, the starkest contrast that can be drawn is between those campaigns that framed gay marriage as a legal matter versus those that framed gay marriage as a moral issue. It is such distinctions in the rhetorical framing

6 Framing Equality

of gay marriage—which are rooted in different political environments, historical experiences, and ideological traditions—that I argue matter most for understanding the other factors separating gay marriage wars, especially the severity of the conservative backlash and the legacy for LGBTQ equality.

Framing, as scholars have defined the concept, points to the way that social movement messages guide the public's attention.[12] As noted by a review essay on how framing operates, "Given the focusing, articulation, and transformative functions of frames, it is arguable that how we see, what we make of, and how we act toward the various objects of orientation that populate our daily lives depend, in no small part, on how they are framed."[13] But framing does more than help the public focus on any given issue. It delineates what is essential about the issue and why it deserves priority over other issues vying for the public's attention. Framing can also identify a new problem, propose remedies to that problem, and rally the public in support of these remedies. Along the way, framing can advance any issue by garnering favorable media attention.

A much less discussed point about framing highlighted in this book is that it can also impact the fate of the opposition to any movement seeking social change—in other words, the backlash. In the case of the gay marriage campaign, an effective framing strategy can neutralize the attacks from gay marriage detractors. It can also undermine the detractors' framing strategies for defeating the marriage equality movement by offering a "counter-framing," understood as a direct challenge to the opposition's framing strategies. These opposition framing strategies include the claims that gay and lesbian couples seeking to marry want "special rights," that gay marriage is a threat to the family and religious freedom, and that homosexual unions are inferior to heterosexual unions because only heterosexual unions can create new life. That last view, often referred to as the "procreation" argument, is a favorite of religious conservatives.

Whether framing proves successful in shaping public perceptions and neutralizing the opposition hinges on the skills of social movement activists to craft messages (often called "frames") that resonate with the public. In the case of the gay marriage campaign, resonance can come from making the

---

[12] See, especially, Francesca Polletta and M. Kai Ho, "Frames and Their Consequences," in *The Oxford Handbook of Contextual Political Analysis*, eds. Robert E. Goodin and Charles Tilly (New York: Oxford University Press, 2006).

[13] David A. Snow, Rens Vliegenthart, and Pauline Ketelaars, "The Framing Perspective on Social Movements: Its Conceptual Roots and Architecture," in *The Wiley Blackwell Companion to Social Movements*, eds. David A. Snow, Sarah A. Soule, Hanspeter Kriesi, and Holly J. McCammon (John Wiley & Sons, 2019), 393.

Introduction   7

issue relatable to the public, such as amplifying the unfairness of denying marriage benefits to same-sex couples, linking gay marriage to markers of national identity, or simply generating interest in the subject among the citizenry. As seen in this book, some of the most successful framing and counter-framing efforts by gay marriage activists were those that focused on how gay marriage would improve society at large rather than those that stressed more narrowly how gay marriage would benefit same-sex couples.

Determining the precise impact of framing on the politics of gay marriage wars requires, first and foremost, disaggregating the variety of framing approaches found in marriage equality campaigns. I contend that these framing approaches conform to one of three ideal types: legal, moral, and political. To be clear, these approaches are not mutually exclusive. Given the plurality of gay rights activism typical of most countries with a matured gay rights movement, some fluidity and overlapping in the claims and appeals that gay marriage campaigns make is to be expected. Unsurprisingly, it is not difficult to identify all three approaches in the same country, as individual groups will likely gravitate toward different approaches. Moreover, it is important to note that gay marriage campaigns are not set in stone. Their rhetorical strategies tend to evolve. Some campaigns may even transition between framing approaches to adjust to changing circumstances, such as the coming of a new government, a change in the composition of the courts, or the arrival of new leadership atop the gay rights movement. That said, one framing approach generally emerges as the defining one and sets the tone for the entire campaign.

The legal framing is the most prominent, if only because it is best embodied by the United States. Anchored on a pure rights-based discourse, it stresses the view of marriage as a civil right that should be available to all couples, regardless of the gender of those entering the union. In the case of the United States, this discourse is anchored on claims of equality under the law found in the Fourteenth Amendment to the US Constitution. Moreover, the legal framing avoids any discussion of the morality of homosexual unions, rooted in the belief that equal rights for homosexuals should not hinge on whether society approves of how homosexuals live their lives, including whom they choose to love. This framing is also likely to skirt any talk of how gay marriage might benefit society or advance the common good. Instead, it is limited to stressing the salutary effects of gay marriage on gay couples and their children.

By contrast, the moral framing regards gay marriage as an ethical matter, rather than as a legal issue, and as a remedy for helping uproot the legacies of homophobia. Its overriding goal is the idealistic objective of "full citizenship" for homosexual couples. As a concept, full citizenship encompasses rights

8 Framing Equality

and responsibilities. But it also incorporates non-legal and ethical dimensions of citizenship—such as dignity, respect, and a sense of belonging.[14] The moral framing also draws upon the language of universal human rights principles, especially the idea that the free expression of sexuality is a fundamental human right. Last but not least, this framing asserts a complete equivalence between heterosexual and homosexual unions that demands that the government place both types of relationships on equal legal footing. In doing that, the moral framing challenges impressions of homosexual unions as immoral or abnormal. At the same time, it stresses the importance of gay marriage in advancing the common good by expanding freedom and equality for everyone.

The political framing freely mixes legal arguments and moral appeals about gay marriage. But this approach also stands on its own by avoiding the purity of the legal framing and the idealism of the moral framing in favor of pragmatism. It upholds the view that the state has the legal and ethical obligation to protect the rights and welfare of gay and lesbian couples and their families but that this protection does not require extending the label of marriage to homosexual unions. This approach is also likely to embrace the view that gay marriage is best achieved in incremental steps. Several factors give rise to this pragmatic discourse about marriage. The most apparent is ambivalence about whether marriage is the best institutional arrangement for same-sex couples. But ultimately, the political framing is informed by political concerns—especially the concern that the struggle over gay marriage will consume political capital that could otherwise be used for securing more attainable goals (such as fighting homophobia and anti-gay violence) and the desire to avoid backlash from conservative forces.

Beyond categorizing varieties of gay marriage framing approaches, this book also theorizes about their political and social consequences. I argue that although all of the aforementioned framing approaches can bring the gay marriage campaign to a successful conclusion, moral arguments and appeals are the most effective for minimizing backlash and bolstering LGBTQ equality. This is a counterintuitive claim. Debating morality can be messy, contentious, and non-conclusive. For this reason, gay marriage activists, at least in the United States, have traditionally kept discussions about the morality of homosexual relationships at bay.[15] But the war over gay marriage, like all culture wars, is ultimately a conflict over different conceptions of

---

[14] On the various conceptions of citizenship, see, especially, David Thunder, *Citizenship and the Pursuit of a Worthy Life* (New York: Cambridge University Press, 2014).

[15] See, especially, Chai R. Feldblum, "Gay Is Good: The Moral Case for Marriage Equality and More," *The Yale Journal of Law and Feminism* 17 (2005), 138–184.

right and wrong. As such, only a robust societal debate about the morality of homosexual unions—one that challenges people's fundamental impressions about LGBTQ people—can change hearts and minds significantly. This debate is less likely to occur under the other two framing approaches. Under the legal framing, the struggle over gay marriage takes place primarily in the courts. As seen already, the political framing is concerned with avoiding conflict and preempting backlash.

Finally, this book has a few things to say about the origins of gay marriage framing approaches. I argue that these approaches reflect the political agency that gay marriage activists bring to their struggles. But political agency does not develop in a vacuum. Any gay marriage campaign is likely to reflect a wide range of structural influences, such as the political environment that surrounds the marriage equality movement, the inspiration that gay marriage activists derive from other social movements (both local and foreign), the ideological foundations embedded in gay rights organizations, and the framing strategies of the opposition to gay marriage. These structural influences do not predetermine the framing of any gay marriage campaign. Still, they provide the context for understanding the making of framing preferences among gay marriage activists and movements. They also reveal the primacy of domestic conditions over international trends in shaping the messaging of gay marriage campaigns. This finding is quite revealing, considering that the marriage equality movement has been broadly affected by cross-national influences.

The Case Studies: An Overview

Of the many national experiences available, this book highlights those of the United States, Spain, and Brazil. This trio of countries is eclectic. It is rare in the extreme for scholars to compare gay politics in the United States to those of other countries. Rarer still is to compare the United States to the nations of the Iberian-Latin world, if only because Spain and Latin America have historically been socially, politically, and economically less developed than the United States. But the cases are not as diverse as they may appear at first glance. Due to an exploding Hispanic population, the United States is currently the fifth-largest Spanish-speaking country worldwide, after Mexico, Colombia, Argentina, and Spain. It also possesses the fourth-largest Catholic population in the world, after Brazil, Mexico, and the Philippines.

It is also the case that the United States probably has more in common with a country like Brazil than it does with the typical Western European nation. The commonalities between these two countries go well beyond being two

10 Framing Equality

of the world's largest and most ethnically and racially diverse democracies. Both countries have a similar religious composition (especially a large and politically influential evangelical population, estimated at 30 percent for each country), have some of the world's worst social and economic inequality, and have recently experienced the political trauma known as "democratic backsliding" (or the weakening of democracy by those elected to protect it).[16] Expanding on the similarities between the United States and Brazil, *The Economist* wrote in 2010:[17]

> Think of two continent-sized countries built on gold rushes and cowboys, on sugar and slaves. Think of the United States being the first country to recognise Brazilian independence. Above all, think of the two countries' topographies. Both consist basically of big cities on the coast where most of the people live; a vast, spectacularly beautiful and largely empty wonder of the natural world in the deep interior (the Rockies for America and the Amazon for Brazil); and, in between, endless savannahs where all the food grows. In either place, it's soybeans as far as the eye can see. Looking down from an airplane as it traverses the flyover states, you would be hard-pressed to know whether you were crossing South Dakota or Goias, Mato Grosso, or the corn belt.

All of this said, my main interest in the American, Spanish, and Brazilian experiences rests in what they reveal about gay marriage wars. For starters, these experiences demonstrate the rich diversity of gay marriage wars, especially concerning the severity of the conservative backlash and the legacy for LGBTQ equality. The United States stands out for the long duration of the struggle and the toxicity of the conservative backlash. Organized gay marriage activism began in earnest in the mid-1990s after Hawaii's Supreme Court ruled that nothing in the state's constitution precluded gay marriage. But it was not until 2015 that gay marriage activists claimed outright victory when the US Supreme Court ruled in *Obergefell v. Hodges* in favor of gay marriage nationwide. Behind the prolonged struggle was a massive gay marriage moral panic orchestrated by the pugnacious culture warriors of the "defense of marriage movement," a coalition of evangelical leaders, family values organizations, and red-state lawmakers.

---

[16] See Nancy Bermeo, "On Democratic Backsliding," *Journal of Democracy* 27, no. 1 (2016), 5–19. For a contrasting analysis of democratic backsliding in the United States and Brazil, see Omar G. Encarnación, "Democratic Backsliding: Comparative Reflections on the American Experience," *Political Science Quarterly* 138, no. 3 (Fall 2023), 407–423.

[17] J. P., "American Brothers: Comparing Brazil and the United States," *The Economist*, April 13, 2010. Available at https://www.economist.com/americas-view/2010/08/13/american-brothers.

Introduction **11**

The United States is the only developed democracy to have enacted a law as ignoble as DOMA, or the Defense of Marriage Act. A counterreaction to developments in Hawaii, this law was pure political backlash. DOMA barred the federal government from recognizing gay marriage, never mind that when enacted in 1996, no locality in the United States and indeed anywhere in the world allowed gay couples to marry. It also freed individual states from the responsibility of recognizing gay marriages performed in other states. DOMA also helped usher in some thirty gay marriage bans across the United States. The United States is also alone among developed democracies in having attempted to amend its national constitution to ban gay marriage by defining marriage as the exclusive union of one man and one woman. It is little wonder that by the time gay marriage was legalized in the United States nationwide in 2015, some two dozen nations had already done so, making the United States a gay marriage laggard. Among the nations that got ahead were other multiracial democracies such as Brazil and South Africa and bastions of Catholicism such as Spain and Ireland.

In Spain, by contrast, the war over gay marriage was comparatively brief, lasting only from 1998, when gay activists declared gay marriage their primary objective, to 2005, when the Spanish Parliament enacted a national gay marriage law. This law made Spain only the third country in the world to legalize gay marriage (ahead of other countries with longer histories of gay rights activism, such as the United States, Britain, Germany, and France) and the first heavily Roman Catholic nation to do so. Less known is that Spain was the first country anywhere in the world to place homosexual and heterosexual marriages on the same legal footing by granting same-sex couples adoption rights. More important, perhaps, is that the conservative backlash in Spain was relatively tame, at least when compared to the situation in the United States. The most daring strategy for defeating gay marriage employed by the Spanish Episcopal Conference, which quickly emerged as the face of the opposition to gay marriage in Spain, was to mobilize the faithful. Although this mobilization failed to derail gay marriage, it generated some of the largest public demonstrations in recent Spanish history. Unlike the United States, the courts limited their intervention to a 2012 ruling from the Constitutional Tribunal asserting the constitutionality of the gay marriage law.

At least concerning the gay marriage backlash, the Brazilian case falls somewhere between the American and Spanish experiences. Gay rights activists in Brazil fought for same-sex civil unions from the mid-1990s until 2011, when the Federal Supreme Court declared that the state could not discriminate against same-sex couples. With civil unions under their belt, gay activists set their sights on gay marriage, which they obtained quickly through the courts

12 Framing Equality

in 2013. Evangelical leaders denounced these rulings as judicial activism in protests around the country. They also attempted to legislate a change in the definition of the family for federal purposes as the exclusive union of one man and one woman. But these efforts did not bear any fruit. There's no Brazilian version of DOMA. And no Brazilian administration entertained a gay marriage ban.

The cases also provide evidence of the unpredictability of gay marriage politics. When viewed through theoretical and historical lenses, the politics of the war over gay marriage in the United States, Spain, and Brazil are genuinely surprising, even paradoxical. On the theoretical side, the cases upset the scholarly understanding of the rise of gay rights in the West, including same-sex marriage. It is a veritable truism in the study of gay rights that social and economic development promotes societal tolerance of homosexuality and sexual diversity in general.[18] This truism draws from modernization theory and its assumption that economic progress goes hand in hand with the rise of "post-material values."[19] These values emphasize self-expression and quality-of-life issues over economic and physical security and include concerns for racial and gender discrimination and tolerance for alternative lifestyles.

Paradoxically, the United States, long regarded as one of the world's most advanced states and, by extension, a good example of the proliferation of post-materialism, had a much harder time welcoming gay marriage than the comparatively less-developed states of Spain and Brazil.[20] Clearly, the experience of the United States reveals the propensity of nations to hold on to hostility (if not outright animus) toward LGBTQ people in the presence of all of the markers of modernity. For their part, the cases of Spain and Brazil suggest that the receptivity of countries to gay rights and gay marriage in particular may not be that closely tied to the cultural changes thought

---

[18] See, especially, M. V. Lee Badgett, Shela Nezhad, Keen Waaldijk, and Yana van der Meulen Rodgers, "The Relationship between LGBT Inclusion and Economic Development," (Los Angeles: The Williams Institute, UCLA School of Law, November 2014): 1. Available at https://williamsinstitute.law.ucla.edu/wp-content/uploads/LGBT-Inclusion-Economic-Dev-Nov-2014.pdf. This study concluded that "the macro-level analysis reveals a clear positive correlation between per capita GDP and legal rights for LGBT and transgender people across countries, as measured by the Global Index on Legal Recognition of Homosexual Orientation (GILRHO) and the Transgender Rights Index (TRI) respectively."

[19] See Ronald Inglehart, *The Silent Revolution: Changing Values and Political Styles among Western Publics* (Princeton, NJ: Princeton University Press, 1977); Ronald Inglehart and Pipa Norris, *Rising Tide: Gender Equality and Cultural Change around the World* (New York: Cambridge University Press, 2003); and Ronald Inglehart and Wayne E. Baker, *Modernization, Cultural Change and Democracy: The Human Development Sequence* (New York: Cambridge University Press, 2005).

[20] In 2005, when Spain legalized gay marriage, ten years ahead of the United States, the country's GDP per capita was $26, 451, versus $44,123 for the United States. The contrast with a developing country like Brazil is more striking. When the federal courts legalized gay marriage in Brazil in 2013, with less backlash than in the United States, Brazil's per capita GDP was $12,458, compared to $53,409 in the United States when the US Supreme Court ruled in favor of gay marriage. Source of Data: The World Bank. Available at https://databank.worldbank.org/indicator/NY.GDP.PCAP.CD/1ff4a498/Popular-Indicators.

Introduction **13**

to flow from social and economic development. These changes could well emanate from other sources, such as the type of advocacy embraced by gay rights activists.

As for historical trajectories, the United States endured the longest and most toxic gay marriage war in the West despite being the cradle of the contemporary gay rights movement. Writing about the "American pioneer pattern" in gay rights that developed following the 1969 Stonewall uprising, David Rayside noted, "In the decades following World War II, the United States was witness to political activism concerning issues of sexual orientation, and later gender identity, on a scale with few parallels in other countries. The Netherlands was home to a visible movement throughout that time, but by the 1970s American activism was more widespread and visible than its counterparts in any other country and concerned a wider set of issues."[21] The United States also pioneered domestic partnerships for same-sex couples, and American gay activists were among the first to make gay marriage a component of their advocacy. Both trends date to the late 1980s.

Spain's gay marriage campaign was met with considerably less political backlash than the American and Brazilian campaigns. Yet few countries can match Spain's long and dark history of repression of homosexuality. The country was home to the Inquisition, an institution infamous for burning "sodomites" at the stake during the Middle Ages. In more recent times, the Spanish community endured the brutal repression of the Francisco Franco dictatorship, in place from 1939 through 1975. Homophobia was one of the hallmarks of this political regime—a reflection of Franco's devotion to the ideology of National Catholicism. It imposed Catholic doctrine on all aspects of private and public life. Not surprisingly, under Franco, Spain had some of the vilest anti-homosexuality laws ever enacted in the Western world, including the 1954 *Ley de Vagos y Maleantes* (Law of Vagabonds and Thugs). This infamous law, which analogized homosexuality to a wide range of criminal activities, including drug use, vagrancy, and prostitution, is responsible for sending thousands of LGBTQ people to prison and mental institutions to undergo reparative therapies. Spain was also one of the last countries in the West to decriminalize homosexuality. It was not until 1979, after the country's return to full democracy, that homosexuality ceased to be a crime under the Spanish penal code.

The strong echoes of the virulence of the American gay marriage backlash in Brazil stand in striking contrast to the country's storied image as a

---

[21] David Rayside, "The United States in Comparative Context," in Craig A. Rimmerman and Clyde Wilcox, eds., *The Politics of Same-Sex Marriage* (Chicago: The University of Chicago Press, 2008), 349.

gay-friendly nation. Remarking on this image, the *New York Times* noted that Brazil's "near-mythic reputation for tolerance is not without justification."[22] Since gaining its independence from Portugal in 1822, Brazil has never enacted any law restricting homosexual behavior, not even during the country's most recent experience with military dictatorship (1964–1985). Brazil was also the first country in the world to ban "gay conversion" therapy, on orders from the federal government, in 1999. It is also telling that Brazilian machismo contradictorily coexists with a culture that unabashedly celebrates sexual diversity, freewheeling sexuality, and gender nonconformity. It is not for nothing that Rio de Janeiro's carnival, famous for its debauchery, including cross-dressing, is, in much of the world's eyes, the essence of Brazilian culture. São Paulo's gay pride parade is routinely ranked as the world's largest celebration of LGBTQ culture.

Ultimately, however, what makes the United States, Spain, and Brazil ideally suited for the research agenda outlined in this book is that they cover the gamut of gay marriage framing approaches. In doing so, they provide excellent empirical laboratories for testing my arguments about how framing has shaped the politics of gay marriage wars. By heartily embracing the view that gay marriage is a fundamental civil right protected by the US Constitution, the American gay marriage campaign became a paradigmatic example of legal framing. It emphasized the hundreds of rights and benefits, such as tax deductions, inheritance provisions, and hospital visitation privileges, unavailable to gay and lesbian couples as a way to expose the discrimination prevalent in existing marriage laws. This purely legalistic framing was quite adequate for securing court victories all the way to the US Supreme Court but woefully inadequate for mitigating political backlash and expanding LGBTQ equality.

Designed primarily to support litigation, the "rights and benefits" messaging did not generate the kind of societal debate about gay marriage that changes hearts and minds. It also did not find much resonance with the general public. On the contrary, it backfired by sending the message to the public that gay people wanted marriage for political and material reasons. Worst yet, the rights and benefits messaging enabled a robust backlash. For the most part, the American gay marriage campaign did not engage the opposition with arguments about the morality of gay unions and homosexuality in general. Nor did the campaign confront the attacks on gay marriage by the Christian right and its conservative allies. These failures and oversights suggest that the gay marriage campaign missed a significant opportunity to do more to move

---

[22] Andrew Jacobs, "Brazil Is Confronting an Epidemic of Anti-Gay Violence," *The New York Times*, July 5, 2016. Available at https://www.nytimes.com/2016/07/06/world/americas/brazil-anti-gay-violence.html.

Introduction   15

the needle in how Americans feel about same-sex relationships and LGBTQ people.

In the absence of compelling non-legal arguments about gay marriage to counter the visceral appeal of the Christian right's framing of gay marriage as a threat to the family and religious freedom, this menacing view of gay marriage was able to enter the public's consciousness without any effective challenges. A replacement messaging to rights and benefits, which emphasized love and commitment, was introduced late in the campaign, in 2012. It broadly stressed the humanity of homosexuals and the morality of gay unions by suggesting that homosexual couples wanted marriage for the same reasons as heterosexual couples. While effective in changing hearts and minds, this new messaging did not challenge Americans' preconceived notions about gay and lesbian couples. It also arrived too late to prevent an all-out assault on the gay community. By 2012, the American gay community had endured years of dehumanizing and demonizing attacks by the Christian right. The gay community had also been subjected to the humiliation of DOMA and some thirty bans on gay marriage enacted from the late 1990s through 2012. These bans included Proposition 8, which overturned a court mandate legalizing gay marriage in that state. Because of this referendum, thousands of existing gay marriages in California were thrown into legal limbo.

It is hard to find a more compelling example of moral framing than Spain. Its idealistic gay marriage campaign was waged as a crusade for full citizenship for gay and lesbian couples. Spanish gay marriage activists fought for not only the rights and benefits of marriage but also for dignity and respect. In pursuit of this ambitious agenda, the campaign demanded complete legal parity between homosexual and heterosexual unions. The campaign's main slogan clarified this demand: "The same rights with the same name." More revealing, Spanish gay marriage activists held gay marriage as redemption for Spain's past sins against the gay community. To that end, the campaign leveraged Spain's dark history with homosexuality to stress the need for the state to make amends to the gay community. This history, together with the painful memory of the Spanish Civil War, had been buried during the country's successful return to democracy that followed Franco's passing in 1975. Lastly, gay marriage activists promoted gay marriage as a modernizing vehicle that would make Spain more tolerant and humane.

Framing gay marriage as a moral cause was critical to Spain's successful management of the conservative backlash. It sparked a robust debate about the status of sexual minorities in the country. Taking place in all corners of Spanish society, the debate helped change people's perceptions of homosexuality by prompting many gays and lesbians to come out to friends and relatives

16 Framing Equality

while at the same time encouraging a desire among Spaniards to leave behind the rigid perceptions of sex, gender, and family promoted by the Franco regime with the complicity of the Catholic Church. The moral framing also helped build bridges between the gay marriage campaign and the human rights community, feminist organizations, and the trade union movement. No less important is that the moral framing acted as a powerful antidote to the apocalyptic messaging of the Spanish Episcopal Conference, which framed gay marriage as an attack on procreation. Having successfully neutralized the opposition, the gay marriage campaign was able to usher in a dramatic expansion of gay rights that made Spain a global leader in efforts to expand LGBTQ equality. The country introduced one of the world's first gender identity laws and pioneered efforts to offer reparations to anyone prosecuted by laws that criminalized homosexuality.

Brazil is an outstanding example of political framing. Brazilian gay activists simultaneously mixed legal and moral arguments when making the case for same-sex civil unions and gay marriage. They argued that civil unions deserved the protected status of "stable unions," a legal category of relationships that honors a history of unmarried cohabitation in Brazil. But they also contended that recognizing same-sex couples was a fundamental human right that was in keeping with the human rights aspirations that Brazil set for itself after the transition to democracy in 1985. These human rights arguments found broad resonance with the Brazilian judiciary (which ultimately approved gay marriage in 2013), civil society, and the Brazilian Catholic Church, which has a tradition of standing up for marginalized communities. They also grounded gay rights in universal human rights principles, especially the concept of dignity. This grounding influenced other gay rights victories that came in the wake of the legalization of gay marriage, especially the criminalization of homophobia on orders from the Federal Supreme Court.

Less apparent is that the pragmatic rhetoric of gay rights leaders also influenced the framing of gay marriage in Brazil. To avert backlash from the Catholic Church and the evangelical movement, gay activists kept their demands squarely focused on same-sex civil unions, even after gay activists in other countries were already campaigning for gay marriage. Indeed, Brazilian gay activists studiously avoided the word marriage in their activism until 2011, the year that the Federal Supreme Court declared that same-sex relationships deserved the constitutionally protected label of stable unions. Brazilian activists also insisted that equality for same-sex couples could be attained without the label of marriage, an argument intended to put some rhetorical distance between the gay rights movement and marriage. These rhetorical maneuvers delivered mixed results. On the positive side, they helped to blunt the conservative backlash by forcing an incremental approach to implementing gay marriage, with the arrival of same-sex civil unions in 2011 paving the way for the legalization of gay marriage in 2013. They also deprived the opposition of the claim, quite widespread in the United States, that gay activists "were out to destroy the institution of marriage." On the negative side, the cautious and pragmatic rhetoric around gay marriage denied Brazil the robust societal debate about gay marriage experienced by Spain and, to a lesser extent, by the United States.

The Organization of the Book

The book is structured as follows. Chapter 1 examines some of the most-discussed factors driving the politics of gay marriage wars. It emphasizes the institutional means by which gay marriage is introduced into the nation, especially legislation versus litigation; the surprising progressivism of the Catholic world on the issue of gay rights; and the organizational capacities of the opposition to gay marriage, including the skill to engineer a moral panic around gay marriage. That discussion continues with an expanded analysis of the varieties of gay marriage framing approaches and their consequences for minimizing backlash and expanding LGBTQ equality. Of particular concern to this analysis is the concept of backlash. Despite its popularity in the gay rights scholarship, the term "backlash" is rarely defined. As understood in this book, backlash is a form of contentious politics fueled by emotion, infused by nostalgia, and driven by retrograde objectives.[23] Although generally associated with conservative activism, backlash may arise from either the right or the left. The most successful outcomes of any backlash include changing the course of public opinion and reversing the policy the "backlashers" are targeting.

Chapters 2 through 4 comprise the empirical backbone of the book. These chapters cover a lot of historical background about the struggle for gay marriage in the United States, Spain, and Brazil. Still, their overarching purpose is analytical: to suggest how different framing approaches shaped the severity of the gay marriage backlash and the legacy for LGBTQ equality. There's no apparent chronological order to the cases because it is not easy to date when the struggle for marriage equality began in each case. That said, there were groups devoted to the legalization of same-sex unions in all three cases by the early 2000s. I start with Spain because, among the cases, it was the

---

[23] This definition of backlash borrows from Karen J. Alter and Michael Zürn, "Conceptualizing Backlash Politics," *The British Journal of Politics and International Relations* 22, no. 4 (November 2020).

18 Framing Equality

first one to make gay marriage the law of the land. As such, it allows for the most extended time frame to gauge the impact of the campaign's framing on the conservative backlash and LGBTQ equality. I continue with the United States. Its legal framing offers a direct counterpoint to the moral framing of the Spanish campaign. I conclude with Brazil, whose political framing combines elements of the legal and moral framing approaches.

Chapter 5 places the study's main findings in a broad comparative perspective. A key concern is explaining why gay marriage activists pursuing the same goal adopt different framing approaches. It starts with an overview of the cases of Argentina and Ireland, two other countries with high-profile gay marriage wars. My intention in exploring these additional cases is to validate further the importance of moral arguments for advancing gay marriage while minimizing backlash and expanding LGBTQ equality. A discussion of the roots of the different gay marriage framing approaches examined in this book follows. As might be expected, the legal framing of the American gay marriage campaign shows the broad influence of the civil rights movement and its struggle to end racial discrimination in the United States. It was from this historical example that gay marriage activists borrowed the idea that gay marriage could be justified under the US Constitution. But other factors played a key role as well. Because of the popularity of the view of marriage as an oppressive, patriarchal institution among gay activists influenced by gay liberation ideology, a legal framing was likely the only framing around which the American gay rights community could rally around.

In Spain, the moral framing of the campaign mirrors the origins of the Spanish gay rights movement in the long struggle against the Franco dictatorship. It was from this struggle that gay rights activists developed a concern for expanding democratic citizenship as part of the struggle for gay liberation. This struggle also gave gay rights organizations a deep grounding in civil society, especially the human rights movement. A lot about political framing in Brazil stems from the political incorporation of the gay rights movement into the Workers' Party and, by extension, the various agencies of the Brazilian state. For much of its history, the gay rights movement has operated as a branch of the Workers' Party alongside the labor movement, feminist organizations, and the Afro-Brazilian movement. This affiliation conditioned a sense of political pragmatism and incrementalism in gay rights advocacy.

The chapter closes with a broad discussion of the main takeaways about the politics of gay marriage wars suggested by this book for future scholarship on gay marriage movements and LGBTQ rights more generally.

Chapter 1
On Gay Marriage Wars

When thinking about gay marriage wars, one question looms large above the rest: what explains the stunning success of the marriage equality movement? It was not that long ago that religious leaders in the United States were warning about apocalyptic scenarios if gay marriage were ever to be made legal (from another civil war to the extinction of gender differences to the disappearance of marriage altogether).[1] For their part, politicians, even liberal ones, were keeping gay marriage activists at arms' length. They knew full well that gay marriage was electoral poison. In 1996, when Gallup first polled Americans on gay marriage, only 27 percent agreed that "gay marriage should be valid."[2]

Scholars, gay activists, and political commentators have offered a wealth of explanations for the remarkable turnaround in the fortunes of the marriage equality movement. Prominent among them is the effective use by gay marriage activists of slogans such as "love is love," "love wins," and "equality for all" to make gay marriage relatable to the public; the support of the marriage equality campaign by straight politicians, the media, business corporations, and liberal churches; and a generational change that sparked a fundamental shift in society's understanding of homosexuality.[3] Much less explored, and therefore less understood, are the differences in the severity of the conservative backlash generated by the war over gay marriage across countries, as well

---

[1] See, especially, Omar G. Encarnación, "Pope Francis' Latin Lessons: How Latin America Shaped the Vatican," *Foreign Affairs*, May 14, 2014. Available at https://www.foreignaffairs.com/articles/central-america-caribbean/2014-05-14/pope-francis-latin-lessons.

[2] See "U.S. Support for Gay Marriage," Gallup, June 5, 2023. Available at https://news.gallup.com/poll/506636/sex-marriage-support-holds-high.aspx.

[3] For a sampling of the massive scholarship generated by the marriage equality movement, especially in the United States, see George Chauncey, *Why Marriage: The History Shaping Today's Debate over Gay Marriage* (New York: Basic Books, 2005); Craig A. Rimmerman and Clyde Wilcox, eds., *The Politics of Same-Sex Marriage* (Chicago: University of Chicago Press, 2007); Michael J. Klarman, *From the Closet to the Altar: Courts, Backlash, and the Struggle for Same-Sex Marriage* (New York: Oxford University Press, 2013); Nathaniel Frank, *Awakening: How Gays and Lesbians Brought Marriage Equality to America* (Cambridge, MA: Harvard University Press, 2017); Peter Hart-Brinson, *The Gay Marriage Generation: How the LGBTQ Movement Transformed American Culture* (New York: NYU Press, 2018); and William N. Eskridge Jr. and Christopher R. Riano, *Marriage Equality: From Outlaws to In-Laws* (New Haven: Yale University Press, 2020).

Framing Equality. Omar G. Encarnación, Oxford University Press. © Oxford University Press (2025).
DOI: 10.1093/9780190880330.003.0002

20 Framing Equality

as the legacies that the conflict left behind for LGBTQ equality. Explaining
these differences is not as easy as one might think.

For one thing, the paradigm that scholars have long relied upon to explain
the rise of gay rights in the West—post-materialism, which suggests how
social and economic development creates an environment that is conducive
to the extension of rights to sexual minorities—explains very little about the
political dynamics of gay marriage wars.[4] While the global spread of gay rights
reveals that social and economic development is a good indicator for predict-
ing when countries are likely to embrace gay rights, this variable does not have
much to say about how the actual struggle for gay rights will play itself out.
Spain and the United States are developed societies with high levels of urban-
ization and educational attainment and thriving LGBTQ communities. It is
not surprising, therefore, that both countries were swept up in the marriage
equality revolution.

But there does not appear to be a correlation between the level of socioe-
conomic development, on the one hand, and the timing of the advent of gay
marriage and/or the intensity of the war over gay marriage, on the other hand.
As seen in this book, the United States, one of the world's most economically advanced states, witnessed a virulent legal and political backlash against
the gay community. By contrast, a country like Spain, a social and economic
backwater for much of its history, emerged as a marriage equality pioneer
by becoming the first nation to place gay and straight marriages on the same
legal footing. Brazil, as noted recently, has experienced "remarkable advance-
ments on LGBT rights while remaining relatively religious, poorly educated,
and socially conservative."[5]

Furthermore, although ubiquitous across democratic societies, gay marriage wars have not generated a robust scholarship. In making this claim, I am
not suggesting that the marriage equality revolution lacks scholarly attention.
On the contrary, the subject has generated a voluminous literature, especially
in the United States. Instead, my point is that this scholarship is relatively thin
in comparative theories and conceptual tools to explain the diverse political

[4] See, especially, Ronald Inglehart and Wayne E. Baker, *Modernization, Cultural Change and Democracy: The Human Development Sequence* (New York: Cambridge University Press, 2005); Louisa L.
Roberts, "Changing Worldwide Attitudes toward Homosexuality: The Influence of Global and Region-
Specific Cultures, 1981–2010," *Social Science Research* 80 (May 2019), 114–131; M.V. Lee Badgett, Shela
Nezhad, Keen Waaldijk, and Yana van der Meulen Rodgers, "The Relationship between LGBT Inclusion and Economic Development," The Williams Institute, UCLA School of Law, November 2014;
and Achim Hindebrandt, Eva-Maria Trüdinger, and Dominik Wyss, "The Missing Link? Modernization, Tolerance, and Legislation on Homosexuality," *Political Research Quarterly* 72, no. 3, (2019):
539–553.
[5] Lucas de Abreu Maia, Albert Chiu, and Scott Desposato, "No Evidence of Backlash: LGBT Rights in
Latin America," *The Journal of Politics* 85 (1), January 2023, 50.

experiences evident in gay marriage wars, especially differences in the severity of the conservative backlash and the legacies for LGBTQ equality.

None of this is surprising, perhaps, considering that American gay rights scholars rarely reference the experience of other countries in their work.[6] It is rare for the scholarship on the development of gay rights in the United States to make note of how more arduous the struggle for gay marriage was in the United States than in peer democracies. Little has been said about why so many other countries outpaced the United States in legalizing gay marriage. The same can be said about the lack of attention to how the strategies of the American gay marriage campaign differed from those of their foreign counterparts.

Fortunately, as with any subject that combines sex, politics, and religion, there is no shortage of compelling angles from which to approach the comparative study of gay marriage wars. As I suggest in this chapter, many of them can be considered counterarguments since they appear to challenge my argument about the primacy of framing in shaping gay marriage wars. I begin with a discussion of the institutional pathway used to introduce gay marriage into the nation, especially whether this is done via legislation or litigation. An examination of the role of culture follows that discussion. The relevance of this factor rests on the causal connection that can be drawn between societal acceptance of homosexuality and the religious environment. Reams of polling data, for example, point to Catholic-majority nations as being more accepting of homosexuality than Protestant-majority nations. I then turn my attention to the resources of the opposition to gay marriage and its capacity to generate "moral panics." I conclude with a discussion of the concept of framing and how I theorize it shapes gay marriage wars, as reflected by the experiences of Spain, the United States, and Brazil.

Legislation Versus Litigation

Probably no other subject has dominated discussions about the political dynamics of gay marriage wars more than whether gay marriage arrives in the country by means of a law or a court mandate.[7] Although national

---

[6] Of course, there are exceptions to this generalization. See, especially, David Rayside, "The United States in Comparative Context," in *The Politics of Same-Sex Marriage*, eds. Craig A. Rimmerman and Clyde Wilcox (Chicago: University of Chicago Press, 2008); and Barry D. Adam, "The Defense of Marriage Act and American Exceptionalism: The 'Gay Marriage' Panic in the United States," *Journal of the History of Sexuality* 12, no. 2 (2003): 259–276.

[7] This conventional wisdom is supported by the large scholarship that posits litigation as the most prominent factor behind the rise of a severe political and legal gay marriage backlash in the United States.

gay marriage laws can be controversial and divisive, they can also serve to minimize political backlash because of the legitimacy that the law-making process confers to gay marriage. For starters, the public is more likely to see a law as more legitimate than a court mandate, if only because legislators are less likely than the courts to act against public opinion. A more critical point is that legislation and all that it entails—lobbying, media attention, public debates, hearings, and testimony from both sides of the issue—creates an opportunity for a robust societal debate about the merits of opening the institution of marriage to gay and lesbian couples, the role of sexual minorities in society, and ways in which the government and civil society can go about addressing expanding LGBTQ equality.

National gay marriage laws, however, are not created equally. They vary significantly in terms of what they allow. This variance could shape the intensity of the controversy surrounding gay marriage. For example, the earliest gay marriage laws, those of the Netherlands and Belgium, enacted in 2001 and 2003, respectively, placed limitations on adoption (Belgium did not allow them at all) to make the law as palatable to as many legislators as possible. This particular limitation in gay marriage laws began to change with Spain's gay marriage law, enacted in 2005, the first one to make no distinction whatsoever between homosexual and heterosexual marriages. It made Spain's gay marriage law more controversial than peer laws in the Netherlands and Belgium.

Some national gay marriage laws are also more expansive than others in how they regulate the extension of marriage rights to same-sex couples. Britain's gay marriage law, which went into effect in 2014, has twenty-one sections that outline a host of religious exemptions and accommodations that void or expand previous laws regulating same-sex relationships. Others, by contrast, are a model of brevity. The best examples are the Spanish and Argentine gay marriage laws. (They are very similar since Spain's gay marriage law served as a blueprint for Argentina's.) In both countries, the gay marriage law entailed removing all references to gender in the portion of the civil code about marriage. The intention behind this action was to allow all the rights and benefits of marriage to be automatically conferred to the individuals entering the marriage. There are also no religious exemptions in the Spanish and Argentine laws.

See, Carlos A. Ball, "The Backlash Thesis and Same-Sex Marriage: Learning from Brown v. Board of Education and Its Aftermath," *William & Mary Bill of Rights Journal* 14 (2006): 1–48; Jane S. Schacter, "Courts and the Politics of Backlash: Marriage Equality Litigation, Then and Now," *California Law Review* 82 (2009): 1153–1224; William N. Eskridge, Jr., "Backlash Politics: How Constitutional Litigation Has Advanced Marriage Equality in the United States," *Boston University Law Review* 93 (2013): 275–322; and Klarman, *From the Closet to the Altar.*

By contrast, legalizing gay marriage through the courts poses a wide range of potential negative consequences. Because litigation generally takes place behind closed doors and often with little input from the general public, it does not provide much of an opportunity for groups in society to weigh in on the pros and cons of gay marriage. Not surprisingly, court rulings favoring gay marriage rarely yield anything resembling closure. Litigation is also, by design, contentious and divisive, allowing very little room for compromise among the warring parties. It can also be unpredictable and likely to result in a prolonged legal struggle. In the United States, the legal battle for gay marriage lasted decades. The first gay marriage victory in an American court arrived in Hawaii in 1993, when the state's highest court determined that denying marriage to same-sex couples violated the state's constitution and its guarantee of equal protection under the law. But gay marriage did not arrive to every part of the United States until 2015, when the US Supreme Court issued a sweeping ruling that simultaneously voided gay marriage bans across the United States and legalized gay marriage in every jurisdiction under the US Constitution, including territories like Puerto Rico.

In other countries, the courts acted relatively quickly—at least faster than the US Supreme Court—but their rulings nonetheless created a lot of confusion. In 2011, the Federal Supreme Court of Brazil ruled that it was a violation of the Brazilian Constitution to treat gay families differently than heterosexual families. The court ruled this way because it was not deliberating the legality of gay marriage but rather the conception of the family in the Brazilian Constitution. But it was left up to notary publics across the country how to interpret the ruling, with some choosing to issue marriage permits to same-sex couples while others refused to do so. To rule out any ambiguity, in 2013, the National Judicial Council, a body that supervises the Brazilian judiciary and that is headed by the Chief Court of the Federal Supreme Court, ruled that the Federal Court intended to erase any discrimination in the treatment of homosexual couples. The ruling also compelled all notary publics to issue a marriage license to any same-sex couples that asked for one and to convert a same-sex civil union into marriage if that was the wish of the couple. This effectively legalized gay marriage in Brazil.

Yet, in other cases, the high court ruled in favor of gay marriage but gave the government a fixed time frame to enact a gay marriage law, thereby throwing gay marriage into political limbo. A case in point is Colombia. In 2011, the Colombian Constitutional Court ruled unanimously that gay and lesbian couples had the right to a family and to have that family recognized by the state. The Court gave the national legislature two years to legalize gay marriage and/or same-sex civil unions. If the legislators failed to act, the Court

24 Framing Equality

ruled that same-sex couples would automatically be able to register their relationship with a notary public. After the legislators failed to pass any law, the country began issuing marriage licenses to same-sex couples. In 2016, the Court ruled in favor of gay marriage, noting that banning gay marriage is unconstitutional and discriminatory. The Court was responding to a petition by Colombia's inspector general to invalidate all the gay marriages that had been approved up until that point, arguing that the Colombian Constitution did not provide for the legality of such unions.

Finally, political backlash thrives whenever litigation takes center stage. For one thing, the losing side in any legal struggle over gay marriage is likely to attempt to delegitimize a court mandate by denouncing it as an act of "judicial activism." In the American context, this claim is politically charged. It echoes Richard Nixon's law and order presidential campaign of 1968 and its attacks on court rulings (especially concerning busing) as a means to appeal to White southerners. After the Supreme Court of Hawaii ruled that the state had no compelling reason for denying same-sex couples the right to marry, the conservative Family Research Council said that "once again, an activist judge has flouted public opinion and a perfectly reasonable law and imposed his own agenda."[8] After George W. Bush decided to back the ill-fated 2004 federal constitutional amendment to ban gay marriage, his White House remarks stressed "that he was acting because activist judges had made aggressive efforts to redefine marriage." Hearings on the amendment were titled "Judicial Activism vs. Democracy."

But cries of judicial activism are just the start of how gay marriage litigation fuels political backlash, an argument especially popular with American legal scholars. Jane Schacter blames gay marriage litigation for nationalizing the conflict over marriage by noting that the local battle in Hawaii "quickly went national, as organized groups associated with traditional values joined the fray to preserve traditional marriage."[9] William Eskridge Jr. writes, "As a result of litigation, same-sex couple proponents face legislative and constitutional obstacles on both the state and federal level that did not exist before they turned to litigation."[10] Michael J. Klarman blames litigation for a host of problems, such as mobilizing opponents, undercutting moderates, and scrambling the logical progression of gay rights in a way that prevented the building of steady public support for gay marriage.[11] John D'Emilio, the dean of American gay historians, has called the American gay marriage campaign

---

[8] This and other quote passages in this paragraph come from Jane S. Schacter, "Courts and the Politics of Backlash: Marriage Equality Litigation, Then and Now," *California Law Review* 82 (2009): 1208.

[9] Ibid., 1185.

[10] William N. Eskridge Jr., "Backlash Politics: How Constitutional Litigation Has Advanced Marriage Equality in the United States," *Boston University Law Review* 93 (2013): 217.

[11] Michael J. Klarman, "Brown and Lawrence (and Goodridge)," *Michigan Law Review* 104 (2005): 431.

"a disaster," citing the many political and legislative setbacks that the pursuit of gay marriage through the courts triggered.[12]

Most damming of them all, however, is Gerald N. Rosenberg, who concluded that "the battle for same-sex marriage would have been better served if activists had never brought litigation, or had lost their cases."[13] The reasoning behind Rosenberg's conclusion is that court rulings are generally not a source of social change. He noted that "courts can almost never be effective producers of significant social reform. At best, they can second the social reform acts of the other branches of government."[14] For him and others, one of the main problems of pro-gay marriage court rulings is that these rulings are often ahead of public opinion. When the courts began to rule in favor of gay marriage in the United States in 1993, the very idea of gay marriage was "audacious and improbable," "many gay people were deeply closeted," and "most Americans reported that they did not personally know a homosexual person and condemned sex between gay couples, whatever the circumstances, while less than a third of Americans thought that heterosexual sex between unmarried people was always wrong."[15]

Of course, none of this is to say that courts cannot play a significant role in advancing gay marriage, even in instances where litigation triggers backlash. Ellen Andersen's study of gay marriage litigation accepts Rosenberg's premise that the courts are limited in their capacity to promote social change; nonetheless, she contends that "litigation has produced some favorable shifts in the legal and cultural frames surrounding gay rights."[16] Even a decision as controversial as *Baehr v. Lewin*, the 1993 decision from Hawaii's highest court that triggered so much backlash, is credited with "a direct influence" on *Goodridge v. Department of Public Health*. This ruling made Massachusetts the first state in the United States to recognize gay marriage.[17] Klarman adds that despite the backlash that judicial rulings generated, gay marriage litigation "has also had several beneficial consequences for the gay community," including "making same-sex marriage a salient topic" and "forcing Americans to discuss and form opinions about a social reform that previously

---

[12] John D'Emilio, "Will the Courts Set Us Free? Reflections on the Campaign for Same-Sex Marriage," in *The Politics of Same-Sex Marriage*, eds. Craig A. Rimmerman and Clyde Wilcox, (Chicago: The University of Chicago Press, 2007), 39.

[13] Gerald N. Rosenberg, "Courting Disaster: Looking for Change in All the Wrong Places," *Drake Law Review* 54 (2006): 795–813.

[14] Gerald N. Rosenberg, *The Hollow Hope: Can Courts Bring About Social Change?* 2nd ed. (Chicago: University of Chicago Press, 2008), 339–419.

[15] Michael Sant'Ambrogio and Sylvia A. Law, "Baehr v. Lewin and the Long Road to Marriage Equality," New York University School of Law, Public Law & Legal Theory Research Paper Series, Working Paper No. 11–37 (June 2011): 706.

[16] Ellen Ann Andersen, *Out of the Closets and Into the Courts: Legal Opportunity Structure and Gay Rights Legislation* (Ann Arbor: University of Michigan Press, 2005), 216.

[17] Sant'Ambrogio and Law, "Baehr v. Lewin and the Long Road to Marriage Equality," 727.

26 Framing Equality

would have struck most of them as incomprehensible."[18] He also notes that the backlash did not stop public opinion from evolving in favor of gay marriage.

Catholicism's Surprising Progressivism

Another powerful explanation for the political dynamics of gay marriage wars is the cultural-religious environment. Of the many paradoxes of the global spread of gay rights, none is more surprising than the apparent ease with which so many Catholic countries have adjusted to gay marriage, including historic bastions of Roman Catholicism, like Spain and Ireland, with relatively recent histories of ostracizing LGBTQ people and criminalizing homosexual behavior. By 2015, when Ireland made history by becoming the first nation in the world to legalize gay marriage via a popular vote, half of the twenty nations that had legalized gay marriage were "countries with a Catholic majority."[19] This is a striking happening considering the Catholic Church's teaching that homosexuality is a sin and that gay unions represent an existential threat to the family.[20] In fact, Catholic-majority nations like Spain, Portugal, Brazil, Uruguay, and Argentina legalized gay marriage ahead of Protestant nations such as the United States, Australia, and Britain. Moreover, in many Catholic-majority countries, like Spain, the advent of gay marriage came without the toxic backlash experienced by many Protestant nations, especially the United States.

The Catholic world's surprising embrace of gay marriage is broadly mirrored in the polling data. It pointedly and consistently shows that Catholics are more tolerant of homosexuality and gay marriage than other Christians, mainly Protestant evangelicals. According to a 2013 Pew survey on "The Global Divide on Homosexuality," which examined acceptance of homosexuality across the world, the leading scorers were Catholic-majority

---

[18] Klarman, *From the Closet to the Altar*, Introduction.

[19] "On Same-Sex Marriage Catholics Are Leading the War," Crux, May 27, 2015. Available at https://cruxnow.com/life/2015/05/on-same-sex-marriage-catholics-are-leading-the-way.

[20] The Congregation for the Doctrine of the Faith explicitly states that "respect for homosexual persons cannot lead in any way to approval of homosexual behaviour or to legal recognition of homosexual unions.... Legal recognition of homosexual unions or placing them on the same level as marriage would mean not only the approval of deviant behaviour, with the consequence of making it a model in present-day society, but would also obscure basic values which belong to the common inheritance of humanity." The document also states that Catholic politicians are "obligated to defend the church's beliefs in their public duties." See https://www.vatican.va/roman_curia/congregations/cfaith/index.htm. For theological analyses of homosexuality and Catholicism see, Mark D. Jordan, *Homosexuality and Modern Catholicism* (Chicago: University of Chicago Press, 2000); John J. McNeill, *The Church and the Homosexual* (Beacon Press, 1993); and Louis J. Cameli, *Catholic Teaching on Homosexuality: New Paths* (Ave Maria Press, 2012).

societies. Spain topped the study, with an impressive 88 percent of respondents answering in the affirmative.[21] Not too far were other Catholic-majority nations, including France (77 percent), Argentina (74 percent), and Italy (74 percent). The United States registered 60 percent. More comparative studies have shown Catholics surpassing other Christians when it comes to acceptance of homosexuality and gay marriage. A 2013 survey on acceptance of homosexuality among Latin American nations found a marked difference between Catholics and non-Catholics: Chile (77 percent vs. 56 percent); Brazil (65 percent vs. 50 percent); Argentina (75 percent vs. 69 percent); and Mexico (61 percent vs. 58 percent).[22]

Another survey from Pew on support for gay marriage in Latin America from 2014 mirrors the findings of the study on acceptance of homosexuality.[23] Almost without exception, support for gay marriage was highest among the religious unaffiliated, followed by Catholics, and then by Protestants, which in Latin America generally means evangelical. In Mexico, 75 percent of unaffiliated people, 59 percent of Catholics, and 35 percent of Protestants supported gay marriage. For Argentina, it was 75 percent for unaffiliated, 53 percent for Catholics, and 32 percent for Protestants. For Chile, it was 67 percent for unaffiliated, 46 percent for Catholics, and 26 percent for protestants. For Brazil, it was 54 percent for unaffiliated, 51 percent for Catholics, and 25 percent for Protestants. For US Hispanics, the numbers were 67 percent for unaffiliated, 49 percent for Catholics, and 25 percent for Protestants.

The data from the United States shows similar findings. A 2011 study from the Public Religion Research Institute found that "Catholics are more supportive of legal recognitions of same-sex relationships than members of any other Christian tradition and Americans overall."[24] Nearly three-quarters of Catholics favor either allowing gay and lesbian people to marry (43 percent) or allowing them to form civil unions (31 percent). Only 22 percent of Catholics said there should be no legal recognition of gay relationships. By contrast, 37 percent of the general population approved of same-sex

---

[21] "The Country That's Most Accepting of Homosexuality; Spain," Pew Research Center, June 4, 2013. Available at https://www.pewresearch.org/global/2013/06/04/the-country-thats-most-accepting-of-homosexuality-spain/.

[22] "Before Pope's Comments, Latin American Catholics Expressed Acceptance of Homosexuality," Pew Research Center, July 30, 2013. Available at https://www.pewresearch.org/short-reads/2013/07/30/popes-comments-on-gays-have-support-within-his-flock/.

[23] "Religion in Latin America: Widespread Change in a Historically Catholic Region," Pew Research Center, November 13, 2014. Available at https://www.pewresearch.org/religion/2014/11/13/religion-in-latin-america/.

[24] "Catholic Attitudes on Gay and Lesbian Issues: A Comprehensive Portrait from Recent Research," Public Religion Research Institute, March 2011. Available at https://www.prri.org/wp-content/uploads/2011/06/Catholics-and-LGBT-Issues-Survey-Report.pdf.

marriage, while approval was 36 percent for mainline Protestants. A Pew study from 2023 on American support for gay marriage had similar findings.[25] It reported that religious unaffiliated Americans (85 percent) are the most likely to support gay marriage, followed by White non-evangelical protestants with 70 percent, Catholics with 65 percent, and White non-Hispanic evangelical Protestants with 30 percent. A Gallup study from 2020 concluded that "Catholics, who constitute more than one-fifth of American adults, have been consistently more supportive of same-sex marriage than the population as a whole over more than a decade—much like young adults and Democrats."[26]

Several factors account for the surprising progressivism that Catholic-majority countries have shown toward gay marriage, starting with the arrival at the Vatican of Pope Francis in 2013. Francis introduced a new tone of acceptance of homosexuality, a reflection of the gay rights advances made in his home country of Argentina.[27] When he was asked in 2013 about gay people in the clergy, Francis famously said: "If a person is gay and seeks God and has good will, who am I to judge?" In 2020, news outlets reported that in a biographical documentary titled *Francesco*, Francis declared his support for same-sex civil unions. The documentary quotes him as saying that "homosexual people have the right to be in a family. They are children of God." He added, "What we have to have is a civil law, that way they are legally covered."[28] Shortly thereafter, in 2023, Francis announced that priests would be allowed to bless same-sex couples. This announcement is "his most definitive step yet to make the Roman Catholic Church more welcoming to LGBTQ Catholics."[29]

Another compelling reason is the view that Catholics do not put homosexuality on the same plane as other sins dictated by their faith, such as abortion. According to Pew, although 67 percent of Catholics in Argentina and 76 percent of Catholics in Brazil believe that abortion is never justifiable, only 39 and 55 percent, respectively, believe the same about homosexuality.[30]

---

[25] Jacob Poushter, Sneha Gubbala, and Christine Huang, "How People in 24 Countries View Same-Sex Marriage," Pew Research Center, June 13, 2023. Available at https://www.pewresearch.org/short-reads/2023/06/13/how-people-in-24-countries-view-same-sex-marriage/.

[26] Kristjan Archer and Justin McCarthy, "U.S. Catholics Have Backed Same-Sex Marriage Since 2011," Gallup, October 23, 2020. Available at https://news.gallup.com/poll/322805/catholics-backed-sex-marriage-2011.aspx.

[27] See, especially, Omar G. Encarnación, "Pope Francis' Latin Lessons: How Latin America Shaped the Vatican," *Foreign Affairs*, May 14, 2014. Available at https://www.foreignaffairs.com/articles/central-america-caribbean/2014-05-14/pope-francis-latin-lessons.

[28] Nicole Winfield, "Francis Becomes 1st Pope to Endorse Same-Sex Civil Unions," Associated Press, October 21, 2020. Available at https://apnews.com/article/pope-endorse-same-sex-civil-unions-eb3509b30ebac35e91aa7cbda2013de2.

[29] Jason Horowitz, "Pope Francis Allows Priests to Bless Same-Sex Couples," *The New York Times*, December 18, 2023. Available at https://www.nytimes.com/2023/12/18/world/europe/pope-gay-lesbian-same-sex-blessing.html.

[30] "The Global Catholic Population," Pew Research Center, February 13, 2013. Available at http://www.pewforum.org/2013/02/13/the-global-catholic-population/.

Another widely shared view is that Catholics regard issues involving sexuality, like homosexuality, as a matter of personal morality that is independent of the church's institutional teachings. As explained by Phil Attey, executive director of Catholics for Equality, "Our families have already dealt with this issue at a personal level, and Catholics largely base their moral understanding of the world through their personal relationships, not the dictates of institutional forces, be they from our church hierarchy in Rome or conservative political groups. We see healthy, happy gay and lesbian families within our families, parishes, and communities, and we know love and commitment when we see it."[31]

Attey's sentiments are especially popular among so-called cultural Catholics, generally defined as people who identify themselves with some of the teachings of Catholicism, primarily because of their upbringing, but who are not active in the Church or conduct their lives according to Catholic theology. For these Catholics, their Catholic identity is defined more by "culture, ancestry, ethnicity or family tradition."[32] Data on the percentage of Catholics who are thought to fall under the category of cultural Catholics is hard to come by. This is primarily the case because who falls under the category depends on how the term cultural Catholicism is defined. However, one study about American Catholics estimates that cultural Catholics comprise just over half of self-identified Catholics in the United States.[33] The phenomenon of cultural Catholics may be as widespread, if not more, in Catholic-majority countries in Western Europe and Latin America, especially in Spain, Argentina, and Ireland.

Finally, due to a host of scandals and ethical lapses, the Catholic Church has in recent decades experienced an acute loss of moral authority.[34] It has vastly diminished the capacity of Catholic leaders to attack gay marriage as a threat to the family and society. Ireland has been the site of the most high-profile child sex abuse scandals involving the Catholic Church. After years of ignoring complaints about child abuse at Catholic-run schools, in 1999 the Irish government organized a commission to study child abuse.[35] Lasting nine years and covering a sixty-year period, the inquiry focused on some thirty-five thousand children placed in a network of reformatories,

---

[31] Jonathan Capehart, "Catholic Lead the Way on Sex-Sex Marriage," *The Washington Post*, March 21, 2011. Available at https://www.washingtonpost.com/blogs/post-partisan/post/catholics-lead-the-way-on-same-sex-marriage/2011/03/04/ABQJQb6_blog.html.

[32] "Catholics Who Aren't Catholics," *The Atlantic*, September 8, 2015. Available at https://www.theatlantic.com/politics/archive/2015/09/catholics-who-arent-catholic/404113/.

[33] See, especially, Maureen K. Day, *Cultural Catholics: Who They Are, How to Respond* (Collegeville, MN: Liturgical Press, 2024).

[34] See, especially, Anna Grzymala-Busse, *Nations under God: How Churches Use Moral Authority to Influence Policy* (Princeton, NJ: Princeton University Press, 2015).

[35] The full report is available at https://wayback.archive-it.org/all/20110613223403/http://www.childabusecommission.com/rpt/01-01.php.

30   Framing Equality

industrial schools, and workhouses up to the 1980s. Its final report, released in 2009, left no doubt as to the severity of the problem. As summarized by the BBC, "The schools were run in a severe, regimented manner that imposed unreasonable and oppressive discipline on children, even on staff."[36] The report further alleged that the children were subjected to beatings and rapes and forced into oral sex. Equally shocking is that the report concluded that church officials at the highest levels knew of the abuse and did little to stop it.

In Spain and across Latin America, child abuse scandals could not have come at a more inopportune time for the Catholic Church. For much of the Cold War era, an association with bloodthirsty right-wing dictatorships tainted the Church with rampant human rights abuses. In Spain, this association began with the Church's complicity with the policy of *limpieza,* or cleansing, the attempt by General Francisco Franco to rid Spain of all left-wing influence. Implemented most vigorously after the end of the Civil War in 1939, but lasting well into the 1950s, the policy of cleansing entailed the execution of some twenty thousand people and the imprisonment in concentration and labor camps of many more. The enormity of the bloodshed and suffering caused by this policy explains references to it as "the Spanish Holocaust."[37]

More recently, the Catholic Church in Spain has been accused of being complicit with the Franco regime in stealing thousands of infants born to left-wing mothers from 1939 through the end of the dictatorship in 1975. The infants were taken from their biological mothers and given to conservative families to raise. Like other crimes of the Francoist era, this one was obscured by the so-called Pact of Forgetting. Negotiated by the leading political parties around the time of the transition to democracy that followed Franco's death in 1975, it granted a blanket amnesty to former Franco officials. It also called for avoiding any public policy, like a truth commission, that could reawaken the memory of the Civil War and the Franco dictatorship while a new democratic regime was under construction. But, as fate would have it, the pact began to fall apart around the time when the campaign for gay marriage was launched in the late 1990s.[38] Needless to say, the many scandals swirling around the Catholic Church, especially those concerning children, encouraged gay marriage activists to stress that it was the Church

[36] "Irish Church Knew Abuse Was Endemic," BBC News, May 20, 2009. Available at http://news.bbc.co.uk/1/hi/world/europe/8059826.stm.

[37] Paul Preston, *The Spanish Holocaust: Inquisition and Extermination in Twentieth-Century Spain* (New York: Norton, 2013).

[38] See Omar G. Encarnación, *Democracy without Justice in Spain: The Politics of Forgetting* (Philadelphia: The University of Pennsylvania Press, 2014).

rather than two people of the same sex getting married that threatened the family.

In Argentina, the Catholic Church became complicit with the Dirty War, a conflict infamous for having caused the disappearance of thousands of political dissidents during the military regime in place between 1976 and 1983. This regime claimed to be "a Catholic government."[39] The Church's complicity with the military regime is part of the public record. According to the 1984 report of the National Commission on the Disappeared, which recorded the disappearance of some ten thousand people during the period of military government, "some of the torturers were convinced they were fighting a holy war and considered themselves sent by God to recover subversives (through torture) for the Christian West."[40] The report further noted that "witnesses mentioned that the priests took part in the torture and denied assistance to the families of the disappeared, claims that were repeated years later during the Trials of the Juntas." As a consequence of these actions, writes sociologist Gustavo Morello, "the image of Catholicism in Argentina has been that of an institution that was an accomplice of, or at the very least did not condemn terrorism by the state."[41]

Coming as close as they did to the rise of the gay marriage movement, the Church's child abuse and political scandals made Catholic officials sound hypocritical when they attacked gay marriage as a threat to the family and faith—to say nothing of trying to demonize homosexuals as criminals, deviants, and predators. Paul Lundrigan, a Catholic dissident priest from Newfoundland, who gained substantial media attention at the time when the Canadians were debating gay marriage, best expressed the predicament of the Catholic Church when confronting gay marriage: "The church should have spoken out on so many other tragic issues and didn't. . . . The church, in recent years, has had thousands of children paraded across the same television screens telling horror stories of how their lives have been shattered by the abuse they suffered in Catholic-run orphanages and residential schools. I think that the hierarchy of our church has lost the moral ground to make a judgment on how best to raise children."[42]

A related development is that the loss of moral authority endured by the Catholic Church has emboldened legislators, judges, and politicians to openly defy the Church on gay marriage. One of the best examples (maybe the best)

---

[39] Gustavo Morello, *The Catholic Church and Argentina's Dirty War* (New York: Oxford University Press, 2015), 1.

[40] Ibid., 4. Human rights activists have put the number of those who disappeared at thirty thousand.

[41] Ibid.

[42] Grzymala-Busse, *Nations under God*, 326.

of this situation comes from Mexico City, which in 2009 became the first locality in Latin America to legalize gay marriage by action from the Mexico City Assembly.[43] Predictably, Catholic leaders lashed out by threatening to excommunicate "any member of the Assembly who voted in favor of the law." But the threat fell on deaf ears. After the Mexican Supreme Court upheld the constitutionality of the actions of the Assembly, the Church tried to delegitimize the ruling. Cardinal Juan Sandoval Iñiguez of Guadalajara accused Mexico City Mayor Marcelo Luis Ebrard, who signed gay marriage into law, of bribing the justices. Ebrard responded by filing a defamation suit against the Church and publicly chastising Cardinal Iñiguez. He noted that the Cardinal "failed to grasp that we live in a secular state, and in it, whether we like it or not, the rule of law prevails—the Cardinal must obey the law like any other citizen in the country." In a very unusual move, the Mexican Supreme Court censured the Cardinal in a unanimous decision supported even by the justices who had dissented from the gay marriage decision.

Conservative Organizing and Moral Panic

Yet another compelling explanation for the politics of gay marriage wars can be found in the scholarship on the conservative opposition to gay rights.[44] A significant portion of this scholarship sees the success of the anti-gay marriage movement in the United States in erecting political and legal roadblocks to gay marriage as a reflection of the movement's organizational prowess, political connections, and framing skills. Of special concern to this scholarship is the capacity of conservative actors to engineer a "moral panic" about gay marriage that exploits society's worst fears and anxieties about homosexuality and same-sex marriage. Coined by British sociologist Stanley Cohen, the term moral panic is a reaction to something seen as a threat to society. In his landmark book *Folk Devils and Moral Panics*, Cohen wrote, "Societies from time to time appear subject, every now and then, to periods of moral panic. A condition, episode, person or group of persons emerges to become defined as a threat to societal values and interests."[45]

---

[43] Omar G. Encarnación, *Out in the Periphery: Latin America's Gay Rights Revolution* (New York: Oxford University Press, 2016), 58.

[44] See, especially, Didi Herman, *The Antigay Agenda: Orthodox Vision and the Christian Right* (Chicago: University of Chicago Press, 1998); Tina Fetner, *How the Religious Right Shaped Lesbian and Gay Activism* (Minneapolis, MN: University of Minnesota Press, 2008); Martha Nussbaum, *From Disgust to Humanity: Sexual Orientation and Constitutional Law* (New York: Oxford University Press, 2010); and Michael Cobb, *God Hates Fags: The Rhetorics of Religious Violence* (New York: New York University Press, 2006).

[45] Stanley Cohen, *Folk Devils and Moral Panics*, 3rd ed. (London: Routledge, 2002), 1.

Cohen's original work concerned "mods and rockers." By the late 1960s, they had become an obsession for the English media, police, and education system. Cohen argued that the press had selectively chosen a few random examples of misbehavior to create a narrative about youth deviance and delinquency. In typical fashion, this particular moral panic was exploited by specific individuals as an issue of ethical importance. This required identifying and demonizing behavior deemed a threat to society's values or norms. Cohen referred to these individuals as moral entrepreneurs. Their job in any moral panic is to enlist the support of those actors and institutions with the power and resources to address the outrage being generated by the moral panic, such as the courts, the media, business enterprises, and the political system. In almost no time, these moral entrepreneurs bandy together to hurry legislation to abate the furor instigated by the moral panic and to get credit for addressing the public's concern.

Further theoretical work on moral panic has insisted that the threat underpinning the moral panic must be disproportionately exaggerated or even distorted. According to Erich Goode and Nachman Ben-Yehuda, "In a moral panic, the reactions of the media, law enforcement, politicians, action groups, and the general public are out of proportion to the real and present danger a given threat poses to the society."[46] They added that "the fear and heightened concern are exaggerated, that is, are above and beyond what a sober empirical assessment of its concrete danger would sustain." Moral panics also target populations on the margins of society or those that are the source of considerable societal anxiety. As argued by Gilbert Herdt, moral panics "provoke a cultural anger in the service of moral regulation that targets the vulnerable in societies."[47] More often than not, the intention is to exploit tendencies already prevalent among the public. As noted by Drislane and Parkinson, "Moral panics gather converts because they touch on people's fears and because they also use specific events or problems as symbols of what they feel to represent 'all that is wrong with the nation.'"[48]

Among democratic states, the United States endured a peerless gay marriage moral panic. It commenced earnestly with the Defense of Marriage Act (DOMA), signed into law on September 21, 1996. DOMA banned federal recognition of same-sex marriage by defining marriage in federal law as the union of one man and one woman and released the individual states of the

---

[46] Eric Goode and Nachman Ben-Yehuda, "Moral Panics: Culture, Politics, and Social Construction," *American Review of Sociology* 20, no. 1 (1994): 156.

[47] Gilbert Herdt, "Moral Panics, Sexual Rights, and Cultural Anger," in *Moral Panics, Sex Panics: Fear and the Fight for Sexual Rights*, ed. Gilbert Herdt (New York: NYU Press, 2009), 2.

[48] R. Drislane and G. Parkinson, "Moral Panic," *Online Dictionary of the Social Sciences*. Open University of Canada, 2016. Available at http://bitbucket.icaap.org/dict.nl.

34 Framing Equality

responsibility of having to accept gay marriages from other states. President Bill Clinton, who signed DOMA into law, declared it "divisive and unnecessary," a reflection of the fact that in 1996 same-sex couples could not marry legally anywhere in the United States and would be unable to do so for another eight years until the legalization of gay marriage in the state of Massachusetts. Nonetheless, Clinton signed the law under the threat of a veto by both houses of the US Congress. The law enjoyed broad bipartisan support and was passed with veto-proof majorities in the US Senate and the US House of Representatives. Years later, in 2013, Clinton denounced DOMA as "unconstitutional" and urged the US Supreme Court to overturn it.[49] That year, the Court struck most of its provisions in *United States v. Windsor*.

Writing about DOMA from a broad comparative perspective and through the lens of the concept of a moral panic, Barry Adam noted that "the speed and success of the passage of this law and the 'mini DOMAs' at the state level show many of the earmarks of a moral panic, especially when swept into law through referenda. What is especially noteworthy about this trend is the degree to which it is exceptional on the world scene."[50] This statement captures DOMA's extraordinary journey, especially the speed at which its sponsors could translate an idea into law. DOMA's origins can be traced to the national campaign to protect marriage, a political rally held in Des Moines, Iowa, on February 10, 1996. At this event, four Republican presidential candidates, including eventual winner Bob Dole, signed and pledged to protect marriage between one man and one woman and urged the federal government to take steps to prevent the coming of same-sex marriage.[51]

George W. Bush's 2004 re-election campaign can be deemed the height of the moral panic triggered by the marriage equality movement in the United States. During that campaign, no fewer than eleven gay marriage referendums were on the ballot across the United States. According to Herdt, the campaign in support of these popular votes on gay marriage, which featured "sexual and religious conservatives tirades against gay marriage," set the stage for "a classic moral panic provoked by sexual politics and assisted by the media, except that in this case, it was clear that the rights of individuals (gay men and lesbians) were at stake and were the object of a well-coordinated effort to scapegoat them."[52] He added that the moral panic helped send Bush back to the White

---

[49] Bill Clinton, "It's Time to Overturn DOMA," *The Washington Post*, March 7, 2013.

[50] Barry D. Adam, "The Defense of Marriage Act and American Exceptionalism: The 'Gay Marriage' Panic in the United States," *Journal of the History of Sexuality* 12, no. 2 (2003): 259–260.

[51] A transcript of this event is available at https://www.c-span.org/video/?69857-1/campaign-protect-marriage-rally.

[52] Gilbert Herdt, "Gay Marriage: The Panic and the Right," in *Moral Panics, Sex Panics: Fear and the Fight for Sexual Rights*, ed. Gilbert Herdt (New York: NYU Press, 2009), 157.

House by "frightening the Christian Right and fundamentalist voters in red states" with sermons denouncing the "devil practice" of gay marriage.[53]

In typical fashion, the moral panic that produced DOMA was fueled by the excessive, exaggerated attention that the Christian right and its conservative allies devoted to the issue of gay marriage. One study of the publicity materials produced by the Family Research Council, a major family values organization based in Washington, DC, concluded that its press releases devoted to marriage exceeded the frequency for all other issues combined. (These other issues included "abortion, school prayer, sex education, bioethics, euthanasia, pornography, and a host of other issues unrelated to gay rights," and one-third concerned marriage.)[54] The content of this publicity material was of questionable scientific value. An independent review of some three hundred Family Research Council publications concluded that they display a discourse that "enables homophobic understandings that appear grounded in scientific truth."[55]

A long and rich history of "gay panics" preceded the gay marriage panic in the United States. By far, the most notorious of these gay panics was "Save Our Children," a norm-busting extravaganza of insults, falsehoods, and conspiracy theories from 1977 about the supposed threat that homosexuality poses to American society headed by singer and beauty queen Anita Bryant, widely remembered to this day as the face of the anti-gay rights backlash.[56] Triggering the crusade was an ordinance passed by Dade County, Florida, on January 28, 1977, banning discrimination in housing, employment, and public accommodation based on sexual orientation. As the first gay rights ordinance for a southern municipality, the Dade County ordinance caught Bryant's attention, the spokesperson for the Florida Citrus Commission. A 2016 profile of Bryant in *The Advocate* that traced the history and legacy of her activism noted that Bryant "ended up conducting an antigay crusade driven by a vitriolic rhetoric that had never been heard before and has rarely been matched since."[57]

Front and center in the Save Our Children crusade were outlandish claims linking homosexuals, whom Bryant famously referred to as "human garbage,"

---

[53] Ibid., 158.

[54] Gary Mucciaroni, *Same Sex, Different Politics: Success and Failures in the Struggles over Gay Rights* (Chicago: University of Chicago Press, 2008), 44–45.

[55] David Peterson, "The 'Basis for a Just, Free, and Stable Society: Institutional Homophobia, and Governance at the Family Research Council," *Gender and Language* 4, no. 2 (2011): 257.

[56] See, especially, Fred Fejes, *Gay Rights and Moral Panic: The Origins of America's Debate on Homosexuality* (New York: Palgrave, 2008) and Gillian Frank, "'The Civil Rights of Parents': Race and Conservative Politics in Anita Bryant's Campaign against Gay Rights in 1970s Florida," *Journal of the History of Sexuality* 22, no. 1 (January 2013): 126–160.

[57] Carlos A. Ball, "When the State Discriminates," *The Advocate*, September 27, 2010; https://www.advocate.com/politics/2012/09/27/chronicling-lgbt-familes-who-used-court-system-change?pg=full.

36 Framing Equality

to child abuse and pedophilia, and arguments conflating civil rights rhetoric, religious claims, and the language of child protection.[58] "God gave mothers the divine right to reproduce and a divine commission to protect our children, in our homes, business, and especially our schools," Bryant told supporters.[59] In appearances on nationally syndicated television shows, like *Donahue*, and in ads that ran in Dade County newspapers, she claimed that "the recruitment of our children is absolutely necessary for the survival and growth of homosexuality—for since homosexuals cannot reproduce, they must recruit, must freshen their ranks."[60] Time after time, she argued that "if homosexuality were the normal way, God would have made Adam and Bruce."[61] By all signs, the campaign proved wildly successful. According to the *New York Times*, "Slightly more than 40 percent of eligible voters went to the polls, an unusually high turnout for a referendum." And they rejected the measure overwhelmingly: by a margin of two to one.[62]

Save Our Children would go on to impact gay rights politics far beyond Florida's borders. According to *The Advocate*, "Not only did Anita mobilize an army of haters to combat the great Satan of sodomy, but she also laid the groundwork for the modern religious right that planted the seeds of intolerance on school boards, city councils, and local and state ballots across the country—and that led to pronouncements that AIDS was a judgment from God when the epidemic struck." Furthermore, the magazine added, "You can trace a blood-red line directly from Anita to the likes of Jerry Falwell, the Moral Majority, and the Tea Party in our own day. Echoes of the movement even resound in Donald Trump's scapegoating of the menacing 'other' in the form of immigrants and potential terrorists."[63]

Most notably, Bryant's activism inspired Falwell's 1979 "Declaration of War on Homosexuality." This fundraising campaign offered religious condemnation of homosexuals via Falwell's massive media empire, including a publishing company and a television network. Attacking homosexuality and gay rights was atop the agenda of Falwell's media empire. "This show is one of the few major ministries in America crying out against militant homosexuals," Falwell wrote in 1981 about *The Old Time Gospel Hour*, a radio and television

---

[58] John D'Emilio and Estelle B. Freedman, *Intimate Matters: A History of Sexuality in America* (Chicago: The University of Chicago Press, 2012), 346.

[59] Frank, "The Civil Rights of Parents," 127.

[60] Ball, "When the States Discriminates."

[61] B. Drummond Ayres, Jr., "Miami Votes 2 to 1 to Repeal Law Barring Bias against Homosexuals," *New York Times*, June 8, 1977.

[62] Ibid.

[63] Robert Whirry, "Understanding Anita Bryant, the Woman Who Declared War on Gays," *The Advocate*, August 18, 2016. Available at https://www.advocate.com/commentary/2016/8/18/understanding-anita-bryant-woman-who-declared-war-gays.

program that was broadcast in hundreds of stations across the United States.[64] Both Bryant and Falwell implicitly or explicitly claimed that "homosexual marriage" was the logical endpoint of society's acceptance of homosexuality even though at the time no gay rights organization had gay marriage on its radar.

Just before the onset of the gay marriage panic, the United States endured the moral panic over Acquired Immune Deficiency Syndrome (AIDS).[65] In quintessential moral panic mode, the promoters of this particular moral panic blamed the AIDS pandemic on the sinful sex lives of homosexuals. In a 1983 piece for the *New York Post* titled "Awful Retribution," conservative commentator Pat Buchanan noted that "the sexual revolution has begun to devour its children. And among the revolutionary vanguard, as gay rights activists, the mortality rate is highest and climbing. The poor homosexuals—they have declared war upon nature, and now nature is exacting an awful retribution."[66] Because AIDS affected people of color disproportionately, the AIDS moral panic also had a distinct racial dimension. In particular, the AIDS moral panic used the threat of nonwhite sexual transmission to legitimize a harsh approach to disease control. As noted by one study, "The moral panic associated with AIDS fulfilled racial and political objectives, capitalizing on the terror of nonwhite sexual transmission to wield neoliberal technologies of social control."[67]

Those behind the AIDS moral panic had plenty to say about how public authorities should handle the pandemic. In 1986, Lyndon LaRouche, a far-right member of the Democratic Party who ran for president eight times, secured a place on the ballot for a measure "to quarantine all Californians who have been exposed to AIDS."[68] This was the most significant referendum on AIDS policy in the United States. While promoting the referendum, LaRouche's organization (aptly named Prevent AIDS Now Initiative Committee, or PANIC) claimed that "AIDS is a plot by the Soviet war machine to conquer America—or else a plot by the International Monetary Fund to wipe out the excess eaters from starving Africa." The referendum met defeat, with

---

[64] "Letter from Jerry Falwell on Keeping Old Time Gospel Hour on Air," August 31, 1981. Available at The Portal to Texas History, https://texashistory.unt.edu/ark:/67531/metadc177440/.

[65] See, especially, Gary W. Dowsett, "The Gay Plague Revisited: AIDS and Its Enduring Moral Panic," in *Moral Panics, Sex Panics: Fear and the Fight for Sexual Rights*, ed. Gilbert Herdt (New York: NYU Press, 2009).

[66] Igor Volsky, "Buchanan: AIDS Is Nature's 'Awful Retribution' against Homosexuality," Think Progress, May 24, 2011, https://archive.thinkprogress.org/flashback-buchanan-aids-is-natures-awful-retribution-against-homosexuality-2049a2734cfb/.

[67] René Esparza, "Black Bodies on Lockdown: AIDS Moral Panic and the Criminalization of HIV in Times of White Injury," *The Journal of African American History* 104, no. 2 (Spring 2019): 256.

[68] David L. Kirp, "LaRouche Turns to AIDS Politics," *The New York Times*, September 11, 1986.

38   Framing Equality

only 29 percent of voters approving it. But this amounted to some two million voters. Also in 1986, *National Review* editor William F. Buckley Jr., writing in the *New York Times*, urged that "everyone detected with AIDS should be tattooed in the upper forearm, to protect common-needle users, and on the buttocks, to prevent the victimization of other homosexuals."[69]

According to conventional wisdom, the propensity of the United States for moral panics concerning homosexuality is rooted in the country's puritanical origins.[70] These exact origins are also thought to account for the persistence of the criminalization of homosexual sex in several parts of the United States through the early 2000s.[71] A closely related factor is the phenomenon of "American exceptionalism." According to Adam, the social conservatism of American evangelicals combined with that of conservative allies (Mormons, Roman Catholics, and Orthodox Jews) plays a factor in American exceptionalism. Quoting sociologist Seymour Martin Lipset, Adam writes, "Polls indicate Americans are the most churchgoing in Protestantism and the most fundamentalist in Christendom . . . Americans are utopian moralists who press hard to institutionalize virtue, to destroy evil people, and eliminate wicked institutions and practices . . . Americans, in harmony with their sectarian roots, have a stronger sense of moral absolutism than Europeans and even Canadians."[72]

Adam's assertions are supported by public opinion data on the issue of "religiosity," or the importance of religion in people's lives. Traditionally, it has been higher in the United States than in other developed democracies. A report by Pew conducted in 2009, at the peak of the gay marriage wars in the West, found the United States had the highest percentage of people claiming that religion was either "very important in your life" (58 percent) or "somewhat important in your life" (82 percent) among developed countries.[73] By contrast, in Spain, only 19 percent of the public deemed religion very important in their lives, and only 46 percent thought that it was somewhat important. Only South Korea, Britain, Japan, and France registered lower rates of religiosity than Spain. Polls also found that Protestants, evangelicals in particular, the largest religious group in the United States, are more conservative than Catholics (predominantly European and Latin American Catholics)

---

[69] William F. Buckley Jr., "Crucial Steps in Combating the Aids Epidemic: Identify All the Carriers," *The New York Times*, March 18, 1986.

[70] Herdt, "Gay Marriage: The Panic and the Right," 1.

[71] See, especially, Joey L. Mogul, Andrea J. Ritchie, and Kay Whitlock, *Queer (In)Justice: The Criminalization of LGBT People in the United States* (New York: Penguin Random House, 2012).

[72] Adam, "The Defense of Marriage Act and American Exceptionalism," 263.

[73] "Global Attitudes and Trends: Religiosity," Pew Research Center, September 17, 2008. Available at https://www.pewresearch.org/global/2008/09/17/chapter-2-religiosity/.

on a whole host of social issues, including homosexuality. Protestants are also less supportive than Catholics of gay rights, including gay marriage.[74]

In recent decades, the United States has undergone relentless secularization. Indeed, the country is no longer an outlier in suggesting that wealthy countries can also be very religious. According to Ronald Inglehart's *Religion's Sudden Decline*, the United States currently ranks as the twelfth least religious country in the world.[75] He also reported that religious decline in the United States has been the deepest of the forty-nine countries examined in his book. However, the increasing secularization of the United States has not diminished the importance of religion in the culture wars. As recent scholarship suggests, there is a strong tendency among religious Americans to define their faith in political terms, especially alongside Republican Party orthodoxy on social issues such as guns, abortion, and gay marriage.

The right's politicization of religion, as noted by political commentator Fareed Zakaria, "is not unique to America or Christianity." He writes, "You can see it in Brazil, El Salvador, Italy, Israel, Turkey, and India, among other places."[76] In the United States, the phenomenon reflects the success of the Christian right to adapt to a changing religious landscape. According to sociologist James Davison Hunter, "Evangelicals grew their numbers by adapting to an America that had become much less religiously observant and devout. The old Protestant Fundamentalism had been filled with warnings against sin, heresy, Catholicism, adultery, divorce, materialism, and any deviation from strict Christian morality. But preachers such as Jerry Falwell made the religion more user-friendly and less doctrinally demanding. What filled the place of religious doctrine was politics."[77]

Hunter's reference to Falwell is especially appropriate since it recalls the long history of the Christian right to weaponize gay marriage.[78] This is one advantage that gay marriage foes in the United States had over their

[74] "The Global Catholic Population," Pew Research Center, February 13, 2013. Available at http://www.pewforum.org/2013/02/13/the-global-catholic-population/.

[75] Ronald Inglehart, *Religion's Sudden Decline: What's Causing It and What Comes Next?* (New York: Oxford University Press, 2020).

[76] Fareed Zakaria, "How Trump Fills a Void in an Increasingly Secular America," *The Washington Post*, April 5, 2025. Available at https://www.washingtonpost.com/opinions/2024/04/05/trump-religion-secularism-authoritarian-populism/.

[77] Ibid.

[78] On the origins of the Christian right's attack on homosexuality and gay rights see William C. Martin, *With God on Our Side: The Rise of the Religious Right in America* (New York: Broadway Books, 2006); Daniel K. Williams, *God's Own Party: The Making of the Christian Right* (New York: Oxford University Press, 2010); Michael Sean Winters, *God's Right Hand: How Jerry Falwell Made God a Republican and Baptized the Religious Right* (New York: Harper Collins, 2012); Seth Dowland, "Family Values and the Formation of a Christian Right Agenda," *Church History* 78 (September 2009):606–631; and Doug Banwart, "Jerry Falwell, The Rise of the Moral Majority, and the 1980 Election," *Western Illinois Historical Review* V (Spring 2013): 133–157.

40 Framing Equality

counterparts in peer democracies when undertaking to defeat the marriage equality movement. Weaponizing gay marriage was an early strategy of the Christian right to fight the rise of gay rights. Historians have traced the roots of the gay marriage moral panic to the activism of conservative icon Phyllis Schlafly, famous for spearheading the successful campaign against the Equal Rights Amendment. This amendment to the US Constitution was initially passed by the US Congress in 1972 to guarantee equal rights to all American citizens regardless of gender. But it failed to be ratified by the required number of states. According to Gillian Frank, drawing from "longstanding opposition to racial integration, interracial marriage, mixed race families," Schlafly pamphlets warned about "sex mixing," "homosexual marriage," and the "threat of homosexual school teachers."[79] Echoing Frank, historian George Chauncey wrote that Schlafly argued that the Equal Rights Amendment "would not just end sex discrimination but also challenge the very notion of difference between men and women by rendering unconstitutional the legal recognition of such differences"; this, in turn, would "subvert everyday common sense about gender differences by requiring unisex toilets, drafting women into the military, and recognizing homosexual marriage."[80]

Framing the Case for Gay Marriage

In the remainder of this book my focus is on gay marriage framing approaches. My purpose is not to dismiss what has been said already, but rather to make the case for framing as a decisive and underappreciated variable in shaping gay marriage wars. I also want to highlight the importance of social movement rhetoric, which is often overshadowed by other factors. This all said, the counterarguments discussed in this chapter are not unimpeachable. It is worth noting that Brazil also experienced a significant amount of gay marriage litigation (up to the highest court in the land, in fact) without witnessing anything approaching the severity of the American gay marriage backlash. There is no Brazilian equivalent of DOMA. When thinking about the role of powerful religious institutions in enabling a gay marriage moral panic in the United States, one cannot ignore the fact that in Spain, the first gay marriage battleground in the Roman Catholic world, gay marriage activists had to contend with the Spanish Episcopal Conference, one of the most powerful Catholic establishments in Christendom, and with the resources of the

---

[79] Gillian Frank, "Phyllis Schlafly's Legacy of Anti-Gay Activism," *Slate*, September 6, 2016. Available at https://slate.com/human-interest/2016/09/phyllis-schlaflys-legacy-of-anti-gay-activism.html.
[80] Chauncey, *Why Marriage*, 146–147.

Vatican. Yet, compared to the United States, the gay marriage moral panic in Spain was muted.

As understood by the social movement scholarship, framing stands for "action-oriented sets of beliefs and meanings that inspire and legitimate the activities and campaigns of a social movement organization (SMO)."[81] More specifically, it refers to the construction of "interpretative packages" or "frames" that social movement activists develop and deploy to shape the public's understanding of any given issue.[82] These frames include "diagnostic frames," which recognize a problem that needs addressing; "prognostic frames," which involve the "articulation of a proposed solution to the problem, or at least a plan of attack"; and "motivational frames," which provide a call to arms or a rationale for engaging in ameliorative collective action, including the construction of appropriate vocabularies of motives.[83]

By focusing on rhetorical strategies, framing stands apart from other social movement paradigms that seek to explain the success and failure of social movements, especially the very influential scholarship known as "resource mobilization."[84] This scholarship highlights the organizational resources that contribute to the success of any social movement—especially financial means, a large membership base, policy networks, and connections to the political system. In particular, these organizational resources allow social movements to exploit "political opportunity structures," those historical circumstances and junctures that shake up the political environment and serve to invigorate collective action.

Although compelling, the resource mobilization paradigm is quite problematic when enlisted to account for the success of the marriage equality movement. It is the case that the movement owes some of its success to organizational resources, especially political connections. But, historically, gay rights organizations, even in rich democracies like the United States, have been plagued by a host of organizational weaknesses—at least relative to other social movements like organized labor, the human rights movement, and feminist groups. The homophobia prevalent in the culture has

---

[81] Robert Benford and David Snow, "Framing Processes and Social Movements: An Overview and Assessment," *Annual Review of Sociology* 26 (2000): 614.

[82] Francesca Polletta and M. Kai Ho, "Frames and Their Consequences," in *The Oxford Handbook of Contextual Political Analysis*, eds. Robert E. Goodin and Charles Tilly (New York: Oxford University Press, 2006), 190.

[83] Benford and Snow, "Framing Processes and Social Movements," 617–618.

[84] See John D. McCarthy and Mayer N. Zald, "Resource Mobilization and Social Movements: A Partial Theory," *The American Journal of Sociology* 82 (1977): 1212–1241; Steven M. Buechler, "Beyond Resource Mobilization? Emerging Trends in Social Movement Theory," *The Sociological Quarterly* 34, no. 2 (May 1993):217 235; and Sidney Tarrow, *Power in Movement: Social Movements and Contentious Politics* (New York: Cambridge University Press, 1998).

42 Framing Equality

traditionally depressed membership in gay rights organizations. Political parties and business corporations for years shunned gay activists, which forced many of them to operate on the margins of the political arena.

Framing advances the goals of any social movement in several mutually supporting ways, starting with making those goals relatable or accessible to the public. In other words, framing allows activists to shape the public's perception of an issue in a manner that is favorable to the activists. According to Mucciaroni, "Because politics is a struggle over alternative realities, how advocates define or frame issues is a crucial part of their strategy to win public policy battles."[85] All of this hinges on crafting frames that can find "resonance" with the public.[86] Framing can also popularize a cause or an issue, a point emphasized by scholars working on "framing effects." It points to how people's understanding of any issue comes from how the mass media spins it.[87] A study of news coverage of the legalization of gay marriage in the United States found that frames and tones differed by medium. For the most part, television presented more negative coverage of the campaign, whereas print provided more favorable coverage.[88]

A decidedly less apparent way framing advances the advocacy of any social movement is by affecting the activism of the opposition. A framing strategy that resonates broadly with the general public can assist a social movement in demobilizing and even demoralizing detractors. It can also weaken the detractors' resolve by acting as a counter-frame to the framing adopted by the detractors. This clash of frames between social movements and their opposition creates what some scholars have called "framing contests."[89] If successful, the counter-frame can effectively blunt the impact of any political and legal backlash. This outcome is particularly salient to the politics of gay marriage. Most marriage equality movements generally trigger a powerful backlash movement devoted to either freezing or derailing progress toward legalized gay marriage, to say nothing of demonizing same-sex couples and even their children. More often than not, these gay marriage backlash movements are attached to religious institutions, especially the Catholic Church and evangelical churches. Curiously, these backlash movements generally avoid religious condemnation of gay marriage. Instead, they tend to stick to

---

[85] Mucciaroni, *Same Sex, Different Politics*, 48.

[86] See David A. Snow and Robert Benford, "Ideology, Frame Resonance, and Participant Mobilization," *International Social Movement Research* 1 (1988): 197–217.

[87] Mucciaroni, *Same Sex, Different Politics*, 48.

[88] Rita Colistra and Chelsea Betts Johnson, "Framing the Legalization of Marriage for Same-Sex Couples: An Examination of News Coverage Surrounding the U.S. Supreme Court's Landmark Decision," *Journal of Homosexuality* 68, no. 1 (2019): 88–111.

[89] Benford and Snow, "Framing Processes and Social Movements," 626.

secular arguments against gay marriage, such as the framing that all children need a mother and a father.

Understanding the connection between framing and backlash politics requires unpacking the meaning of "backlash," a term most frequently encountered in the media. As used primarily by pundits, backlash stresses a conservative counterreaction to progressive policies like gay rights and women's rights.[90] It also emphasizes that backlash takes place when powerful interests are challenged by historically underrepresented groups, such as women and sexual minorities.[91] Concerned that this understanding of backlash lacks analytical rigor, political scientists have traditionally kept the concept at bay. As observed by Karen Alter and Michael Zürn, "The study of backlash is not new. Yet, perhaps, because political scientists are so skeptical about pundit backlash claims, existing scholarship on the causes, nature, or consequences of political backslashes is surprisingly sparse and vague."[92]

Hoping to make the term backlash useful to comparative political analysis, in 2017 Alter and Zürn organized a workshop on "backlash politics" from which this book originated.[93] Its main accomplishment was establishing a working definition of backlash, a task expertly handled by Alter and Zürn's framing essay.[94] It defined backlash as "a distinct form of contentious politics" that can come from either the right or the left, and that includes the following three necessary elements: (1) "a retrograde objective of returning to a prior social condition," which "may be an actual earlier situation, or a condition that is mostly an imagined or white-washed nostalgia"; (2) "extraordinary goals and tactics that challenge dominant scripts"; and (3) "a threshold condition of entering into mainstream political discourse."[95]

According to Alter and Zürn, when combined with frequent companion accelerants—such as nostalgia, emotional appeals, taboo-breaking, and institutional reshaping—backlash politics can bring about results that are unpredictable, contagious, transformative, and enduring. In particular, they recognize three different outcomes that can result from backlash politics: (1) "no change," a situation in which the backlash peters out;

---

[90] See, especially, Susan Faludi, *Backlash: The Undeclared War against American Women* (New York: Broadway Books/Random House, 1991).

[91] See, especially, Edward Lempinen, "Attack on LGBTQ+ Rights: The Politics and Psychology of a Backlash," *Berkeley News*, May 2, 2011.

[92] Karen J. Alter and Michael Zürn, "Conceptualising Backlash Politics: Introduction to a Special Issue on Backlash Politics in Comparison," *The British Journal of Politics and International Relations* 22, no. 4 (November 2020): 565.

[93] The workshop met in Berlin in 2017 to outline the main goals of the project, and a year later at Northwestern University, in Evanston, Illinois, to present the final papers. In November 2020, a special issue of *The British Journal of Politics and International Relations* published the workshop papers.

[94] Alter and Zürn, "Conceptualising Backlash Politics" 564–571.

[95] Ibid.

(2) "fundamental change," which entails the creation of new cleavages that incorporate backlash elements and objectives into ordinary politics; and (3) "social reversion," an outcome in which the backlash succeeds in reconstituting the polity to fit the vision of the movement. This short list of outcomes implies that backlash can occur even in the absence of a reversal in policy and/or a significant change in public opinion on the issue triggering the backlash.

In my paper for the workshop, a comparison of gay rights politics in the United States and Latin America, I characterized the gay marriage backlash as "a textbook case of backlash politics."[96] I emphasized the retrograde and nostalgic objectives of this particular backlash, a point underscored by the conservative Christian slogan "God made Adam and Eve, not Adam and Steve." When making this claim, anti-gay marriage activists are inferring that heterosexual unions are the only unions that are legitimate in the eyes of God and the only ones that are morally defensible. Another closely related objective of the gay marriage backlash is the desire to return society to a prior condition when homosexuality was viewed as a sin, an illness, and an aberration, if not a crime, and when heterosexuality was upheld as the norm for everyone in society. This desire is reflected in what is known as the "procreation argument," or the depiction of opposite-sex unions as superior to same-sex unions because only opposite-sex unions can procreate. Because of this essential difference, critics of gay marriage argue that the state has a legitimate rationale for limiting the institution of marriage to heterosexual couples.[97] Otherwise, these critics argue, marriage is reduced to a romantic relationship between two adults. The clear intention behind these retrograde objectives is to undermine the growing acceptance of homosexuality and gay unions in Western societies, a telling example of the "backlashers" trying to flip the script on gay rights.

I also argued for paying close attention to the framing strategies of the target of the gay marriage backlash when looking at the outcomes of the backlash. I contended that the outcomes of the gay marriage backlash depend as much on the activism of those fronting the backlash as on the counterreaction to the backlash. In particular, I noted the ability of the target of the backlash to construct counter-framing strategies and competing narratives that can undermine and even blunt the effects of any backlash. As seen in

---

[96] For a revised version of this paper, see Omar G. Encarnación, "The Gay Rights Backlash: Contrasting Views from the United States and Latin America," *The British Journal of Politics and International Relations* 22, no. 4 (November 2020): 654–665.

[97] See, especially, Sherif Girgis, Robert George, and Ryan T. Anderson, "What Is Marriage?" *Harvard Journal of Law and Public Policy* 34 (2010):245 287.

the next chapter, this point about counter-framing strategies and narratives in the context of gay marriage wars is most powerfully suggested by the Spanish experience, where the core framing of the gay marriage campaign was a direct counterreaction to the arguments against gay marriage advanced by the Spanish Episcopal Conference.

In the forthcoming chapters about the war over gay marriage in Spain, the United States, and Brazil, I explore three arguments about gay marriage framing and gay marriage wars. The first and most important is that gay marriage framing approaches tend to conform to one of three types: legal, moral, and political. To be sure, these framing approaches are ideal categories, which means that they may not always be perfectly realized in the real world. As might be expected, there's some fluidity in them. Indeed, given the great variety of gay rights activism prevalent in most democratic states, these approaches may coexist in the same country. In the case of the United States, for instance, all three approaches were embodied by different gay rights organizations during the life of the gay marriage campaign. It is also the case that gay marriage campaigns are not set in stone: they can abandon one approach and embrace a new one as they adjust to changing political circumstances. In two of our cases—the United States and Brazil—a shift to a moral framing is evident late in the campaign. All of this said, one framing approach usually sets the tone for the entire campaign.

The legal framing is anchored on a pure rights-based discourse that stresses that marriage is a civil right that should be available to all couples, regardless of the gender of those entering the union. When justifying gay marriage, this framing rarely references universal human rights principles or the ethical components of citizenship. Instead, it emphasizes legal arguments rooted in domestic laws, usually the national constitution. Moreover, the legal framing makes a very modest case about the impact of gay marriage on society. Almost no reference is made to any impact gay marriage may have in advancing the common good; instead, the emphasis of the campaign is on expanding civil rights for gay and lesbian couples. As a reflection of all of this, the legal framing generally skirts debates about the morality of homosexual relationships and families, deeming this issue to be a private matter of no concern to public policy.

Indeed, the legal framing adopts a neutral stance on the morality of private relationships inspired by liberal political theory. Legal scholar Chai R. Feldblum has summarized this view as follows: "Public and especially legal discourse should be concerned with rights and not with conceptions of the good." Feldblum added that according to this view, "Individuals living in a pluralist society will inevitably hold divergent normative and moral beliefs, and the role of law and government is to equally and adequately safeguard the rights necessary for each individual to pursue his or her own normative view of 'the good life'—not to affirmatively advance one moral, normative view of 'the good' over others. Thus 'bad people,' so long as they are not criminally bad (and very often even then), have the same rights as 'good people.'" Feldblum concluded that "the morality to be advanced by the state is thus the morality of pluralism—that is, the explicitly non-judgmental moral values of equality, freedom, and choice."[98]

Rooted in theories of political morality—understood as the "practice of making moral judgments about political action and political agents"—the moral framing makes the idealistic claim that gay marriage is a moral imperative, rather than a legal matter, one intended to correct a great historical injustice. It does so by extending full citizenship to homosexuals.[99] This type of citizenship encompasses legal rights and ethical aspects, such as dignity, respect, and a sense of belonging.[100] Achieving this level of acceptance for gay and lesbian couples requires doing away with the moral opprobrium that has traditionally been attached to homosexual conduct. More specifically, it requires drawing a moral equivalence between heterosexual and homosexual relationships. This claim implies that the love and commitment that two people of the same sex profess for one another should, in the eyes of the state, be no different from that expressed by a heterosexual couple. Not surprisingly, the moral framing generally insists on the state's willingness to extend the designation of marriage to gay unions.

Moral equivalence also aims to undermine the "traditional conservative" view on same-sex relationships. According to legal scholar Carlos Ball, this view rests on three premises: (1) that "same-sex relationships, unlike different-sex relationships, are intrinsically problematic"; (2) "that it is proper for the State to rely on moral considerations in deciding which intimate relationships to recognize"; and (3) that "the State should not recognize same-sex relationships."[101] Ball added that these arguments are grounded in the notion that heterosexual unions are more valuable than those of same-sex couples because heterosexual relationships can generate new life. For those upholding the traditional conservative position on same-sex relations, "the fact that

---

[98] Chai R. Feldblum, "Gay Is Good: The Moral Case for Marriage Equality and More," *The Yale Journal of Law and Feminism* 17 (2005): 147.

[99] Dennis F. Thompson, "Political Ethics," in *International Encyclopedia of Ethics*, ed. Hugh LaFollette (Oxford: Blackwell Publishing, 2013).

[100] See David Thunder, *Citizenship and the Pursuit of a Worthy Life* (New York: Cambridge University Press, 2014).

[101] Carlos A. Ball, "Against Neutrality in the Legal Recognition of Intimate Relationship," in *Moral Argument, Religion, and Same-Sex. Marriage: Advancing the Common Good*, eds. Gordon A. Babst, Emily R. Gill, and Jason Pierceson (Lexington Books, 2010), 78.

gay sex lacks a reproductive component means that there is no purpose to that sex other than the pursuit of physical pleasure, which makes it morally problematic."[102]

The moral framing also posits that gay marriage should do more than bring rights and benefits to gay and lesbian couples. It should also serve to advance the common good. This argument is in keeping with the view popularized by human rights activists that no society can be entirely free as long as the state endorses discrimination against any of its citizens.[103] Not surprisingly, many gay marriage activists who use moral arguments rely on the principles stipulated in the 1948 Universal Declaration of Human Rights, especially dignity, rather than on civil rights claims such as those found in any national constitution. It is worth noting that human rights are widely regarded as "the lingua franca of global moral thought."[104]

Gay activists embracing the political approach typically mix legal and moral arguments about gay marriage. However, this approach is also noted by a very pragmatic discourse around marriage. It upholds the view that the state has the moral and legal obligation to protect the rights and welfare of gay and lesbian couples and their families. In doing so, this framing combines some of the claims and appeals that characterize the legal and moral approaches, like the call for equality under the law and the defense of the morality of same-sex unions. But unlike the legal and moral approaches, the political approach is quite flexible regarding whether the state's recognition of same-sex unions needs to be accompanied by the designation of marriage. Gay rights activists operating under this approach are less likely to insist on the term "marriage" from the outset. They may prefer to do without it altogether. Or they may choose to defer demanding gay marriage until after the right to civil unions, or other priorities, have been secured.

Several factors anchor the pragmatic nature of the discourse about marriage prevalent in the political framing. Certainly, ambivalence about marriage is an issue. For many gay activists, especially those under the influence of the ideology of gay liberation, marriage is a patriarchal, oppressive institution, regardless of the gender composition of those choosing to enter into it. But for others, unhappiness with marriage is more practical than ideological. They object to the prospect of spending a lot of political capital on a struggle for something (gay marriage) that may never materialize. They are also cognizant that even if the battle for marriage proves successful, it may come with a very

---

[102] Ibid., 78.

[103] See Michael J. Perry, *The Idea of Human Rights* (New York: Oxford University Press, 2000).

[104] Stefan-Ludwig Hoffmann, ed., *Human Rights in the Twentieth Century* (New York: Cambridge University Press, 2010), Introduction.

48 Framing Equality

high price, such as compromising other priorities for the gay community. Lastly, there's the concern for avoiding backlash from conservative forces.

My second argument is that while all the framing approaches discussed above can bring the gay marriage campaign to a successful conclusion, the moral framework does the most for minimizing backlash and advancing LGBTQ equality. This framing puts the struggle for gay marriage squarely within the political sphere and the culture at large. As such, it is the approach most likely to generate a robust debate about the rights of sexual minorities. Moreover, by engaging with the morality of homosexual unions, this framing is the most likely to offer an effective counter-framing to the arguments by the opposition to gay marriage. Only when confronted, can these arguments be thoroughly debunked. Most of these arguments concern morality since all culture wars are conflicts over moral judgments.

My third and final argument holds that the variety of gay marriage framing approaches outlined above generally reflects the agency that gay rights activists bring to their struggles. But this agency does not emerge in a vacuum. Instead, it is broadly influenced by a host of domestic factors, including the political context in which gay activists operate, the ideological orientations of gay rights activists and the institutional legacies embedded in gay rights organizations (especially "foundational moments"), and the strategies of the opposition to gay marriage. More often than not, the framing of the gay marriage campaign is a reflection of the framing of the campaign in opposition to gay marriage.

Chapter 2
Spain

A Moral Framing

The scene in the Congress of Deputies on June 30, 2005, was unlike any other in this august nineteenth-century law-making chamber where some of the most momentous chapters in Spanish history have been written. On that day, Spanish legislators voted on a controversial bill that made Spain only the third country in the world and the first Roman Catholic–majority nation to legalize same-sex marriage. Less known is that Spain was, as reported in the *New York Times*, "the first nation to eliminate all legal distinctions between same-sex and heterosexual unions."[1] While the Netherlands and Belgium, which legalized gay marriage ahead of Spain in 2001 and 2003, respectively, enacted gay marriage laws with "separate rights for same-sex couples that do not fully match those of heterosexuals on issues like adoption," Spain's marriage law called for complete equality for homosexual couples from the outset. Spain also did without a conscience clause that would allow public employees, private individuals, and religious institutions to opt out of facilitating same-sex marriages. All of these things point to a gay marriage law that is broadly recognized as historic and pathbreaking.

Emotions were on full display when the legislators voted decisively in favor of gay marriage: 187 for and 147 against, with four abstentions. According to *El País*, Spain's paper of record, the chamber erupted in cheers when the final vote was announced, with some activists crying and hugging each other while others were waving and blowing kisses to the lawmakers.[2] The cheering and the clapping drowned the many expressions of anger and dissatisfaction coming from the losing side of the vote. "Shameful" and "disgraceful," shouted the members of the conservative People's Party, or PP, which fiercely opposed the bill. As a reminder to everyone in attendance that this historic vote was taking place in one of the world's bastions of Catholicism, among those in the

---

[1] Renwick McLean, "Spain Legalizes Gay Marriage: Law Is among the Most Liberal," *The New York Times*, July 1, 2005. Available at https://www.nytimes.com/2005/07/01/world/europe/spain-legalizes-gay-marriage-law-is-among-the-most-liberal.html.

[2] "El Congreso aprueba la ley del matrimonio gay," *El País*, June 30, 2005. Available at https://elpais.com/sociedad/2005/06/30/actualidad/1120082402_850215.html.

Framing Equality. Omar G. Encarnación, Oxford University Press. © Oxford University Press (2025).
DOI: 10.1093/9780190880330.003.0003

50 Framing Equality

chamber was a gay male couple carrying a sign that read in Latin *Habemus Matrimonium* (We have marriage), a reference to *Habemus Papam* (We have a Pope), the phrase used by the Vatican to announce the election of a new pope.

Befitting Spain's emergence as the first gay marriage battleground in the Catholic world, the Spanish Episcopal Conference (Spain's national conference of bishops), one of the most powerful Catholic establishments in Christendom, put up a spirited fight. The bishops pressured the legislators into opposing gay marriage by claiming that this was the duty of all Catholics. They also mobilized the public against gay marriage, hoping to intimidate the government and the gay marriage movement. When all of this failed, the bishops joined the PP in a suit claiming that the gay marriage law violated the Spanish Constitution's understanding of marriage. The Conference also argued that the law violated the human rights of children by denying them "the joy of enjoying a father and a mother in the context of a stable family environment."[3]

In 2012, after dragging its feet for years, Spain's Constitutional Tribunal upheld gay marriage in an eight to three vote, with one member of the Tribunal abstaining from voting for having already stated his position on gay marriage in his previous job. The Tribunal cited the Spanish Constitution's protection of "dignity and personality" and argued about "the need to accommodate modern life."[4] In the Tribunal's view, the Spanish Constitution is like a living tree, which demands that it be interpreted to reflect the present time. This ruling removed all uncertainty about the constitutionality of gay marriage in Spain. After the constitutional challenge ended, the conservative opposition to same-sex marriage in Spain, and by extension, Spain's gay marriage war, came to a dramatic and decisive conclusion. By then, however, gay marriage had ceased to be a polarizing issue in Spain, and the country had become something of an international trailblazer in expanding LGBTQ equality. Indeed, the opposition to gay marriage had fizzled out well before the Tribunal's ruling.

As seen in this chapter, Spain's success in legalizing gay marriage ahead of other countries with significantly larger and more experienced gay rights movements, such as France, Germany, and the United States, owes a lot to the strong support that the gay marriage campaign enjoyed from Prime Minister

---

[3] "Los obispos Españoles quieren que se modifique la ley del matrimonio gay," *La Sexta*, November 19, 2012. Available at https://www.lasexta.com/noticias/nacional/obispos-espanoles-quieren-que-modifique-ley-matrimonio-gay_2012111957285a0c6584a81fd8859e5d.html.

[4] Carmen Garcimartin, "The Spanish Law on Same-Sex Marriage: Constitutional Arguments," *Brigham Young University Journal of Public Law* 27, no. 2 (2012): 456.

José Luís Rodríguez Zapatero of the Spanish Socialist Workers' Party, or PSOE. This support for gay marriage was unprecedented for any leader. Gay marriage became a key component of Zapatero's 2004 electoral platform, and during his inauguration he urged Spaniards to end the exclusion of same-sex couples from marriage. Once in office, Zapatero made gay marriage a top legislative priority. Most political parties on the left, including Zapatero's own, questioned why he was risking other policy projects by prioritizing gay marriage. But he forged ahead, determined to put Spain on the cutting edge of LGBTQ rights.

Spain's gay marriage campaign also benefited from one of the most significant social changes to have taken place in the country in recent decades: the transition from a confessional state under the Francisco Franco dictatorship (in place between 1939 and 1975) to a secular society. As reported by *The Economist* in 2021, "In the past four decades, Spain has become a secular society with astonishing speed, perhaps faster than anywhere else in Europe."[5] Secularization in Spain is being fueled by the usual set of factors—hectic lifestyles that leave very little time for attending Church, the sense that the Catholic Church's views on issues like abortion, divorce, and gay marriage are antiquated, and an aging population. Making things worse in Spain, however, is the Church's acute loss of moral authority resulting from its complicity with the Franco regime's repression of Spanish society.

But the overall dynamics of Spain's gay marriage war, especially the failure of the conservative opposition to push back more vigorously and the success of the marriage equality movement in making gay marriage a platform for advancing LGBTQ equality, stem primarily from the moral framing of the gay marriage campaign. As seen already, this framing stands apart from the two other gay marriage framing approaches examined in this book: legal and political. It is distinguished by, among other things, a call to arms to society to correct a great injustice that needs addressing, not because it contravenes the law but because it offends decency and could be deemed immoral. This approach also provides diagnostic solutions for redressing injustice and morally based arguments to demobilize and defeat the opposition.

Spain's gay marriage campaign was structured as a crusade for "full citizenship" for gay and lesbian couples. This understanding of citizenship emphasizes the ethical dimensions of citizenship, especially dignity, respect, and a sense of belonging. Accordingly, the rhetoric of the campaign drew a moral equivalence between homosexual and heterosexual couples and

---

[5] "The Lingering Influence of Catholicism in Increasingly Secular Spain," *The Economist*, May 1, 2021. Available at https://www.economist.com/europe/2021/05/01/the-lingering-influence-of-catholicism-in-increasingly-secular-spain.

insisted that same-sex unions be granted the designation of the word "marriage." Anything else would be akin to treating gay and lesbian couples as second-class citizens. More unconventionally, the Spanish campaign emphasized the idea of gay marriage as redemption for how society had traditionally treated homosexuals by stripping them not only of their rights but also of their dignity. Last but not least, the moral framing promoted gay marriage as a common good intended to make Spain more humane, tolerant, and progressive.

Among the many ways in which the moral framing of the gay marriage campaign helped blunt political backlash while at the same time boosting LGBTQ equality was by ushering in a robust debate about the state of sexual minorities in Spanish society. It proved to be decisive in changing hearts and minds about gay marriage and homosexuality in general. This change is reflected in the public opinion data. By the time gay marriage was legislated, support for gay marriage exceeded a clear majority of Spaniards. In particular, the moral framing found considerable resonance with the general public by tapping into the desire of Spaniards to leave their dark history behind and reimagine their country as a beacon of social liberalism. The moral framing of the campaign also helped build solidarity with other social movements in civil society, including the human rights movement, feminist organizations, and organized labor.

Finally, the moral framing provided a powerful antidote to the bleak and dispiriting messaging about gay marriage coming from the hierarchy of the Spanish Episcopal Conference. Indeed, it served as a very effective counterframing strategy. The main argument by Spain's bishops against gay marriage was that it was family-phobic, a retrograde messaging that proved to be no match for the positive, uplifting, and forward-looking messaging of the pro-gay marriage side. Moreover, the moral arguments made by the gay marriage campaign cast a very harsh light on the Church's moral failures, including its complicity with the Franco regime in repressing homosexuality. It also put the Church in the uncomfortable position of standing against universal principles such as democracy, citizenship, and human rights.

Spain's morally framed gay marriage campaign, including its ambition and idealism, grew out of the country's long and difficult history with homosexuality. Throughout the campaign, gay activists leveraged Spain's repression of homosexuality—going back to the Middle Ages—to make the case for gay marriage as redemption for past transgressions against the gay community. The gay marriage campaign was also firmly rooted in the origins of the Spanish gay liberation movement in the struggle against authoritarianism. Aside from inspiring future generations of gay activists, the long struggle against the Franco dictatorship helped fold gay rights into a broader struggle for democratic citizenship. It also created lasting bonds between the gay rights movement and other groups in civil society, especially human rights organizations. Finally, the inspiring message that gay marriage was a bridge to the future served as a counterpoint to the antiquated views on gender and sexuality inherited from the Francoist dictatorship, a political regime defined by National Catholicism. This ultra-conservative ideology calls for all aspects of life to adhere to the most dogmatic elements of Catholic theology.

Gay Politics before Gay Marriage

Organized gay activism in Spain dates only to 1970, with the organization of the *Movimiento Español de Liberación Homosexual* (MELH), founded in Barcelona by gay rights pioneer Armand de Fluvià.[6] The most remarkable thing about the MELH is that it emerged during Franco's authoritarian regime, one of Western Europe's long-standing dictatorships in the twentieth century. Franco emerged victorious from the Spanish Civil War (1936–1939) by defeating the defenders of the popularly elected Second Republic (1931–1936), Spain's short-lived attempt to live under democracy during the interwar years. Although illegal at the time, the MELH managed to publish the gay monthly journal *AGHOIS*, or *Agrupación Homosexual para la Igualdad Sexual* (Homosexual Group for Sexual Equality), which was printed in France and then shipped to Spain for distribution. According to historian Geoffroy Huard, the circulation of such a publication suggested the strange mixture of tolerance and oppression of homosexuality that marked the late Franco period, especially in Barcelona, historically Spain's most socially progressive city.[7] Around the time of Franco's passing in 1975, which opened the way for a transition to democracy, there were some twenty "exclusively homosexual bars" in Barcelona.[8]

---

[6] For a more extensive look at the history of the Spanish gay rights movement, see Armand de Fluvià, "El Movimiento Homosexual en el Estado Español," in *El homosexual ante la sociedad enferma*, ed. José Ramón Enriquez (Barcelona: Tusquet, 1978); Paul Julian Smith, *Laws of Desire: Questions of Homosexuality in Spanish Writing and Film, 1960–1990* (Clarendon Press, 1992); Richard Cleminson and Francisco Vásquez García, *Los Invisibles: A History of Male Homosexuality in Spain, 1850–1939* (Cardiff: University of Wales Press, 2007); Kerman Calvo, *Pursuing Membership in the Polity: The Spanish Gay and Lesbian Movement in Comparative Perspective, 1970–1997* (doctoral dissertation, Instituto Juan March, Madrid, and University of Essex, 2004); and Geoffroy Huard, *Los Antisociales: Historia de la Homosexualidad en Barcelona y Paris, 1945–1975* (Marciel Pons, 2014).

[7] Author's electronic communication with Mr. Huard (July 28, 2020).

[8] Geoffroy Huard, "Los homosexuales en Barcelona bajo el franquismo: Prostitución, clase y visibilidad entre 1956 y 1980," *Revista d'Historia i de Cultura* 4 (2016): 142.

54 Framing Equality

In 1977, the MELH folded itself into the *Front d'Alliberament Gai de Catalunya* (Gay Liberation Front of Catalonia), or FAGC, also founded by de Fluvià. In keeping with its original Marxist orientation, the FAGC described itself as "a revolutionary force."[9] A FAGC manifesto from 1977 argued, "Our struggle is focused fundamentally toward the formation of a conscience within the working class of our oppression and about our plans to achieve liberation and about the importance of our demands to redefining a future society that is free of class distinctions and that pushes for radical change in all the levels of ordinary life."[10] But it was the longstanding oppression of homosexuality in Spanish history, culture, and law that drove the emergence of Spain's gay liberation movement.

As might be expected, the Inquisition, a medieval institution notorious for burning, stoning, and castrating "sodomites," was a point of reference for Spanish gay liberation activists.[11] Another statement from the FAGC's 1977 manifesto noted, "Until the year 1822, homosexual or sodomites, as they were called then, were, by disposition of the law, burned alive at the stake. The marked confusion that existed then between rights and ethics and crimes and sins persists in the minds of our legislators and jurists, who place the law to the service of their morality and the norms of behavior considered as 'normal,' that is to the service of sexual ideology (machista, sexist and heterosexist) of the dominant classes."[12]

A more immediate concern for gay liberation activists was Franco's persecution of homosexuals. We may never know how many homosexuals perished during the Civil War "since many homosexuals were also left-wing sympathizers," according to Severiano Hernández Vicente of the National Civil War Archive in Salamanca.[13] Still, plenty is known about the rampant homophobia of Franco's nationalist, right-wing crusade. Tellingly, the most famous killing of the Civil War was a known homosexual: the poet and playwright Federico García Lorca, author of such seminal works as *Yerma*, *Blood Wedding*, and *The House of Bernarda Alba*. For years, Franco officials argued that Lorca died a victim of the mayhem of the Civil War. But newly discovered documents reveal that in 1936 Lorca was arrested and taken into custody

---

[9] Kerman Calvo and Gracia Trujillo, "Fighting for Love Rights: Claims and Strategies of the LGBT Movement in Spain," *Sexualities* 14, no. 5 (2011): 566.

[10] Jordi Manel Monferrer Tomás, "La construcción de la protesta en el movimiento gay español: la Ley de Peligrosidad Social (1970) como factor precipitante de la acción colectiva," *Revista Española de Investigaciones Sociológicas* 102 (2003): 191.

[11] Byrne Fone, *Homophobia: A History* (New York: Henry Holt, 2000), 201. According to this source, "In Barcelona, Valencia, and Saragossa, over sixteen hundred persons were prosecuted for sodomy and bestiality between 1540 and 1700. About 20 percent were actually executed."

[12] Monferrer Tomás, "*La construcción de la protesta en el movimiento gay* español," 195.

[13] Author's interview with Mr. Hernández Vicente (Salamanca, August 14, 2024).

by a Francoist militia. Following a forced confession, he was executed and buried in an unmarked grave. He was charged with being "a Socialist and a Freemason, about whom rumors swirled about homosexual and abnormal practices."[14]

According to recent scholarship, after the Civil War ended in 1939 thousands of homosexuals (or suspected homosexuals) were rounded up and sent to institutions designed to treat "sexual perverts."[15] One such place, reported to be a "concentration camp," was the agrarian colony of Tefía, in Fuerteventura, in the Canary Islands. A report by *Público* noted that Tefia prisoners were "tortured and required to perform hard labor as a form of punishment for their sexual orientation."[16] This repression was part of *limpieza*, or cleansing, a policy premised on the view that Spain was infected by the virus of radicalism. Referred to by historian Paul Preston as "the Spanish Holocaust," this policy resulted in the execution of thousands of political dissidents and the imprisonment of many more in concentration and labor camps.[17] The engine behind this sinister policy was psychiatrist Antonio Vallejo Nágera, an official in Franco's army and the architect of the popular theory of the "red gene."[18] It famously contended that there was a link between Marxism and deviancy.[19]

Among the factors that scholars have offered for the Franco regime's overt hostility toward homosexuality is the glorification of masculinity. According to historian Mary Vincent, "Notions of gender were used both explicitly and implicitly in the construction of the Francoist crusade ... ideas of masculinity were imbued with those of militarism."[20] Another factor was Franco's embrace

[14] Ashifa Kassam, "Federico García Lorca Was Killed on Official Orders, Say 1960s Police Files," *The Guardian*, April 23, 2015. Available at https://www.theguardian.com/culture/2015/apr/23/federico-garcia-lorca-spanish-poet-killed-orders-spanish-civil-war.

[15] See, especially, Arturo Arnalte, *Redadas de violetas: la represión de los homosexuales durante el franquismo* (Madrid: Esfera de los Libros, 2003); Lucas Jurado Marín, *Identidad: represión hacia los homosexuales en el franquismo* (La Calle, 2014); and Estefanía Sanz Romero, *Silenciadas: represión de la homosexualidad en el franquismo* (LES Editorial, 2021).

[16] María Serrano Velázquez, "Los campos de concentración que Franco abrió en los 50s para reformar al colectivo homosexual en Canarias," *Público*, November 29, 2019. Available at https://www.publico.es/sociedad/franco-canarias-campos-concentracion-franco-abrio-50-reformar-colectivo-homosexual-canarias.html.

[17] Paul Preston, *The Spanish Holocaust: Inquisition and Extermination in Twentieth Century Spain* (New York: Norton, 2013).

[18] Juan María Terradillos Basoco, "Homofobia y ley penal: la homosexualidad como paradigma de peligrosidad social en el derecho penal español (1933–1995)," *Revista de Estudios Jurídicos y Criminológicos* 1 (2020): 69.

[19] Vallejo Nágera's pseudo-scientific theory became the basis for Franco's repression of homosexuality but also for taking the babies of Republican mothers at the time of their birth. Vallejo Nágera argued that this was the only option for eradicating the red gene that the babies inherited from their radical mothers.

[20] Mary Vincent, "The Martyrs and the Saints: Masculinity and the Construction of the Francoist Crusade," *History Workshop Journal* 47 (Spring 1999): 70–71.

56 Framing Equality

of the ideology of National Catholicism.[21] After gaining control of Spain, Franco developed a transactional relationship with the Catholic Church, which was made official with the concordat that the Church signed with the Vatican in 1953. In exchange for recognizing the regime's legitimacy, Franco restored Catholicism as Spain's official religion. With this designation, the Church was entitled to state subsidies, control of the education system and parts of the welfare state, and a commitment from the Franco regime that all laws had to conform to Catholic doctrine, such as new laws abolishing divorce and criminalizing homosexuality.

Yet another factor was a concern by the psychiatric community with "sexual inverts," which played a prominent role in shaping policy toward homosexuality under Franco.[22] By the 1920s, Spanish psychiatrists, led by Antonio Navarro Fernández, the editor of the journal *Sexualidad* (1925–1928), stigmatized homosexuality across the Spanish-speaking world. The journal highlighted a "kind of social panic" in Spanish society about the visibility and actions of "sexual inverts."[23] Around the same time, Spanish criminologists began to theorize about the phenomenon of *la mala vida*, literally the sinful life and, figuratively, the seedy underworld, which tied homosexuality to criminality.[24] Such views, which were popularized in such studies as José M. Llanas Aguilaniedo's *La mala vida en Madrid* (1901) and Max Bembo's *La mala vida en Barcelona* (1912), led to the criminalization of homosexuality under the Primo de Rivera dictatorship, in power from 1923 to 1930.[25] In 1931, under the Second Republic, homosexuality was decriminalized and re-criminalized again by Franco after 1939.

Whatever the case, during its remarkable longevity, the Franco regime developed a legal framework deemed "one of the most hostile to gay rights in the Western world."[26] Franco's assault on homosexuality began in earnest in 1954, with the revamping of the *Ley de Vagos y Maleantes* (Law of

---

[21] See, especially, Stanley G. Payne, *Spanish Catholicism: An Historical Overview* (Madison, WI: University of Wisconsin Press, 1984).

[22] This is a central theme of Richard Cleminson and Francisco Vásquez García, *Los Invisibles: Una Historia de la Homosexualidad Masculina en España, 1850–1939* (Granada: Comares, 2011).

[23] Richard Cleminson, "The Review of Sexualidad (1925–1928), Social Hygiene, and the Pathologisation of Male Homosexuality," *Journal of Iberian and Latin American Studies* 6, no. 2 (2000): 122.

[24] The concept *La Mala Vida* was imported to Spain, and later to Latin America, from Italy, where it originated as *La Mala Vita*, in the late nineteenth century. See Ricardo Campos, "Pobres, Anormales, y Peligrosos en España (1900–1970): De la Mala Vida a la Ley de la Peligrosidad y Rehabilitación Social," XIII Coloquio Internacional de Geocrítica: En control del espacio y los espacios de control, University of Barcelona, May 5–10, 2014.

[25] For a useful analysis of these works see, Richard Cleminson, "Transnational Discourse on the Mala Vida: Male Homosexuality in Madrid, Buenos Aires and Barcelona," *Journal of Spanish Cultural Studies* 10, no. 4 (2009): 461–483.

[26] Celia Valiente, "An Overview of Research on Gender in Spanish Society," *Gender and Society* 16 (December 2002): 777.

Vagrancy and Thugs). First enacted in 1933, under the Republican period, this law traditionally dealt with drug users, prostitutes, crooks, gamblers, and vagabonds.[27] But the revised law made homosexuality a crime and labeled homosexuals sick, perverted, and a threat to national security. Those convicted under the law were required to spend time in special institutions that provided for isolation from other inmates and to register with local authorities following their release into society. A study based on oral testimony of individuals treated at one of these institutions found that the "re-education measures" employed included "electroshock and aversion therapy."[28] Electroshock consisted of electrical charges at the bottom of the feet, which were favored because burn marks could be covered. Aversion therapy involved forcing the patient "to regurgitate by injecting him with or forcing him to ingest substances that would induce vomiting (apomorphine or emetine) at the same time that he was exposed to homosexual stimuli such as pornographic magazines."[29]

A new phase in the repression of homosexuality began in 1970 with the *Ley de Peligrosidad y Rehabilitación Social*, or Law of Social Menaces and Rehabilitation. This new law called for sentences ranging from three months to five years for those convicted of homosexual activities and for compulsory "reparative treatment."[30] It responded to the unintended consequences of economic liberalization policies implemented by Franco's technocrats in 1959. Economic liberalization, especially the opening of Spain to foreign visitors since the end of the Civil War, brought about more relaxed attitudes toward sex and the emergence of thriving countercultural communities across the Spanish mainland. According to sociologist Oscar Guasch, the development of spaces of leisure and recreation in urban centers such as Madrid, Barcelona, and Valencia created a "sexual market" that promoted and facilitated sexual interaction among males. "Erotic satisfaction took a new face in these spaces: flirting and seduction were sidelined in favour of easy and fast ways of achieving sexual pleasure."[31]

Remarkably, the Franco regime persecuted homosexuals until its very end in 1975. One of the regime's last homosexual victims was a lesbian, identified in court papers only by her initials: MCD. She was arrested in 1974 at

---

[27] On the origins of this law and its legacy, see Basoco, "Homofobia y ley penal: la homosexualidad como paradigma de peligrosidad social en el derecho penal español (1933–1995):" 63–102.

[28] Gema Pérez-Sánchez, *Queer Transitions in Contemporary Spanish Culture: From Franco to La Movida* (Albany: SUNY Press, 2007), 30.

[29] Ibid.

[30] See Monferrer Tomás, "La construcción de la protesta en el movimiento gay español."

[31] Oscar Guasch Andreu, "Social Stereotypes and Homosexualities: The Spanish Case," *Sexualities* 14, no. 5 (2011): 533.

58 Framing Equality

just seventeen years of age. After a trial in which her state-appointed attorney provided no defense and threw her at the mercy of the court, she was sentenced to between four months and three years in prison and to undergo a program of "re-education."[32] Rehabilitation centers for homosexuals, including the best-known one in Huelva, in the southern region of Andalusia, did not close until 1978, one year before Spain decriminalized homosexuality and enacted a new democratic constitution. According to the reporting by the Barcelona newspaper *La Vanguardia*, the Huelva center, which today stands as "a symbol of Francoist repression towards homosexuals," housed male prisoners found guilty of engaging in "public scandal," including "wearing make-up and cross-dressing."[33]

During the democratic transition triggered by Franco's death of natural causes in November 1975, the picture for gay rights was downright bleak. Homosexuals were not covered by the blanket pardon issued by King Juan Carlos I on November 25, 1975, which commuted the sentences of "thousands of ordinary criminals."[34] Homosexuals were also excluded from the amnesty for political prisoners issued by the Spanish Parliament on July 31, 1976. The royal criminal pardon and the political amnesty preceded Spain's 1977 general elections, the country's first free elections in nearly four decades. The exclusion of homosexuals from the pardon and amnesty of the democratic transition prompted gay activists to tell *El País* in 2004 that "we are the forgotten ones of the transition."[35]

Despite the repression of homosexuals that carried over from the Franco dictatorship, gay activists were part of the massive mobilization of the public that forced the authoritarian regime to abandon a plan for "Francoism without Franco," or the continuation of the dictatorship under another dictator.[36] On June 26, 1977, only days after the first general elections of the democratic era, some four thousand people took to the streets of Barcelona carrying banners that read "sexual amnesty" and "we are not dangerous," an apparent reference to those individuals still in prison because of their sexual orientation and to the labeling of homosexuality by the old regime as a

---

[32] Fiona Govan, "Spanish Lesbian to Seek Damages over Franco Persecution," *The Telegraph*, October 24, 2012. Available at https://www.telegraph.co.uk/news/worldnews/europe/spain/9630986/Spanish-lesbian-to-seek-damages-over-Franco-persecution.html.

[33] Irene Barahona, "La antigua cárcel de Huelva, símbolo de represión franquista contra los homosexuales," *La Vanguardia*, July 31, 2020. Available at https://www.lavanguardia.com/vida/20200731/482589550976/la-antigua-carcel-de-huelva-simbolo-represion-franquista-contra-homosexuales.html.

[34] "Spain Announces Clemency Move," *The New York Times*, November 26, 1975. Available at https://www.nytimes.com/1975/11/26/archives/spain-announces-clemency-move.html.

[35] Emilio De Benito Cañizares, "5,000 vidas fichadas," *El País*, December 20, 2004. Available at https://elpais.com/diario/2004/12/20/sociedad/1103497204_850215.html.

[36] On this mobilization see José María Maravall, *Dictatorship and Political Dissent: Workers and Students in Franco's Spain* (London: Routledge, 1978).

threat to society.[37] Such a public sign of defiance by Spain's gay community was a significant affront to what was still a very conservative Catholic society. Recalling the shock of that day for much of Spanish society and public officials on the demonstration's fortieth anniversary, de Fluvia told *El País*, "We were the scandal of Catholic Spain." He added, "In addition to being dangerous, we were the very definition of a child molester. For the medical field, we were mental patients; for the Church, we were the worst sinners; and for society, the worst of the worst. We were the men who had abandoned their virility to become little women."[38]

Spain's first democratic government, headed by the Union of the Democratic Center, a center-right coalition of parties, deferred all policies related to homosexuality to the Catholic Church. This action prompted gay activists to undertake a public relations campaign to undo decades of stigmatization of homosexuality by the Franco regime that also served as a prelude for the campaign to decriminalize homosexuality.[39] A 1975 cover story in the magazine *Guadiana* titled "The Spaniards and Homosexuality" provided a glimpse of how darkly ordinary Spaniards viewed homosexuality at the time of the start of democracy.[40] When asked to answer the question, "Should homosexuality be allowed by society or should it be made to disappear?" three percent thought that it should be allowed, 83 percent thought it should be made to disappear, and 15 percent had no opinion. When asked if they would support a law to prohibit homosexuality, 80 percent agreed. More than 80 percent of Spaniards deemed homosexuals "sick, delinquent, and sinners." The survey was based on 1,363 interviews covering all Spanish provinces.

In 1978, de Fluviá and Jordi Petit, both members of FAGC, went on television and became the first persons in Spain to identify as gay publicly. (They did so on the Catalan television shows *De bat a bat* and *Vostè pregunta*.) Their main intention was to put a face to gay activism and cultivate empathy with the public. They also hoped to entice a nascent independent media to cover the repression of homosexuals under the old regime and to expose the lingering discrimination of homosexuals prevalent in the new democracy. These goals were broadly achieved in scores of stories that appeared in the Spanish media during the 1980s, especially in Catalan newspapers such as

---

[37] Pablo Candel, "El día que Barcelona salió del armario," *El País*, June 30, 2017. Available at https://elpais.com/ccaa/2017/06/28/catalunya/1498647028_431114.html.

[38] Ibid.

[39] This section draws from Jordi Petit, *Vidas del arco iris* (Barcelona and Madrid: Editorial Egales, 2016); and Jordi Petit and Empar Pineda, "El movimiento de liberación de gays y lesbianas durante la transición," in *Una discriminación universal: La homosexualidad durante el franquismo y la transición*, ed. Javier Ugarte Pérez (Madrid: Espasa, 2004).

[40] Jordi Petit, *25 Años Más: Una perspectiva sobre el pasado, presente y futuro del movimiento de gays, lesbianas, bisexuales y transexuales* (Barcelona: Editorial Iracaria, 2003), 17–18.

60 Framing Equality

Tele/Express, Mundo Diario, Correo Catalán, Diario de Barcelona, and *Avui*, as well as in national papers such as *El País* and *El Mundo*.[41]

When it came to petitioning rights, gay activists in the new democracy developed an early reputation for making unrealistic and idealistic demands that, according to sociologist Kerman Calvo, made the activists seem like "utopian creatures."[42] This behavior reflected a trait of Spanish gay rights advocacy that would endure through the gay marriage campaign and beyond: that the emancipation of homosexuals was intrinsically tied to the liberalization of Spain as a whole. Among the demands made by gay activists during the early years of the new democracy were "free abortion, the end of the compulsory military service, free divorce, welfare rights against sexually transmitted diseases, no discrimination against transgender people, the elimination of the age of consent for sexual relations, and finally the reduction of the working day to enjoy a more pleasant sexual life!"[43] When Calvo asked a member of the Homosexual Democratic Movement to justify his idealistic demands, the activist noted, "We were carried away by a kind of revolutionary euphoria that made us work from an endless sense of possibility. Did we really think that all of that could be achieved? I do not know what to say; this was our ideological project, and we had to state and fight for it."[44]

In the new democracy, gay rights activists looked to universal human rights principles rather than domestic laws, like the new Spanish Constitution, as the inspiration for their struggles. In 1978, when calling for the abrogation of the Law of Social Menaces, gay activists argued that the law contravened the European Convention on Human Rights and its stipulation for respect for the dignity of all human life, which Spain was seeking to ratify at the time. The conjoining of gay and human rights encapsulated in this argument put Spanish gay activists in the vanguard of international gay rights activism. It was not until the late 1980s that many international and national LGBT groups "began to use an explicit human rights frame to promote their cause," and it was not until 1998 that major human rights organizations, such as Amnesty International, began to "recognize sexual orientation as a human rights issue."[45]

On December 26, 1978, the Spanish Parliament removed homosexuality from the list of criminal behaviors covered under the Law of Social Menaces. This action cleared the way for the decriminalization of homosexuality

---

[41] Petit, *25 Años Más*, 20.

[42] Calvo, *Pursuing Membership in the Polity*, 180.

[43] Ibid.

[44] Ibid., 180–181.

[45] Kelly Kollman, "Same-Sex Unions: The Globalization of an Idea," *International Studies Quarterly* 51, no. 2 (2007): 338.

and for the legalization of gay rights organizations such as the Barcelona-based *Coordinadora Gay y Lesbiana de Cataluña* (CGL) and the *Colectivo de Gais de Madrid* (COGAM). These groups ushered in a new approach to gay activism in Spain by replacing Marxism and gay liberation with human rights as their main philosophical framework. Making note of this new ideological emphasis, Calvo wrote, "While the homosexual liberation fronts of the late 1970s and early 1980s reasoned along the lines of class struggles, social revolution, and oppression, the CGL (and the string of reformist groups that followed suit) understood its mission as concerned with legal change, equality, human rights and citizenship."[46] Calvo added that CGL and COGAM made "a concerted effort to achieve legal equality through the systemic employment of human rights discourses."[47] These discourses reflected the influence of the *Asociación Pro Derechos Humanos de España* (APDHE), or Spain's Association for Human Rights, created in 1976. The APDHE published the first study about Spanish public opinion on homosexuality.[48] It also collaborated with gay rights organizations in the struggle to decriminalize homosexuality and in the fight against HIV/AIDS.

Also new to the gay activism ushered in by the CGL and COGAM was engaging with the political system. This engagement meant the end of the mobilization tactics of gay liberation veterans. These new groups found a political home within *Izquierda Unida* (IU), an umbrella organization of left-wing and progressive parties assembled in 1987, "located at the far left of the ideological spectrum."[49] Although never a real contender to govern the country—the party has never garnered more than 6 percent of the national vote in a general election—the IU nonetheless significantly shaped progressive politics in Spain. It was "crucial in introducing the most progressive proposals contributing to the emergence of LGBT policy issues on the political stage."[50] It also helped gay rights organizations compensate for serious organizational shortcomings. During the 1980s, the visibility of the Spanish gay movement masked "the fragility of its militancy base, and also considerable organizational weaknesses" that inhibited the "public representations of homosexuality."[51]

---

[46] Calvo, *Pursuing Membership in the Polity*, 307.

[47] Ibid., 144.

[48] Petit, *25 Años Más*, 18.

[49] Irina Stefuruic and Tània Verge, "Small and Divided Parties in a Multi-Level Settings: The Case of Izquierda Unida in Spain," *South European Society & Politics* 13, no. 2 (2008): 156.

[50] Raquel Platero, "Love and the State: Gay Marriage in Spain," *Feminist Legal Studies* 15 (2007): 332.

[51] Oscar Guasch, "Social Stereotypes and Homosexualities: The Spanish Case," *Sexualities* 14, no. 5 (2011): 534.

62 Framing Equality

Among the factors driving a new approach by gay rights organizations like CGL and COGAM was the HIV/AIDS epidemic, which hit Spain especially hard.[52] Spain's first-ever AIDS case was diagnosed in 1981, in Barcelona, only a few months after other European and US cities reported their first cases. By the 1990s, Spain had the third-highest number of HIV infections in all of Western Europe, after Switzerland and France. Among the factors fueling HIV/AIDS in Spain was a massive heroin epidemic, which explains why, for much of the AIDS epidemic in Spain, drug addicts drove the number of people infected with the AIDS virus. Given Spain's history of repression of homosexuality, there was also widespread distrust among homosexuals in what the government was saying about AIDS. According to Calvo, homosexuals in Spain found "frightening similarities between the mainstream discourse on AIDS and past strategies of social regulation that targeted the homosexual population."[53]

As in other countries, HIV/AIDS unleashed a wave of discrimination against gay people fueled by a tendency among conservatives to blame the epidemic on the "gay lifestyle." "AIDS is a violent backlash by nature, a payback for the sexual revolution, of gay pride, strident pornography in the media, and the tolerance of soft drugs," wrote a columnist in 1990 in *La Vanguardia*.[54] Such attitudes prompted gay activists to pressure the government to take action to remedy this new wave of anti-gay discrimination. These efforts began to bear fruit in 1995 when the Socialist administration of Felipe González reformed the penal code. The reformation banned anti-gay discrimination in Spanish law and made violence against LGBT people a hate crime. But there were limits to González's support of gay rights. In particular, his party (the PSOE) balked at a proposal for a national civil unions law that would cover same-sex couples. PSOE leaders were unwilling to "engage with a divisive issue."[55]

Gay activists were more successful in advancing same-sex civil unions at the regional level. This effort was aided by the decentralization of the state, which was introduced with the creation of seventeen "autonomous" communities, each with ample jurisdiction over education, health, and social welfare, at the time of the transition to democracy in 1977.[56] In 1998, Catalonia became

---

[52] See, especially, Jesús M. de Miguel Rodríguez, "El problema social del SIDA en España," *Revista Española de Investigaciones Sociológicas* 53 (1991): 75 105.

[53] Calvo, *Pursuing Membership in the Polity*, 226.

[54] "El SIDA," *La Vanguardia*, August 29, 1990.

[55] Calvo and Gracia Trujillo, "Fighting for Love Rights: Claims and Strategies of the LGBT Movement," 574.

[56] José Ignacio Pichardo Galán, "Same-Sex Couples in Spain: Historical, Contextual, and Symbolic Factors," in *Same-Sex Partnerships & Homosexual Marriages: A Focus on Cross-National Differentials*, eds. Marie Digoix and Patrick Festy (Paris: INED, 2004), 162.

the first Spanish region to enact a civil unions law. Catalonia's Law of Stable Couples granted most of the rights of marriage to gay couples, save for adoption. It served as a template for other regions. By 2005, when same-sex marriage became legal nationwide, the majority of the autonomous communities (twelve out of seventeen or some 80 percent of the Spanish population) had legalized some form of same-sex civil union, with varying degrees of rights. Five regions (Navarre, the Basque Country, Aragón, Catalonia, and Cantabria) had also legalized adoptions by same-sex couples.

Demands for gay marriage began in earnest in 1998 when gay activists announced a campaign for *matrimonio igualitario* (egalitarian marriage). At the helm of the campaign was the Spanish Federation of LGBT Organizations, or FELGBT, a group formed in 1992 as Spain's first nationwide gay rights organization. As part of Madrid's 1998 gay pride parade, the FELGBT organized a demonstration demanding "civil marriage rights for gay and lesbian couples," with similar demonstrations held in Barcelona, Seville, and Valencia.[57] By 2002, gay marriage had become the FELGBT's primary policy objective. Marriage equality was also in keeping with the idealism that had marked gay rights activism in Spain since its inception in the mid-1970s. For the most part, gay marriage activists operated under the mantra that they should demand what they thought they deserved rather than what they believed they could get.

Unquestionably, the pursuit of gay marriage was outright quixotic—and not just because in 1998 the Spanish government was firmly in conservative hands. In the late 1990s, no country anywhere in the world allowed same-sex couples to marry. The first two countries that got gay marriage legalized ahead of Spain—the Netherlands and Belgium—were small countries well known for their socially progressive policies. Spain, by contrast, was a large, overwhelmingly Catholic nation with a long history of religious involvement in politics, especially in matters concerning homosexuality. Moreover, legalizing gay marriage through the courts was not a realistic option in Spain. Under the new constitution enacted in 1978, the Spanish judiciary continued to display a strong conservative bent, a development related to the very slow pace of the modernization of the judicial system. As recently as 1994, the Constitutional Tribunal, Spain's highest court for solving constitutional controversies, ruled that marriage was "a naturally heterosexual institution."[58]

---

[57] Armando G. Tejeda, "Miles de homosexuales se manifiestan en España por el derecho al matrimonio civil," *El País*, June 29, 1998. Available at https://elpais.com/diario/1998/06/28/sociedad/898984805_850215.html.

[58] Erika Rickard, "Spain Sprint to Marriage Equality," *The Gay and Lesbian Review*, September/October 2012. Available at https://glreview.org/article/spains-sprint-to-marriage-equality/.

64 Framing Equality

More importantly, support for gay marriage among ordinary Spaniards was tenuous at best. In the late 1990s, no organization was polling Spaniards on the issue of gay marriage, but the polling data of the time on public attitudes toward homosexuality were very revealing. In 1992, according to the Center for Sociological Investigations, or CIS, only 17 percent of Spaniards deemed homosexual relationships acceptable, 47 percent unacceptable, and 30 percent indifferent.[59] These impressions help explain why, for much of the 1990s, support for gay marriage among left-wing political parties was lukewarm at best. Indeed, in making gay marriage its chief priority, the FELGBT was disregarding the advice of the left-wing establishment. According to FELGBT leaders, "When we began to demand marriage, PSOE and IU leaders were advising us to put marriage on hold and instead devote our energies to a national same-sex civil unions law or legislation banning anti-gay discrimination."[60]

There were also internal challenges to overcome within the gay activist community. Older groups, such as the CGL and COGAM, were ambivalent about marriage. Activists at these older and more established organizations were skeptical that Spain was ready for gay marriage. They also feared an intense backlash from the Catholic hierarchy, given that in the late 1990s, no Roman Catholic country had yet undertaken any efforts to legalize gay marriage.[61] Spain's feminist-lesbian community presented another challenge. Traditionally, this community had been very hostile to the institution of marriage. In an interview for this book, gender scholar Celia Valiente pointed out that for Spanish lesbian feminists, marriage was the quintessential patriarchal institution. Still, marriage was also tainted in the minds of many lesbian feminists by its association with the old regime. "Under the Franco regime, civil marriage did not exist, and Catholic marriage was mandatory."[62]

Addressing how Spanish gay activists achieved consensus on marriage, Beatriz Gimeno, the lesbian feminist who, as FELGBT president, led the fight for gay marriage, noted in an interview for this book that "we had to confront the part of the gay rights movement that thought that Spain was not ready for same-sex marriage, another part that contended that marriage was a conservative demand and yet another part that thought that civil unions were preferable to marriage." She added that the last group was composed primarily of older homosexual men. "But we prevailed by stressing that we

---

[59] "Barómetro de Junio 2004," Centro de Investigaciones Sociológicas, Madrid. Available at http://www.cis.es/cis/opencm/ES/1_encuestas/estudios/ver.jsp?estudio=3994.

[60] Author's interview with FELGBT President Jesús Generelo (Madrid, June 11, 2018).

[61] Ibid.

[62] Author's electronic communication with Ms. Valiente (October 31, 2018).

were not judging marriage as an institution; instead, we thought of it as an option that is available to heterosexuals and that, as such, it should be available to us as well—that is what equality is all about."[63] She added that the FELGBT was born "precisely to unify the gay community around the idea of marriage equality. That was our foremost objective." Furthermore, Gimeno noted that the new organization operated under the theory that if the gay community had different views on gay marriage, the state would favor the option that was closest to its interests. "For that reason, we thought it was important that the gay movement was united in its demand for marriage. We had other differences, but we were united on the issue of marriage."

In the end, as noted by Jesús Generelo, who presided over the FELBGT from 2015 to 2018, opposition to gay marriage within the gay community was more tactical than ideological.[64] He added that "although there were some gay rights organizations that initially doubted the feasibility of a gay marriage campaign in Spain, there was consensus among all the national and regional gay rights associations on gay marriage; the only debate was whether to go all out for marriage or to work towards it in incremental steps. In the end, we went all in." Unity among gay activists and organizations also helped to get the gay community ready to battle the conservative opposition to gay marriage by avoiding leaving any room within the gay community for the opposition to exploit. According to Generelo, "The internal consensus about gay marriage within the community was critical for preventing the opposition from dividing and conquering the gay community by saying this group wants marriage, but this other one is happy with civil unions."

Generelo added that the biggest concern among gay marriage activists was the dearth of foreign examples for Spanish gay rights activists to emulate. "When we targeted gay marriage as a priority, there were no international models for how to conceive, organize, and frame a marriage equality campaign, especially in a country like Spain, a Catholic nation with a long history of homophobia. We also had no significant financial means to do anything like what was being done in the United States, such as an elaborate public relations campaign and extensive polling operations to test how the public would respond to different messages about gay marriage." But Generelo noted that from its inception the marriage equality campaign was clear about one thing: the desire "to go beyond a legal discourse about rights when talking about marriage and into the realm of expanding citizenship." This desire prompted the realization that any gay marriage campaign had to involve the

---

[63] Author's electronic communication with Ms. Gimeno (September 5, 2017).
[64] This and other quotes from this section come from the author's interview with Mr. Generelo (Madrid, June 11, 2018).

66 Framing Equality

reimagining of marriage, an institution that was critical to Franco's control of Spanish society, especially women.[65]

Framing the Case for Gay Marriage

Going beyond a rights discourse essentially meant framing gay marriage as a moral issue rather than a legal one. To be sure, this framing did not grow out of some well-laid-out strategy. Instead, it developed intuitively. That said, in the years that the gay marriage campaign was active—1998 through 2005— gay activists were very consistent in upholding three guiding principles. The primary one was to cast the campaign as a crusade for full citizenship. This meant emphasizing the ethical components of citizenship, especially respect and dignity. This objective was conveyed in the slogan chosen to anchor the campaign: *Los mismos derechos con los mismos nombres* (the same rights with the same names). That slogan, which in time would become popular across the Spanish-speaking world, was intended to drive a key messaging point of the gay marriage campaign: the complete moral equivalence between homosexual and heterosexual relationships in the eyes of the state and society. According to Generelo, "The slogan emphasized that homosexual unions are deserving of the same rights as heterosexual couples, including having their relationships recognized with the word marriage."

Echoing Generelo's idealism, Gimeno noted, "For us, accepting a law that was not equal and that did not use the term marriage was akin to Apartheid. We always knew that accepting that inequality was surrendering to something immoral. We were as concerned with the symbolism of marriage as we were about marriage itself. Real rights are not real unless they have the same name, connotations, and associations across society."[66] She recalled that during the conservative administration of José María Aznar (1996–2004), he offered to support same-sex unions as long as the name marriage and adoption were not part of the deal. Her organization summarily dismissed this offer. "I was in the Moncloa Palace speaking with Aznar. The very moment he made the

---

[65] Under the Franco regime two types of marriages were created: "ecclesiastical marriage," which was mandatory if the spouses were Catholic, which was the case for the vast majority of Spaniards, and "civil marriage," which was intended for non-Catholic spouses. For much of the life of the regime, women were basically treated as property of their husbands. The age of maturity for women was set at 21, and 25 if they were single and/or in a convent. Many professions, like diplomacy and stock-trading, were off-limits to women, as was entry into some professional and vocational schools. Women were not allowed to have their own checking account and/or to have a drivers' permit without permission from their husbands. Many of these provisions were not lifted until after a new Constitution in 1978 recognized gender parity and divorce was legalized in 1981. See Aurora Morcillo, *True Catholic Womanhood: Gender Ideology in Franco's Spain* (Northern Illinois University Press, 2008).

[66] Author's electronic communication with Ms. Gimeno (September 4, 2017).

Spain **67**

proposal, we turned him down. We had little time to consider the matter, but our struggle was for complete equality. We thought that if we accepted the proposal, it would be years before we could advance complete equality."

Writing in her memoirs about the centrality of citizenship in the gay marriage campaign, a campaign she characterized as "an ethical journey," Gimeno noted that: "We had to change the way people thought about marriage. To separate it from the Church, traditional rites, and family celebrations, and to view it for what it is: a matter of citizenship." She added that "because citizenship has historically been restricted to heterosexual males, citizenship has a special, symbolic meaning for excluded and marginalized groups. So we built a discourse that seeks to replace old principles with the ethical and enlightened principles that constitute the moral spine of the modern concept of democracy: equality, citizenship, and human rights."[67]

Generelo and Gimeno took their cues from Pedro Zerolo, the FELGBT's first president and the PSOE's federal secretary for social movements. Recognized as the architect of the Spanish marriage equality campaign, Zerolo imbued the gay marriage campaign with a highly ethical understanding of citizenship. According to Miquel A. Fernández, Zerolo's former chief of staff and today the executive director of the Pedro Zerolo Foundation, Zerolo's gay marriage advocacy was rooted "in his belief in the dignity of all individuals, regardless of their station in life."[68] He added that Zerolo believed that "how a society treats its most vulnerable, including women, homosexuals, and immigrants, reflects its humanity. He wistfully spoke of Spain as a country that leaves no one behind." Fernández attributed this idealistic thinking to Zerolo's traumatic upbringing. He was born in Carácas, Venezuela, where his father had fled to escape the political repression of the Franco regime and migrated to Spain as a child. After finishing law school, Zerolo immersed himself in Madrid's budding gay rights movement.

Zerolo conceived the lofty goal of making the gay marriage campaign an act of redemption for Spain's historical, moral failures. The conception of gay marriage as redemption would become the second guiding principle of the campaign. In his testimony to Congress on the final vote on the gay marriage bill, which required Congress to lift a veto imposed by the Senate, Zerolo implored the legislators to "make history" by passing a law that promised "equality, freedom, justice, dignity, pluralism, tolerance, solidarity; in other words, full citizenship."[69] Recalling that vote for *El País* before his death of

[67] Beatriz Gimeno, "El matrimonio entre personas del mismo sexo: un recorrido ético y reinvindicativo," November 30, 2008, FALGBT archives, Madrid, consulted June 2018.
[68] Author's online interview with Mr. Fernández (Madrid, July 29, 2024).
[69] Jordi Ortiz Gisbert, *Pedro Zerolo: Una lucha por la igualdad* (Editorial Luhu, 2018), 132.

pancreatic cancer at age 54 in 2015, Zerolo noted, "It was important for Spain to arrive on time for this date with history. We were not the first country to abolish slavery or to recognize the right of women to vote. But Spain was the first country to recognize the dignity of homosexuals by drawing no distinctions between homosexual and heterosexual marriage. This is something to be proud of."[70]

Echoing Zerolo, Gimeno pointed to Spain's long and dark history with homosexuality as the underlying reason for the moral framing of the marriage equality campaign. "It was important that Spain, which had led the world in oppressing homosexuals with the Inquisition, now lead the world in advancing equality, freedom, and justice for homosexuals." This aspiration, she argued, reflected the kind of society that Spain had evolved into after decades of living under Francoism. "Spain endured a forty-year dictatorship and emerged from that dictatorship with enormous desires for freedom, human rights, and equality. This explains why, within a few short years, we managed to get ahead of other countries moving at a slower speed."

The notion of gay marriage as redemption for past wrongs was both a reflection as well as a contributing agent of the changing climate regarding the memory of the Franco regime. For decades after Franco's death in 1975, Spanish politics operated under the Pact of Forgetting, or Pact of Silence. Negotiated during the transition to democracy by the leading political parties of the era, this political agreement granted complete amnesty to the members of the old regime in order not to compromise the chances of a successful transition to democracy.[71] This meant that in Spain, in contrast to many other countries that have undergone a democratic transition in recent decades, there was no truth commission to document the abuses of the old regime or political prosecutions of the former oppressors. But by the early 2000s, the consensus to forget was beginning to crack with the rise of the Association for the Recovery of Historical Memory (or ARMH in Spanish), a human rights organization founded by journalist Emilio Silva in 2000 to excavate and identify the remains of the thousands of bodies dumped and buried in mass graves during the Civil War. Among its achievements is the 2007 Law of Historical Memory. It declared Franco's regime illegitimate, offered financial compensation and moral rehabilitation to those victimized by Franco, including

---

[70] Juan Cruz, "La república transmite los mejores valores ciudadanos," *El País*, July 4, 2014. Available at https://elpais.com/sociedad/2014/07/04/actualidad/1404472882_800397.html.

[71] See Paloma Aguilar, *Memoria y olvido de la Guerra Civil Española* (Madrid: Editorial Alianza, 1996); Omar G. Encarnación, *Democracy without Justice in Spain: The Politics of Forgetting* (Philadelphia: University of Pennsylvania Press, 2014); and Omar G. Encarnación, "Exhuming the Violent Past in Spain," *Human Rights Quarterly* 45, no. 1 (February 2023): 161-166.

LGBTQ people, and removed from public view monuments honoring the Franco regime.

Memory activists like the ARMH awakened the memory of some of the worst human rights abuses of the Francoist period. The most infamous of these abuses concern the vast network of baby trafficking enabled by public officials, doctors, nuns, and priests. It is believed to be responsible for the theft of as many as three hundred thousand babies from mothers deemed by public authorities to be unfit to raise their children because of their political beliefs.[72] The babies were subsequently given to conservative families to raise. This sinister plot began at the end of the Civil War and persisted through the 1980s. Although the first accusations that infants were being sold under Franco came as early as the 1980s, it was not until the early 2000s that those demanding justice began to be taken seriously as part of a national reckoning with the past that led to the 2007 Law of Historical Memory.

As might be expected, the effort to recover the memory of the abuses of the Franco dictatorship eventually grew to incorporate the repression of the homosexual community. Books such as Arturo Arnalte's *Redadas de violetas: la represión de los homosexuales durante el franquismo* (*Violet Raids: The Repression of Homosexuals under Franco*), published in 2003, introduced Spaniards to a history that was unknown to many of them. It offered graphic depictions of the inhumane treatment of homosexual prisoners, including young people, at the hands of Catholic priests. The shocking revelations contained in the book prompted extensive media coverage at the same time that the debate about gay marriage was intensifying in the Spanish Parliament and the culture at large. In 2004, *El País* investigated the Francoist repression of the homosexual community. The paper's key finding was that some five thousand people were detained and arrested in Franco's Spain for "LGBT actions and behaviors."[73] But the paper cautioned that this estimate was conservative since police records are dispersed across Spain.

Gay marriage activists wasted no time in incorporating the repression of homosexuals under the Franco regime as part of the narrative for why Spain needed to legalize gay marriage. The FELGBT championed the work of the Association of Former Social Prisoners, an organization officially formed in 2004 by gay rights activist Antoni Ruiz. In 1976, at age seventeen, Ruiz was imprisoned on homosexual charges at Valencia's Modelo Prison, where he

---

[72] In recent years, this story has been covered extensively by the Spanish and foreign media. See, for instance, Nicholas Casey, "Taken under Fascism, Spain's Stolen Babies Are Learning the Truth," *The New York Times*, September 27, 2022. Available at https://www.nytimes.com/2022/09/27/magazine/spain-stolen-babies.html.

[73] Cañizares, "5,000 vidas fichadas."

was sexually assaulted and tortured. He also spent time at Carabanchel, a prison built by political prisoners after the Civil War notorious for its abuse of gay males.[74] In an interview for this book, Ruiz recalled the origins of his activism, which coincided with launching the struggle for gay marriage. He credited Zerolo, whom Ruiz called "a mentor and a staunch supporter," with recognizing that "the suffering of Franco's social prisoners was the same as that of political prisoners."[75] Ruiz's first victory came in 2001, when the Spanish Parliament "pledged to wipe clean the criminal records of gays locked up by the former dictator" and "to look for ways to compensate them for the years of torture and imprisonment." Zerolo greeted the news by noting that "the rehabilitation of former gay prisoners is part of the process for equality for the LGBT community, including same-sex marriage and adoption."[76]

Zapatero's election as PSOE secretary general in 2000 gave the FELGBT's gay marriage campaign political viability. Less apparent is that Zapatero also significantly boosted the campaign's moral framing. In particular, Zapatero became the most compelling messenger of the view of gay marriage as a common good intended to make Spain a better country. This would be the third and final guiding principle of the moral framing of the campaign. In 2000, Zapatero was tasked with the unenviable job of restoring the political fortunes of Spanish socialism. By then, the PSOE had lost two consecutive general elections to its nemesis, the conservative People's Party. The party's performance in the 2000 general elections was its worst since the restoration of democracy in 1977. The PP secured an absolute majority of seats in the Congress of Deputies and increased its margin of victory over the PSOE by some 2.5 million votes.

At the center of Zapatero's plan for reinvigorating the PSOE was incorporating progressive movements into the party's fold. Over the years, progressives had grown disenchanted with the PSOE partly because of the corruption that drove the party from power in 1996. The alliance of gay activists and Zapatero was a significant step for both sides. The PSOE had a checkered gay rights history. As noted previously, during the 1990s, when the party was in power, it balked at enacting a national civil unions law that would be available to same-sex couples for fear of antagonizing the Catholic Church. Becoming a gay marriage crusader was not a role Zapatero was destined to play either. It took considerable persuasion on the part of gay activists to make Zapatero a gay marriage supporter. In 2015, on the occasion of Zerolo's passing, Zapatero

[74] Author's interview with Mr. Ruiz (Barcelona, August 23, 2019).
[75] Ibid.
[76] Gilles Tremlett, "Gays Persecuted by Franco Lose Criminal Status at Last," *The Guardian*, December 13, 2001. Available at https://www.theguardian.com/world/2001/dec/13/gayrights.gilestremlett.

admitted this much. "Zerolo convinced me to make the law of homosexual marriage. He was a free man who made the rest of us freer."[77]

In Zapatero, gay marriage activists found more than a political ally. They also found a tireless crusader. Gay marriage became the most controversial component of Citizen Socialism, a set of social policies that Zapatero incorporated into his 2004 electoral platform intended to eradicate all forms of inequality in Spanish society.[78] Alongside gay marriage, Citizen Socialism called for gender parity in the workplace, a strict divide between church and state by ending compulsory religious classes in public schools, a path to citizenship for undocumented workers, improving living conditions for the Roma population, liberalizing divorce and abortion laws, and reckoning with the human rights atrocities of the Civil War and the Franco dictatorship. This broad social agenda was inspired by the political ethicist Philip Pettit and his notion of "Civic Republicanism," which emphasizes the interconnection of individual freedom and civic participation with promoting the common good.[79] Civic Republicanism also emphasizes using all the resources available to the state to end discrimination and domination. Zapatero was so taken with Pettit's ideas that he brought him into his administration as a formal advisor. Pettit was also charged with grading Zapatero's record of implementing his agenda.

Ethical considerations aside, Citizen Socialism was also a bold political play by Zapatero. In 2004, Zapatero needed policies to make the PSOE stand out, as he had no significant disagreements on economic issues with the opposition. As noted by Calvo, "the PSOE's strategists considered that the introduction of policy issues that could unambiguously distinguish their party from the ruling PP was the only way to regain power at the national level."[80] Suddenly, gay activists went from being shunned by the Socialist establishment to being lured into the party's inner sanctum in the hopes of re-energizing the Socialist brand among disenchanted liberals, young people, and voters with serious concerns about discrimination in Spanish society. This luring translated into a commitment by the PSOE grandees to put gay marriage at the forefront of the party's policy priorities.

[77] "Zapatero: 'Quien me convenció para hacer la ley del matrimonio homosexual fué Pedro Zerolo,'" *El Diario*, September 6, 2015. Available at https://www.eldiario.es/rastreador/Zapatero-matrimonio-homosexual-Pedro-Zerolo_6_396920312.html.

[78] Bonnie Field, ed., *Spain's "Second Transition"?: The Socialist Government of José Luis Rodríguez Zapatero* (New York: Routledge, 2013).

[79] José Luis Martí and Philip Pettit, *A Political Philosophy in Public Life: Civic Republicanism in Zapatero's Spain* (Princeton: Princeton University Press, 2010).

[80] Kerman Calvo, "Sacrifices That Pay: Polity Membership, Political Opportunities and the Recognition of Same-Sex Marriage in Spain," *South European Society & Politics* 12, no. 3 (September 2007): 304.

72 Framing Equality

Indeed, the boldness (some might say the radicalism) of Citizen Socialism led some to suspect that Zapatero did not believe that he could win the 2004 elections—that the main objective of Citizen Socialism was simply to reboot the Socialist brand.[81] Whatever the case, Zapatero's political fortunes dramatically increased just days before the elections with the bombing of a commuter train at Madrid's Atocha Station by radical Islamic terrorists in retaliation for the Aznar administration's support of the US invasion of Iraq, including sending Spanish soldiers to Iraq. Almost two hundred people perished in the attack, and some eighteen hundred were injured, making the attack the single worst act of terrorism on Western European soil since World War II. In the days following the attack, the PP did itself tremendous damage by putting the blame for the attacks on Basque separatists and then concealing the evidence that linked the terrorist attack to Islamic terrorists. This botched response to the attack exposed the government to criticism from across the political spectrum. It also caused a rush of voters to the polls, especially those who planned to skip the elections, giving Zapatero an unexpected but convincing victory. It also earned Zapatero the moniker of "the accidental prime minister."[82]

The gay marriage bill was among the first the new administration sent to the Congress of Deputies. In support of the bill, gay activists launched a significant public relations effort. According to Generelo, "We aimed for nothing short of *ganar la calle* (winning the street)," an objective borne from the conviction that the public would welcome a radical reimagining of the institution of marriage. He noted that to woo politicians, the media, and the general public, the marriage equality campaign emphasized how gay marriage would serve as a vehicle for burying Spain's image as an ultra-conservative society once and for all and for reimagining Spain as a beacon of progressivism, human rights, and individual liberty. These modernizing messages, Generelo added, were in keeping with the origins of the Spanish gay liberation movement in the fight against Francoism and the traditional role of the Church in dictating social norms. He pointed to how human rights arguments— especially the notion that the free exercise of sexuality is a fundamental human right—had been pivotal to the creation of the gay rights movement in the post-transition era and the decriminalization of homosexuality in 1979.

On June 30, 2005, gay marriage was legalized by the Congress of Deputies by adding a new paragraph to Article 44 of the Civil Code stating that "marriage shall have the same requirements and responsibilities regardless of

---

[81] See, especially, Omar G. Encarnación, "Spain's New Left Turn: Society-Driven or Party-Instigated," *South European Society and Politics* 14, no. 4 (2010): 399–415.

[82] Victoria Burnett, "Zapatero: Spain's Bold Liberal," *The New York Times*, March 10, 2008. Available at https://www.nytimes.com/2008/03/10/world/europe/10zapatero-web.html.

whether the spouses are of the same or of different genders." That simple sentence, according to Juan Fernando López, Zapatero's first justice minister, "signaled the first time that Spain made was in the vanguard of social rights in the European Union."[83] The law (Congress of Deputies Law 13/2005) also replaced the words *marido y mujer* (husband and wife) for the gender-neutral words *cónyuges* (spouses) and the words *padre y madre* (father and mother) for *progenitores* (parents) in the Civil Code. The simplicity of the alteration guaranteed that all the rights, benefits, and responsibilities of marriage were extended to gays and lesbians, such as adoption, reproduction, inheritance, and nationality, from the minute the law became official. "Never in our recent history has such a small legislative change provoked such strong social changes," noted a document from the FELGBT. Curiously, the law did not include a conscientious objection. From the start, the Zapatero government rejected such an objection, noting that its inclusion in the law would imply that homosexual marriages were anything less than equal to heterosexual marriage.

Despite opposition from the Catholic Church, the final vote in the Congress of Deputies was a surprisingly comfortable win for the Zapatero government: 187 to 147, with four abstentions. The Senate vetoed the bill a week earlier, but the Congress of Deputies lifted that veto. Support for the measure came from all the parliamentary groups—the PSOE, the Basque Nationalist Party, the Republican Left of Catalonia, the Canarian Coalition, United Left, and the Mixed Group (two deputies from Convergencia—a center-right party from Catalonia, now defunct—and one from the PP).[84]

The vote in Congress was accompanied by a robust debate about the role of sexual minorities in Spanish society provoked, in no small measure, by the moral arguments raised by the gay marriage campaign. In the months leading to the parliamentary debate, all the major groups in civil society weighed in on the gay marriage bill in reports submitted to Congress, through their allies, by availing themselves of the media, and, especially, by mobilizing the general public in big demonstrations in favor and against gay marriage. These groups included gay rights activists and their allies, the Spanish Episcopal Conference, Protestant and Jewish groups, and the nation's leading trade unions. Even the Royal Spanish Academy—the organization that polices usage of the Spanish language—had its say, opining that it saw no problem whatsoever

---

[83] Álvaro Rigal, "10 Años de Nuevas Familias," El Confidencial.com. Available at https://datos.elconfidencial.com/matrimonio-homosexual4/.

[84] "El Congreso aprueba la ley del matrimonio gay," *El País*, June 30, 2005. Available at https://elpais.com/sociedad/2005/06/30/actualidad/1120082402_850215.html.

74 Framing Equality

in employing the word marriage in the context of same-sex couples.[85] There was also a private side to the debate about homosexuality. In a way, this debate was more important than the gay marriage law in changing public perceptions about gay marriage and gay people in general. It took place in bars, homes, churches, and work areas, often prompted by people coming out of the closet to their friends, neighbors, and relatives.

By far, the most compelling and commanding voice in the debate over gay marriage was that of Prime Minister Zapatero. He did not simply offer support for gay marriage by incorporating it into his political agenda; he also used the bully pulpit to promote the argument that the exclusion of gays and lesbians from the institution of marriage was a great injustice in need of redressing. It certainly helped in framing gay marriage in moral terms that when Zapatero embraced the issue, it was not particularly popular among Spaniards. That immunized Zapatero against the charge that he was pandering to public opinion or doing what was politically convenient, expedient, and popular. On the contrary, in their analysis of Zapatero's public policies, José Luis Marti and Philip Pettit noted that Zapatero's embrace of gay marriage was a bold act of political courage. At the time, gay marriage was "a very controversial initiative," and he chose to put the issue front and center in his election campaign and "in the face of very strong and united criticism. The Catholic Church, the whole Right, and even part of his party on the Left were fiercely opposed to it." Moreover, they added, "Almost everybody, including some of those on the Left who in principle favored the measure, questioned the urgency of such a divisive issue. But Zapatero went ahead with it, presenting the initiative as a means of enlarging rights, protecting freedom equally for all, and defending human dignity."[86]

On April 15, 2004, Zapatero made history by becoming the first world leader to refer to marriage equality during his swearing-in ceremony. In his inaugural speech, he spoke about gay marriage in ways that few heterosexual politicians—and much less a head of government—had before: with unusual moral clarity. "The time has come to end, once and for all, the intolerable discrimination that many Spaniards still suffer for the sole reason of their sexual orientation. I will say it as clearly as I can: homosexuals and transsexuals deserve the right as heterosexuals to live their lives as they see fit." He added, "We will modify the Civil Code to acknowledge their right to marriage and all that it entails in connection to inheritance, labor rights and protection,

---

[85] "El Congreso aprueba el matrimonio entre personas del mismo sexo," *El Mundo*, April 22, 20005. Available at https://www.elmundo.es/elmundo/2005/04/21/espana/1114087944.html.

[86] Martí and Pettit, *A Political Philosophy in Public Life*, 21.

and social security."[87] Once in office, the gay marriage bill was one of the first introduced in parliament by the Zapatero administration.

Zapatero also became the face of the gay marriage campaign and the primary spokesperson for the campaign's moral themes. In 2005, he conducted a media blitz on behalf of the campaign, including a cover story in the gay magazine *Zero* with the headline "A Better Country." He argued that gay marriage "will benefit everyone and make Spain an example of equality, respect, tolerance, and modernity . . . it does so by extending dignity to those who have not been treated justly for many years."[88] His administration also made it clear that gay marriage would be a milestone for Spain. In 2015, in an interview with *El País*, María Teresa Fernández de la Vega, spokesperson and vice president of the government, noted that gay marriage law was "an injection of self-esteem" intended "to situate Spain in a position of pioneer. It was not enough that Spain be among the leaders, we had to be ahead of the pack, and that's why we insisted on complete equality across the board, including gay adoption."[89]

On the day of the final vote on the gay marriage bill in the Congress of Deputies, Zapatero made a surprise visit to deliver a speech that brought together the overarching moral themes of the gay marriage campaign, especially the point that marriage equality was something that was needed as much by a small minority of Spaniards (the gay community) as it was for Spain as a whole. "They are indeed only a minority, but their triumph is everyone's triumph. It is also the triumph of those who oppose this law, even though they do not know this yet: because it is the triumph of liberty. Their victory makes all of us (even those who oppose the law) better people, and it makes our society better." The speech also dwelled on the idea of gay marriage as an extension of democratic citizenship and dignity to the gay community and a recognition of the oppression and injustices of the past.[90]

> We are not legislating, honorable members, for people far away and unknown by us. We are enlarging the opportunity for happiness for our neighbors, our co-workers, our friends, and our families. At the same time, we are making a

---

[87] José Luís Rodríguez Zapatero, "Discurso de Investidura del Candidato a la Presidencia del Gobierno," PSOE, Oficina de Prensa Federal. Available at https://e00-elmundo.uecdn.es/documentos/2004/04/15/discurso.pdf; accessed on March 8, 2019.

[88] "Zapatero asegura en la revista Zero que el matrimonio entre parejas gay beneficiará a toda la sociedad," *El Mundo*, June 28, 2005. Available at https://www.elmundo.es/elmundo/2005/06/27/comunicacion/1119870906.html.

[89] Emilio De Benito, "La ley fué una inyección de autoestima para nosotros," *El País*, June 30, 2015. Available at https://elpais.com/politica/2015/06/23/actualidad/1435061576_853715.html.

[90] A translated version of Zapatero's speech is available from the Gay Liberation Network at http://www.gayliberation.net/opinion/2005/1220zapatero.html.

76 Framing Equality

more decent society, because a decent society does not humiliate its members. Today Spanish society gives its answer to a group of people who for years have been humiliated, whose rights have been ignored, and whose dignity has been offended. Today, Spanish society gives back the respect they deserve, acknowledges their rights, restores their dignity, affirms their identity, and restores their liberty.[91]

Containing the Conservative Backlash

Already up in arms about the Zapatero administration's other social reforms—such as fast-track divorce and the relaxation of abortion—the Spanish Catholic Church invested significant resources in opposing same-sex marriage. As noted by Susana Aguilar, this behavior stood in contrast to that of other Western European churches that have "refrained from belligerently entering into politics." She added, "The church in Spain is one of the few European religious institutions that have opted for an open confrontational strategy when confronted with a morally-liberal agenda." Among the reasons cited by Aguilar for this anomalous behavior is the existence in Spain "of a quasi-monopoly religious market" that facilitates the framing of the church demands in terms of "the Institution that defends the moral values of the broad majority of Spaniards." She also made note of "well-established alliances with certain social groups" and "a privileged church-state relationship."[92]

As a sign of confidence (perhaps arrogance) in its ability to defeat the gay marriage bill, the Spanish Episcopal Conference did not request to meet with government officials to register its objection to the bill, as the Conference had done with Zapatero's education proposals. Instead, Church officials took to the airwaves to denounce the bill as "family phobic."[93] As the bill made its way through the parliament, Church officials escalated their attacks. Speaking to TV3, Cardinal Archbishop Emeritus of Barcelona Ricard María Carles noted, "To obey the law instead of your conscience leads to Auschwitz."[94] Archbishop Juan Antonio Martínez Camino, spokesperson and secretary general of the

---

[91] Ibid.

[92] Susana Aguilar Fernández, "Fighting against the Moral Agenda of Zapatero's Socialist Government (2004–2011): The Spanish Catholic Church as a Political Contender," *Politics and Religion* 5 (2012): 684.

[93] Dale Fuchs, "Spanish Socialist' Proposals Opposed by Church," *The New York Times*, May 30, 2014. Available at https://www.nytimes.com/2004/05/30/world/spanish-socialists-proposals-opposed-by-church.html.

[94] "Carles: Obedecer la ley antes que la consciencia lleva a Auschwitz," *El País*, April 26, 2005. Available at https://elpais.com/diario/2005/04/27/sociedad/1114552801_850215.html.

Episcopal Conference, went on national television to warn that "the legalization of this type of union would be like releasing a virus upon society," which became a key talking point for the Conference.[95]

Hoping to appeal to Catholics, Martínez Camino added that "his intention was not to attack anyone, but rather to help Catholics understand their faith." The Episcopal Conference also contended that Catholic legislators had a moral obligation to oppose gay marriage in keeping with their faith. Just before the final vote in the Congress of Deputies, a statement from the Conference noted, "Catholics are morally not obliged to vote in favor of an eventual law that will make homosexual unions equivalent to marriage because it goes against reason and morality. . . . It is their duty to speak with clarity when Spain seeks to lead a regression in the development of society, with a legal measure that is without precedent and gravely damaging to the fundamental rights of marriage, the family, young people, and teachers."[96]

To influence public opinion, the Episcopal Conference distributed millions of pamphlets warning of the dangers that gay marriage posed to the family, and priests across the Spanish territory gave homilies urging the faithful to oppose the gay marriage bill. A May 25, 2005, advertisement titled "Warning" that appeared in *El País* sponsored by the organization Fathers and Mothers of Spain made the case that if the gay marriage law was approved, "children of homosexual couples would be left vulnerable," "AIDS and other illnesses would spread," and "Spain will become a refuge for the world's homosexual population."[97] Spain's conservative media, especially the papers *El Mundo* and *ABC* and the radio network COPE, amplified these attacks on gay marriage. "We are stepping on slippery and confusing terrain . . . the very word marriage touches the most sensitive and sacred fibers of the heart. Without reproductive couples, civilization will cease to exist or have existed at all," wrote Archbishop Emeritus of Mérida Antonio Montero in the conservative daily *ABC*.[98] This publicity campaign against gay marriage was a prelude to a massive mobilization of Catholics against the gay marriage bill.

On June 18, 2005, anti-gay marriage activists, with the blessing of the Episcopal Conference, organized a demonstration under the slogan of "Madrid, Capital of the Family," which they claim drew half a million people, making it

---

[95] "Los obispos dicen que legalizar el matrimonio homosexual es 'imponer a la sociedad un virus,'" *El País*, September 27, 2004. Available at https://elpais.com/elpais/2004/09/27/actualidad/1096273023_850215.html.

[96] "Spanish Bishops: Catholics Cannot Vote for Homosexual Marriage," *Catholic News Service*, May 8, 2005. Available at https://www.catholicnewsagency.com/news/3846/spanish-bishops-catholics-cannot-vote-for-homosexual-marriage.

[97] "Una publicidad homofoba desata numerosas protestas," *El País*, May 26, 2006.

[98] "El matrimonio gay: batalla inutil?," *ABC*, June 30, 2006.

78 Framing Equality

one of the largest mobilizations in Spain since the demise of the dictatorship.[99] According to media reports, "More than 300 buses from 30 Spanish cities and four chartered planes from the Spanish islands in the Mediterranean and Atlantic came to Madrid for the protest."[100] Covering the distance from Plaza Cibeles to Puerta del Sol, the marchers carried banners that read "Family matters," "To abolish the family is to destroy society," and "Bishops, stay firm; you are not alone."[101]

Intending to intimidate the Zapatero government, the demonstration was attended by a delegation from the opposition party (PP), headed by PP General Secretary Ángel Acebes and PP spokesperson Eduardo Zaplana, ultra-Catholic organizations such as Opus Dei (Work of God), and conservative groups like the Spanish Family Forum, the main organizer of the event. Most surprising, however, was the attendance of nineteen bishops, including Madrid Archbishop Antonio María Rouco Valera and Archbishop Javier Martínez of Granada, and officials from the Spanish Episcopal Conference, including Vice President Antonio Cañizares and spokesperson Juan Antonio Martínez Camino.[102] Explaining his presence at the demonstration, Martínez Camino told *El País*, "We are living in an unprecedented situation in the history of humankind. In 2000 years the Church has never seen a threat like this."[103]

The sight of bishops marching through the streets of Madrid protesting a government policy was striking. Spaniards had not seen anything of this magnitude since the days of the Second Republic (1931–1939), which included the Civil War. That bloody conflict pitted a liberal government with a strong anticlerical bent against a nationalist, right-wing insurrection supported by the Catholic establishment. In the years leading to the war, the burning of churches and convents became commonplace, prompting Church leaders to mobilize against the Republic. This situation radically changed under the Franco regime's embrace of National Catholicism. According to one account, "Bishops and priests occupied a prominent place in any official ceremony, and the authorities attended ex-official religious ceremonies. The intellectual life, media, and school textbooks were subject to government censorship to

---

[99] This figure has been widely disputed. Madrid officials put the figure of those in attendance at one hundred and seventy thousand.

[100] Renwick McLean, "Spaniards Protest Bill on Gay Marriage," *The New York Times*, June 19, 2005. Available at https://www.nytimes.com/2005/06/19/world/europe/spaniards-protest-bill-on-gay-marriage.html.

[101] Marta Lama, "Las bodas gay en España," *Debate Feminista* 32 (October 2005): 120.

[102] Ibid., 121.

[103] "La Iglesia, contra el matrimonio gay porque es un desafío único en la historia de la humanidad," *El País*, June 16, 2005. Available at https://elpais.com/sociedad/2005/06/16/actualidad/1118872803_850215.html.

exclude any criticism of the church."[104] Not surprisingly, as noted shortly, the bishops' participation in the protests against gay marriage became one of the most polarizing events in the battle over gay marriage.

In opposing gay marriage, the Spanish Episcopal Conference enjoyed the full support of the Vatican. It fell to Pope Benedict XVI, already famous as one of the most homophobic popes in recent history, to contend with the legalization of gay marriage in Spain. After the gay marriage law was passed, a Vatican official condemned the law as "an aberration that does not reflect the wishes of the Spanish people."[105] The Vatican also noted that public officials were not obliged to follow "immoral laws," a command that many took to mean that public notaries should refuse to issue marriage permits to same-sex couples. In a 2006 visit to Valencia to address the Fifth World Meeting of Families, Benedict blasted gay marriage as "a threat to the traditional family."[106] Zapatero skipped the event, an apparent rebuke to the Vatican.

In subsequent years, Benedict escalated his war of words with Zapatero in no small measure because he feared that developments in Spain would spill over into other Catholic countries, especially in Latin America. In 2010, while visiting Barcelona to consecrate the city's famed Sagrada Familia Basilica, Benedict compared the "aggressive secularism" suggested by the gay marriage law to the anticlericalism that paved the way for the Civil War. With words that roiled the Spanish political establishment—the Civil War is the third rail of Spanish politics—Benedict noted that "although Spain had been the country that shaped modern Catholicism, the country also birthed a strong and aggressive secularism in the 1930s. This clash between faith and modernity is being recreated in Spain today."[107]

Despite the spirited opposition and the support of powerful political forces, the Catholic Church was unable to stop the gay marriage bill. During the parliamentary debate, future PP Prime Minister Mariano Rajoy accused Zapatero of "dividing the country in a manic effort to appear modern," adding that "marriage has always been an institution between one man and one woman." He also promised to challenge the new law in the Constitutional Tribunal

---

[104] Juan J. Linz, "Church and State in Spain from the Civil War to the Return of Democracy," *Daedalus* 120, no. 3 (Summer 1991): 162.

[105] "El Vaticano dice que la ley es 'aberrante' y 'no refleja la voluntad del pueblo español,'" *El País*, June 30, 2005.

[106] "Benedicto XVI Debuta en España," *El Mundo*, October 25, 2018. Available at https://www.elmundo.es/especiales/2006/07/espana/visita_papa/visita.html.

[107] José Manuel Vidal, "El Papa vincula el laicismo de la España de Zapatero con el anticlericalismo de la II República," *Periodista Digital*, November 7, 2010. Available at https://www.periodistadigital.com/cultura/religion/espana/20101107/papa-vincula-laicismo-espana-zapatero-anticlericalismo-ii-republica-noticia-689401194263/.

80 Framing Equality

"at whatever cost necessary."[108] Although Rajoy kept his word, the constitutional challenge never really stood a chance, with gay marriage enjoying broad approval with the general public and across the ideological spectrum and thousands of gay marriages already in the books. According to the National Institute of Statistics, 22,104 same-sex marriages were registered by 2011.[109] More importantly, even before the ruling from the Constitutional Tribunal in favor of gay marriage was announced, the political opposition to gay marriage had all but evaporated.

In 2012, many within the PP had already accepted the legitimacy of gay marriage. "We will wait and see what the Constitutional Court says, but my opinion is that there is no reason to be declared unconstitutional," said Justice Minister Alberto Ruiz Gallardón to the SER radio network when speaking about gay marriage under the new conservative administration of Prime Minister Rajoy.[110] Following the Tribunal's ruling, opponents of gay marriage in Spain formally accepted defeat. Soon after the decision was announced, Alfonso Alonzo, the PP's parliamentary spokesperson, noted that the decision had "effectively ended the debate about gay marriage" and that Spanish society, including the members of the PP "had overcome the issue."[111] In September 2015, Rajoy attended the same-sex wedding of Javier Maroto, PP's vice-secretary general. Most of the leadership of the PP was also in attendance—a virtual who's who of Spanish conservatives. In explaining to the Spanish public why Rajoy was attending a same-sex marriage, the PP released a statement that read, "In Spain, the right to marry is for everyone to enjoy, and today we want to share that message." The statement added that "societies evolve and parties evolve."[112]

To a large degree, the Catholic Church's failure to stop the gay marriage bill and to sustain an intense backlash against the marriage equality campaign mirrors the success of the campaign in framing the struggle for gay marriage as a moral cause. For starters, the campaign's moral arguments found broad cultural resonance, which helped build support for gay marriage across Spanish society. There's no better indicator of this resonance than the public's

---

[108] Pilar Marcos and Emilio De Benito, "Rajoy afirma que el matrimonio homosexual responde a la manía del gobierno de parecer moderno," *El País*, January 21, 2005. Available at https://elpais.com/diario/2005/01/21/sociedad/1106262006_850215.html.

[109] Garcimartin, "The Spanish Law on Same-Sex Marriage: Constitutional Arguments," 462.

[110] "Gay Marriage Law Should Not Be Overturned, Says Justice Chief," *El País*, February 7, 2012. Available at https://english.elpais.com/elpais/2012/02/07/inenglish/1328595650_850210.html.

[111] Ana Pardo de Vera, "Dirigentes del PP a favor del matrimonio gay sacan pecho y piden 'zanjar' el asunto," *Público*, June 11, 2012. Available at https://www.publico.es/espana/dirigentes-del-pp-favor-del.html

[112] Juancho Dumall, "¡Cielos, Rajoy en una boda gay," *El Periódico*, September 20, 2015. Available at https://www.elperiodico.com/es/opinion/20150920/cielos-rajoy-en-una-boda-gay-4523333.

acceptance of gay marriage. By the time Congress legalized gay marriage in 2005, a clear majority of Spaniards were already in favor of it. A CIS poll of June 2004 reported that 66.2 percent of the public approved of gay marriage, 26.5 opposed it, and 6 percent had no opinion on the matter.[113] The last time that the CIS polled Spaniards on same-sex relationships (not gay marriage), in 1994, only 35 percent of Spaniards deemed such relationships "acceptable."

Explaining how the moral arguments of the campaign helped move public opinion, gay marriage activists such as Generelo noted that making gay marriage "a great moral cause" worked "to undermine the then-popular idea of gay marriage in Spanish society as a whim or a fancy, or as special rights."[114] He added that emphasizing gay marriage as an expansion of citizenship for a historically discriminated and despised minority was an effective means for gay marriage activists to connect with other groups in civil society, especially the trade union movement, which Generelo credits with being among the first civil society actors in Spanish to embrace the view of gay rights as human rights. This embrace by the unions lent legitimacy to the efforts of gay marriage advocates, both in terms of justifying the case for gay marriage to the public and bolstering the view of gay marriage as a means for expanding democracy, given the unions' historic role in the fight against the Franco dictatorship.

In her memoirs, Gimeno argued that moral arguments made it easier for the public to relate to gay marriage. She wrote, "Once we embraced full citizenship as a goal, the campaign's framing changed radically. We stopped talking about rights for gays and lesbians to construct a universal framing; this allowed us to better connect with the citizenry at large, which was more disposed to relate to demands for universal wants than with demands for particular rights, most of them of an economic nature." She added, "Over the years and in every manner possible, conferences, interviews, testimony, articles, we explained that the fight for gay marriage was not about inheritance rights and survivorship benefits—rights that we could have attained through a same-sex civil unions law and in a speedier fashion. It was instead about equality, dignity, legitimacy, and against homophobia."[115]

Framing the debate about gay marriage in moral arguments also helped expand the appeal of gay marriage beyond the confines of the left and the gay community. Indeed, the moral framing enabled straight allies not affiliated with the left and/or the gay marriage movement to voice their support

---

[113] "Barómetro de Junio 2004," Centro de Investigaciones Sociológicas, Madrid. Available at http://www.cis.es/cis/opencm/ES/1_encuestas/estudios/ver.jsp?estudio=3994.

[114] Author's interview with Mr. Generelo (Madrid, June 11, 2018).

[115] Gimeno, "El matrimonio entre personas del mismo sexo: un recorrido ético y reinvindicativo."

82 Framing Equality

for gay marriage. One of the most eloquent supporters of gay marriage was the conservative Spanish-Peruvian novelist Mario Vargas Llosa. Writing in *El País*, Vargas Llosa pointedly linked gay marriage to Spain's democratic aspirations, something he argued was beyond politics. He noted that while a Socialist administration was enacting the gay marriage law, there was nothing Socialist about the law "because Socialism has throughout its history been as puritanical and prejudiced on sexual matters as the Catholic Church." Moreover, Vargas Llosa argued that gay marriage was "profoundly democratic and liberal." That is why, he noted, the discrimination of homosexuals in Communist societies (such as Cuba) was as fierce as it was in Nazi Germany.[116]

It is also the case that the moral framing, especially the idea that gay marriage would make Spain more tolerant, modern, and progressive, tapped into an intense desire to catch up with the future and all that this might entail. Public opinion polls suggest that this desire for "modernity" is one of the most notable markers of Spanish public culture in the post-Franco era.[117] It is rooted in a deeply seated sense of cultural, political, and economic inferiority relative to the rest of Western Europe that goes back at least to the Spanish-American War of 1898 and the loss of the last remnants of a once-massive overseas colonial empire to an upstart power, the United States. Poet and dramatist Ramón del Valle-Inclán, a member of the "Generation of 98," a group of authors whose writings reflected on Spain's decline in the early part of the twentieth century, best captured this sentiment of inferiority with his devastating description of Spain as "a grotesque deformation of European civilization." The sense of Spanish inferiority relative to the rest of Western Europe was exacerbated by the brutality of the Civil War and the longevity of the Franco dictatorship. For one thing, the dictatorship kept Spain outside the European unification project until 1986, when the country joined the European Economic Community, the precursor to the European Union.

In the post-Franco era, many social movements that preceded marriage equality successfully capitalized on the Spaniards' desire for modernity and progressivism; this gave gay marriage activists a historical affinity with older social movements. Such movements include *La Movida Madrileña*, the punk-inspired counterculture movement that spawned from the Spanish capital city around the democratic transition in the mid-1970s. Led by actors, singers, cartoonists, muralists, writers, and filmmakers—most notably Pedro

---

[116] Mario Vargas Llosa, "El matrimonio gay," *El País*, June 26, 2005. Available at https://elpais.com/diario/2005/06/26/opinion/1119736807_850215.html.

[117] See, especially, Peter McDonough, Samuel H. Barnes, and Antonio Lopez-Pina, *The Cultural Dynamics of Democratization in Spain* (Ithaca, NY: Cornell University Press, 1998).

Almodóvar—*La Movida* gave new forms of expression across all aspects of the general culture—from music to film to fashion. It also challenged virtually all of the social conventions of Franco's Spain—including compulsory Catholic education, evening curfews for women, and the criminalization of homosexuality and drug abuse.[118] Marriage equality also followed in the footsteps of other successful social campaigns in Spain that used modernization as a framing tactic, including the fights for the legalization of divorce, prostitution, pornography, and abortion.

Lastly, the moral framing undermined the attacks on gay marriage coming from the Catholic Church, especially the view of gay marriage as "family-phobic." To be sure, that argument was a tough sell in Spain. By the late 1990s, the Catholic Church was in no position to dictate how Spaniards should think about homosexuality and the family. The most obvious reason was the changing composition of the country's religious landscape. Data from the National Institute of Statistics shows that in the decades since the democratic transition Spaniards have been "losing their religion," with a reported 27 percent of the public self-identified as "atheist, agnostic, or non-believers."[119] The majority of self-identified Catholics in Spain also do not see themselves as bound to the Church's teachings on sexuality. But the moral framing of the gay marriage campaign made it especially difficult for Church officials to organize an effective response to gay marriage. Above all, the moral arguments in favor of gay marriage worked as an antidote to the bleak and dispiriting messaging coming from the Church.

For starters, the contention that gay marriage would entail the expansion of citizenship to a marginalized community put a spotlight on the history of the Spanish Church in siding with the political forces that had hindered democracy and social progress. As fate would have it, the revelations of the dark history of the collaboration between the Church and the Franco regime in repressing homosexuals (including teenagers) and women erupted as the nation was debating the merits of gay marriage. Many of the scandals facing the church pointedly underscored the claim by gay activists that the Catholic Church had no credibility accusing anyone of threatening the welfare of children when they were facing a mountain of accusations of having violated the most basic human rights of children and mothers. Indeed, the juxtaposition of the Church's attacks on gay marriage and the historical accusations facing

---

[118] See Eduardo Cimadevila Niño and Ana Cristina Aparicio, *La Movida Madrileña* (Editorial Tebar, 2019).

[119] Alfonso L. Congostrina and Julio Núñez, "Is Spain Losing Its Religion? New Report Shows Spaniards Are Turning Their Backs on Faith," *El País*, April 18, 2018. Available at https://english.elpais.com/elpais/2019/04/12/inenglish/1555056887_664300.html.

84 Framing Equality

the Church made a good foil for gay activists. As Generelo put it, "We knew we had a good chance of passing the gay marriage bill when the Catholic Church became the face of the opposition to gay marriage."[120]

Ironically, the Church's actions and rhetoric facilitated the work of gay activists of discrediting the Church's attacks on gay marriage and tying the Church to the Franco regime. The bishops' march through downtown Madrid became a public relations nightmare for the Spanish Episcopal Conference. Aside from awakening painful memories of the decades-old support that the Catholic Church offered to Franco during the Civil War and its aftermath, it gave fodder to gay activists to accuse the Church of wanting to return Spain to National Catholicism. The bishops' propensity to refer to gay marriage as "a virus in need of containment" boosted the charge by gay rights activists that the Catholic Church was out of step with Spanish society. This medical metaphor echoed the Franco regime's proclivity of using medical terminology like viruses, epidemics, and contagion to demonize the left and almost anything it deemed foreign to Spain. In particular, it recalled the pseudo-scientific theories embraced by the Franco regime as the basis for repressing homosexuality after the Civil War. Reflecting on the bishops' rhetoric, Generelo noted, "It was a war of words, and our side won: while the bishops spoke about viruses and contagion, we stressed dignity and respect."[121]

Becoming the face and the leading voice of the opposition to gay marriage also backfired on the Catholic Church by igniting a debate about the role of the Church in Spanish political life. In 1976, following Franco's death, the Vatican entered into an accord with the Spanish government that allowed the Church to regain the autonomy it lost under Franco, such as the ability to appoint bishops. The Church was also recognized in the 1978 constitution for advancing Spanish civilization. This provision allows the Church to receive state subsidies for its ecclesiastical activities. But the new accord came with the understanding that the Church would not meddle in the affairs of the government. As noted by political observer Santiago Belloch, while some are of the view that the Catholic Church has been "revitalized" by its fights with the Zapatero government to a degree not seen since the transition to democracy, the confrontation has been counterproductive "by giving impetus to demands to renegotiate the Vatican Accords of 1976."[122]

Not surprisingly, some legislators were appalled by the behavior of the Episcopal Conference, and especially by the suggestion that it was a duty for

---

[120] Author's interview with Mr. Generelo (Madrid, June 11, 2018).
[121] Ibid.
[122] Fernán González, "La Iglesia vs. Zapatero," *BBC Mundo*, March 5, 2008. Available at http://news.bbc.co.uk/hi/spanish/international/newsid_7268000/7268643.stm.

Catholic legislators to oppose gay marriage. So were many with close ties to the Church. Enrique Miret, former president of the John XXIII Association of Theologians, said his group disagreed with the Episcopal Conference's support of the protests against gay marriage. "The Church should not be getting involved in questions of civil law," he says. "That's what parliament is for."[123] Joan Carrera, Auxiliary Bishop of Barcelona, told *Catalan Radio* that "there is risk in the Conference's participation in the protest, which is to divide the Church, especially among the faithful. It's worrisome that two poles could emerge and the Church gets boxed into one. It is the most un-Christian thing that can happen."[124] Carlos Agarcia Andoin, a former official with the Diocese of Bilbao, told the *Christian Science Monitor* that "with this support for the demonstration, the Episcopal Conference is making a qualitative leap into the political arena. It establishes an alliance between the conservative PP and the Church."[125]

Finally, taking the higher moral ground allowed gay marriage activists to undercut the capacity of the Catholic Church and its allies to undermine the case for gay marriage by setting boundaries of what was deemed an acceptable or an unacceptable attack on the gay community. After *El País*, a left-leaning paper, ran the aforementioned ad that warned about gay marriage being a threat to children, among other fallacies, the uproar caused by the ad prompted the paper to apologize to its readers. In an article titled "A Homophobic Ad Unleashes Numerous Protests," the paper claimed that the ad reflected a "failure of its control systems."[126] The paper also noted that the ad "will never again run in its pages." Capitalizing on the controversy, gay marriage activists at the FELGBT denounced the ad as "borderline criminal." It also encouraged "all political forces and associations to distance themselves from the ad and those who sponsored it" and to carry out a campaign that was worthy of the values of the Spanish people.

An Inspiring Legacy

A morally framed campaign was not a requirement for making gay marriage the law of the land in Spain. As seen in the coming chapters, other marriage equality campaigns have achieved success by framing their struggles

---

[123] Ibid.

[124] Juan G. Bedoya, "Los obispos dicen que no se ha vivido nada igual en 2000 años como las bodas gays," *El País*, June 17, 2005. Available at https://elpais.com/diario/2005/06/17/sociedad/1118959203_850215.html.

[125] Geoff Pingree and Lisa Abend, "Catholic Leaders in Spain Join Gay Marriage Protests," *The Christian Science Monitor*, June 20, 2005. Available at https://www.csmonitor.com/2005/0620/p07s01-woeu.html.

[126] "Una publicidad homofoba desata numerosas protestas," *El País*, May 26, 2006.

86 Framing Equality

with legal and political arguments. But the victory achieved in Spain by framing gay marriage around moral themes and messages was unique, and so was its legacy. The consensus around this view is quite broad. Kürsad Kahramanoglu, president of the International Lesbian and Gay Organization, hailed the law as a human rights breakthrough, noting that "this law is unique in the world; I hope that in five years the rest of Europe will follow the Spanish example."[127] International human rights activist Carlos Castresana was equally effusive in declaring, "The Spanish law will make reality some of the fundamental elements of social coexistence: freedom, equality, and tolerance. Any justification for discrimination against homosexuals should not exist in a democratic society. Fifty years ago, some societies considered racial segregation natural and normal; in years to come, a prohibition against gay marriage will be probably considered an equally barbaric tradition."[128]

Rightly so, the Spanish law resonated around the globe. Indeed, it became a global game changer in gay marriage politics. It encouraged countries like the Netherlands and Belgium to bring their gay marriage laws in line with Spain's, especially on the issue of adoption. It also boosted the gay marriage campaign in the United States at a critical time: right after the devastating defeats of 2004. During that year's presidential contest, no fewer than eleven states voted on gay marriage. In all of them, gay marriage was defeated, even in liberal states. Remarking on how he drew inspiration from Spain, Evan Wolfson, the founder of Freedom to Marry, the leading organization pushing for gay marriage in the United States, recalls that after gay marriage became legal in Spain he went around saying, "If Spain can do this, why can't we?"[129]

Spain's gay marriage law also proved influential across Latin America. It influenced the arrival of gay marriage in Mexico City in 2009, the first locality in Latin America to legalize gay marriage, and in Argentina, in 2010, the first Latin American nation to enact a national gay marriage law. These developments were assisted by the Zapatero government's decision to make marriage equality promotion a feature of Spanish foreign policy, including providing financial support and advice to nascent marriage equality movements across Latin America. When advising Latin American gay activists, Spanish activists and officials mined the playbook that proved so successful in minimizing political backlash in Spain: unity among the activists in support of gay marriage, privileging the political arena over the courts in advancing gay marriage

---

[127] Emilio De Benito, "Gays, lesbianas y transexuales celebran un día histórico," *El País*, July 1, 2005. Available at https://elpais.com/diario/2005/07/01/sociedad/1120168803850215.html.

[128] Carlos Castresana, "Gay Marriage in Spain," *Peace Review: A Journal of Social Justice* 17 (2005): 136.

[129] Author's interview with Mr. Wolfson (New York City, September, 2018).

demands, and, most of all, framing gay marriage as a moral issue rather than a legal matter.

But the law's most significant impact was at home, by enabling a dramatic gay rights boom. After 2005, the Law of Assisted Reproduction was amended to cover in vitro fertilization for same-sex couples under the national healthcare system. The legislators also enacted another pioneering law: a gender identity law to allow transgender individuals the right to use the name and sex of their choice on official documents regardless of whether the individual has undergone surgery. In 2022, Spain enacted the Equality Law, a landmark legislation that bans all discrimination, including age, gender, religion, nationality, race, ethnicity, health status, sexual orientation, and any other personal or social condition. Known as "Zerolo's Law," after gay activist Pedro Zerolo, this law also removed the diagnosis of gender dysphoria as a condition for an official gender change, expanded access to reproductive services under the public healthcare system to single women and transgender people, and banned conversion therapy intended to change a person's sexual orientation or identity or gender expression.

The legacy of the gay marriage campaign's moral framing can also be seen in the coming of gay "reparations," or policies intended to make amends to the gay community for the harm caused by homophobic policies and laws. With the Law of Historical Memory, enacted in 2007, Spain became the first nation to offer moral rehabilitation and monetary compensation to those persecuted because of their sexual orientation and gender identity. In 2008, the Spanish parliament approved a budget allocation of 2 million euros (or $2.27 million) to finance compensation claims by LGBTQ people. Since 2008, other countries have followed Spain's example, including Britain, Canada, Ireland, and Germany, by issuing official apologies and pardons to those prosecuted for homosexual offenses and by offering compensatory programs.[130]

Transforming Spain, however, was the gay marriage campaign's most important legacy. Today, the country leads the world in acceptance of homosexuality, something almost unimaginable as recently as the 1980s, when the country was seen by many in the international community as a social backwater. In 2013, *The Atlantic*, based on polling data from Pew, declared Spain "the country that is most accepting of homosexuality."[131] It reported that a stunning 88 percent of the population professes acceptance of homosexuality. According to a 2021 YouGov survey, Spaniards are the most likely among

---

[130] See Omar G. Encarnación, *The Case for Gay Reparations* (New York: Oxford University Press, 2021).

[131] Olga Khazan, "The Country That's Most Accepting of Homosexuality?: Spain," *The Atlantic*, June 4, 2013. Available at https://www.theatlantic.com/international/archive/2013/06/the-country-thats-most-accepting-of-homosexuality-spain/276547/; accessed January 10, 2018.

88 Framing Equality

the surveyed nationalities to say that they would be supportive both when it came to a family member coming out as lesbian, gay, or bisexual (91 percent) or transgender/non-binary (87 percent).[132]

Nor is it surprising that gay marriage has become a marker in Spain's evolution as a democracy, even as some groups, like the ultra-conservative Vox, try to challenge the country's undeniable acceptance of LGBTQ rights. While Vox is primarily known for its vicious attacks on immigrants, Vox has called for curtailing gay pride parades and limiting the teaching of homosexuality in schools; it has even "drawn parallels between homosexuality and bestiality."[133] In 2020, on the occasion of the fifteenth anniversary of the passing of the gay marriage law, Socialist Prime Minister Pedro Sánchez offered remarks that echoed the gay marriage campaign's promise to remake Spain into a more tolerant and humane society. "Marriage equality was a before and after in the history of our country, of our democracy. The law was an inflection point that transformed our lives far beyond the confines of the law itself."[134] He added that: "marriage equality created a country where there is room for everybody."

---

[132] Eir Nolsøe, "International Survey: How Supportive Would Britons Be of a Family Member Coming Out?" YouGov, August 31, 2021. Available at https://yougov.co.uk/international/articles/37846-international-survey-how-supportive-would-britons-.

[133] Belen Carreño, "Far-right Vox Challenges Spain's Acceptance of LGBT Rights," Reuters, May 24, 2019. Available at https://www.reuters.com/article/world/far-right-vox-challenges-spains-acceptance-of-lgbt-rights-idUSKCN1SU1OQ/.

[134] Campaña del PSOE por los 15 años del matrimonio homosexual en España. Available at https://www.dailymotion.com/video/x7uqpzi.

Chapter 3
The United States

A Legal Framing

As reported by New York's *Daily News*, the going out of business party for Freedom to Marry—the first organization created specifically to bring marriage equality to every locality in the United States—was "a raucous" affair.[1] Held on July 10, 2015, at Cipriani Wall Street, a high-end restaurant in lower Manhattan, the party was attended by many celebrities and political heavyweights, including then–Vice President Joe Biden. There was a very compelling reason behind the decision by Freedom to Marry to dissolve and celebrate the occasion. On June 26, 2015, with its historic decision of *Obergefell v. Hodges*, the US Supreme Court declared gay marriage a constitutionally protected right. Without question, this ruling is the crowning achievement of the American gay rights movement. Making the ruling sweeter for Freedom to Marry was the traumatic nature of the struggle for gay marriage across the United States. For one thing, in contrast to other countries, the war over gay marriage in the United States entailed more than a conflict between gay rights activists and a well-organized opposition movement. It also involved a war within the gay community itself.

The so-called gay marriage civil war divided the American gay activist community into three camps, each with its own position on gay marriage.[2] In the first camp was the "gay left," the heir to the legacy of the gay liberation movement born in 1969 following the Stonewall uprising, the seminal event in launching the contemporary gay rights movement. For this group, marriage was an oppressive heterosexual institution. Understandably, it deemed

[1] Nicole Hensley, "Vice President Biden Joins Marriage Equality Celebration in Manhattan," *Daily News*, July 10, 2015. Available at https://www.nydailynews.com/news/politics/joe-biden-cheers-gay-marriage-wall-street-event-article-1.2287519. On the history of the freedom to marry, see Marc Solomon, *Winning Marriage: The Inside Story of How Same-Sex Couples Took on the Politicians and the Pundits and Won* (ForeEdge Publishers, 2014).

[2] For a broader overview of the "gay marriage civil war" see Mary Bernstein and Verta Taylor, eds., *The Marrying Kind?: Debating Same-Sex Marriage within the Lesbian and Gay Movement* (Minneapolis: University of Minnesota Press, 2013); Andrew Sullivan, ed., *Same Sex Marriage, Pro and Con: A Reader* (New York: Vintage, 1997); Nathaniel Frank, *Awakening: How Gays and Lesbians Brought Marriage Equality to America* (Cambridge, MA: Harvard University Press, 2017); and Jane S. Schacter, "The Other Same-Sex Marriage Debate," *Chicago-Kent Law Review* 84 (April 2009): 379–402.

Framing Equality. Omar G. Encarnación, Oxford University Press. © Oxford University Press (2025).
DOI: 10.1093/9780190880330.003.0004

90 Framing Equality

gay marriage a betrayal of the legacy of gay liberation. Another group was the "gay rights establishment," the cluster of national organizations that powered the struggle for civil rights for LGBTQ Americans during the 1970s and 1980s. Although not explicitly against gay marriage, this group saw gay marriage as a bridge too far and a potential obstacle to more attainable goals like minimizing anti-gay discrimination and violence, combating the HIV/AIDS epidemic, and creating domestic partnerships and civil unions. Accordingly, for much of the struggle for marriage equality, many establishment organizations chose to stay on the sidelines. Caught between the gay left and the gay rights establishment was the third group: the assortment of gay rights activists who patiently built the marriage equality movement from the ground up, including Freedom to Marry. For years, these activists had to contend with the hostility of the gay left and the skepticism of the gay rights establishment.

More traumatic for gay marriage activists, however, was the massive legal and political backlash unleashed by the marriage equality movement. It has no peers among democratic states. It helps explain why by 2015 the United States had fallen behind some twenty other democracies in allowing same-sex couples to marry nationwide, including several Catholic-majority countries notorious for their homophobic cultures—such as Spain, Argentina, and Ireland. Among the consequences of the backlash was the creation of a patchwork of gay marriage laws that became the source of so much chaos and suffering for the gay community, a situation highlighted by the legal case behind *Obergefell*. The plaintiff in the case was Jim Obergefell, an Ohio resident whose husband, John Arthur, was terminally ill with only a few months to live. But Obergefell's marriage, conducted in Maryland, where same-sex marriage was legal, was not recognized in Ohio, where a ban on gay marriage was enacted in 2004.[3]

The conventional wisdom about the war over gay marriage in the United States, especially the longevity and severity of the backlash, points to the outsized role of litigation in the gay marriage campaign. There's almost a universal consensus among legal scholars that litigating gay marriage fueled a massive counterreaction from social and religious conservatives. When assessing both the virulence of the anti-gay marriage backlash as well as the backlash's complex legacy for LGBTQ equality, historian John D' Emilio observed that "the battle to win marriage equality through the courts has done something that no other campaign or issue in our movement has done: it has

---

[3] See Debbie Cenziper and John Obergefell, *Love Wins: The Lovers and Lawyers Who Fought the Landmark Case for Marriage Equality* (New York: William Morrow, 2016).

created a vast body of new antigay law."[4] Other scholars have blamed litigation for a host of other problems, including nationalizing the conflict over gay marriage, generating pro-gay marriage rulings that were quite unpopular with the public, and preempting a broad debate about the pros and cons about gay marriage in American society.[5] Not surprisingly, perhaps, several legal scholars have drawn parallels between the backlash that greeted the *Obergefell* decision and the backlash unleashed by *Brown v. Board of Education*, the landmark decision from 1954 that desegregated public schools across the United States.[6]

It is also the case that in the United States, in contrast to other democracies, the conservative opposition to gay rights is organized around a unified front, the so-called Christian right. Well before the onset of the marriage equality movement, the Christian right had become skilled at generating moral panics about homosexuality and gay rights. This activism benefited from a long and dark history in the United States of using federal and state laws to criminalize homosexuality and lash out at the gay community.[7] The last remaining laws criminalizing sodomy were not invalidated in the United States until 2003, when the US Supreme Court ruled them unconstitutional. For much of the twentieth century, these laws were used to justify banning gays and lesbians from serving in the military and the federal government and even for removing children from their biological father or mother on suspicion of homosexuality. By the time of the advent of the marriage equality campaign, this history created a strong predisposition for justifying gay marriage bans and other policies intended to "defend" traditional marriage.

Much less observed, and therefore less understood, is how the backlash was shaped by the framing of the gay marriage campaign in the United States, a textbook case of legal framing. This framing stands in contrast to the moral framing evident in Spain and the political framing that prevailed in Brazil. For the most part, gay marriage was framed in the United States as a civil

---

[4] John D'Emilio, "The Marriage Fight Is Setting Us Back," *Gay & Lesbian Review Worldwide*, November–December 2006, 10.

[5] See, especially, Jane S. Schacter, "Courts and the Politics of Backlash: Marriage Equality Litigation, Then and Now," *California Law Review* 82 (2009); 1153–1224; William N. Eskridge, Jr., "Backlash Politics: How Constitutional Litigation Has Advanced Marriage Equality in the United States," *Boston University Law Review* 93 (2013): 275–323; Gerald N. Rosenberg, *The Hollow Hope: Can Courts Bring about Social Change?* 2nd ed. (Chicago: University of Chicago Press, 2008); and Michael J. Klarman, *From the Closet to the Altar: Courts, Backlash, and the Struggle for Same-Sex Marriage* (New York: Oxford University Press, 2013).

[6] See Carlos A. Ball, "The Backlash Thesis and Same-Sex Marriage: Learning from Brown v. Board of Education and Its Aftermath," *William & Marry Bill of Rights and Journal* 14 (2006): 1494–1540.

[7] See, especially, Margot Canaday, *The Straight State: Sexuality and Citizenship in Twentieth America* (Princeton, NJ: Princeton University Press, 2009); Joey L. Mogul, Andrea J. Ritchie, and Kay Whitlock, *Queer (In)Justice: The Criminalization of LGBTQ People in the United States* (Beacon Press, 2012); and Omar G. Encarnación, *The Case for Gay Reparations* (New York: Oxford University Press, 2021).

right guaranteed under the US Constitution's Fourteenth Amendment and its promise of equality under the law. Standing at the center of this framing was the messaging of "rights and benefits," a reference to the hundreds (if not thousands) of rights and privileges that existing marriage laws denied gay and lesbian couples. Minimal effort was made to promote gay marriage as a moral cause and as a platform for expanding citizenship. Not surprisingly, although wildly successful in changing the legal landscape surrounding marriage across the United States, the rights and benefits messaging did little to prevent backlash and advance LGBTQ equality beyond extending marriage rights to same-sex couples.

Intended primarily to advance litigation, the rights and benefits messaging failed to resonate with ordinary Americans. It backfired by giving the impression that gay and lesbian couples wanted marriage for material and political reasons. It also did little to neutralize the opposition by not offering a counter-narrative to the framing of gay marriage by the Christian right as a threat to the family and religious freedom. This menacing view of gay marriage was left to linger in the public's consciousness. Finally, the rights and benefits messaging did not provide much of a foundation for expanding LGBTQ equality, such as extending the respect and dignity to same-sex relationships that are afforded to heterosexual couples. A new message centered around love and commitment, which suggested that homosexuals wanted marriage for the same reasons as straight people, was introduced late in the campaign. While this new messaging succeeded in increasing public support for gay marriage, it arrived too late to avoid the severe backlash unleashed by the Christian right.

As in Spain and Brazil, domestic factors rather than international trends shaped the legal framing of the American gay marriage campaign. For a start, the prominence of litigation as the main strategy for securing gay marriage meant that the primary goal of any messaging strategy was to support the legal efforts underway in the courts. Inspired by the historical precedent set by the African American civil rights movement and its effective use of constitutional arguments to end legalized racial discrimination, this strategy provided something of a roadmap for gay marriage activists. Moreover, marriage has a long and very contentious history among American gay activists. This history made it difficult for the gay community to rally around marriage as anything other than a civil rights issue. Indeed, the notion of gay marriage as a civil right was a rare source of unity among gay rights activists. Finally, decades of moralistic attacks on the gay community by the Christian right encouraged gay marriage activists to steer clear of moral claims and to stick to legal arguments focused on equality under the law.

Gay Politics before Gay Marriage

Pro-gay marriage activism in the United States dates back to the 1950s with the rise of the "Homophiles" (meaning loving the same), the country's first viable gay rights movement, and leading Homophile organizations of the time such as the Mattachine Society, Daughters of Bilitis, and ONE, Inc.[8] At the heart of their activism was educating American society about the need to offer legal protections to the homosexual community. The movement also encouraged gays and lesbians to conform to conventional gender norms as a means for furthering societal acceptance, a reason why organizations like the Mattachine Society developed a reputation for "being timid, conservative, and overly focused on mainstream assimilation."[9] Also contributing to this reputation was the embrace of gay marriage. In June 1963, *ONE* magazine published a cover story titled "Let's Push Homophile Marriage." It made the case for marriage as part of the campaign for gay rights. "It is high time the modern homophile movement started paying more attention to homophile marriage," the article concluded.[10]

Much like the Homophile movement itself, the Homophiles' activism for gay marriage was short-lived and eventually swept away by the gay liberation revolution. Historian George Chauncey's account of the American struggle for gay marriage notes that during the 1970s, "support for gay marriage was a distinctly minority position within the lesbian and gay movement" and that couples seeking marriage were the target of criticism for "imitating the meaningless, bad habits of our oppressors."[11] These critics were cheered by the gay press that "urged men to overcome their sexual shame and to value the diverse pleasures and new friendships made possible by sexual experimentation with many partners."[12] Among the factors sowing disdain for gay marriage was the ideological legacy of the Stonewall uprising of 1969. From this seminal event emerged the Gay Liberation Front (GLF).[13] Capitalizing on the

---

[8] On the history of the American gay rights movement, see Eric Marcus, *Making History: The Struggle for Gay and Lesbian Equal Rights, 1945 to 1990* (New York: Harper Collins, 1992); John D'Emilio, *Sexual Politics/Sexual Communities: The Making of a Homosexual Minority in the United States* (Chicago: University of Chicago Press, 1998); Barry D. Adam, *The Rise of a Gay and Lesbian Movement* (Boston: Tawyne, 1987); and Michael Bronski, *A Queer History of the United States* (Boston: Beacon Press, 2011).

[9] Frank, *Awakening*, 21.

[10] Randy Lloyd, "Let's Push Homophile Marriage," *One* (June 1963). Made available to this author by Charles Francis of the Mattachine Society of Washington, DC.

[11] George Chauncey, *Why Marriage: The History Shaping Today's Debate over Gay Marriage* (New York: Basic Books, 2005), 93.

[12] Ibid.

[13] On the GLF, see Donn Teal, *The Gay Militants* (New York: Stein and Day, 1971) and Terence Kissack, "Freaking Fag Revolutionaries: New York's Gay Liberation Front, 1969–1971," *Radical History Review* 62 (1995): 105–134.

94 Framing Equality

counterculture and free-love movements, the GLF extolled nonconformity in sexual behavior and physical appearance to affirm and promote sexual diversity.

It was the emphasis that gay liberationists placed on nonconformity that shaped the GLF's critical stance toward the institution of marriage. Indeed, a wholesale rejection of marriage was at the very heart of the GLF's identity. A statement from the organization from the early 1970s is revealing. "We expose the institution of marriage as one of the most insidious and basic sustainers of the system. The family is the microcosm of oppression."[14] Others within the GLF objected to the centrality of monogamy in traditional marriage, which they felt was in and of itself oppressive since "monogamy suppresses the sexual liberty that is the aim of gay liberalization."[15] These sentiments about marriage left a strong legacy in the mindset of ordinary homosexuals and, as discussed later, were a significant obstacle to the framing of gay marriage as a tool for advancing freedom, dignity, and equality for the gay community. In an interview for this book, historian Charles Kaiser noted that for "gay men of my generation, a generation shaped by the Stonewall uprising and the counterculture, being gay meant not having to get married and raise a family." He added that "marriage was antithetical to being gay."[16]

The arrival of new gay rights organizations invested in advancing civil rights for gays and lesbians—such as Lambda Legal, the Human Rights Campaign (HRC), and the National Gay Task Force—did not make marriage more popular among gay activists. But, unlike the GLF, opposition to gay marriage by these new groups was more pragmatic than ideological. For decades, national gay rights activists viewed gay marriage as a fool's errand. This was a reasonable view considering that as recently as 2003 dozens of American states still had laws in their books criminalizing gay sex. As noted by Mary Bernstein and Verta Taylor, "Regardless of lesbian and gay feelings about marriage, during the 1970s LGBT people faced such a hostile climate that achieving the legal recognition of same-sex marriage was virtually unthinkable."[17]

Moreover, gay activists doubted that the American public would ever embrace gay marriage. "Oh, no, we're not interested," remembers Vic Basile, the head of the HRC from 1983 to 1989, about his organization's attitude toward gay marriage during the 1980s. He thought that the idea that Americans would broadly accept same-sex marriage seemed "inconceivable

---

[14] William N. Eskridge, Jr., *The Case for Same-Sex Marriage: From Sexual Liberty to Civilized Commitment* (New York: Free Press, 1996), 53.

[15] Ibid., 54.

[16] Author's telephone interview with Mr. Kaiser (November 7, 2018).

[17] Mary Bernstein and Verta Taylor, eds., *The Marrying Kind? Debating Same-Sex Marriage within the Lesbian and Gay Movement* (New York: Oxford University Press, 2013), Introduction.

The United States **95**

at the time" and that "demanding equality on that front seemed strategically unwise. I wanted to deflect the whole issue because I thought that would really set us back."[18]

Once the HRC came on board with marriage equality, under the leadership of Elizabeth Birch (1995-2004), the organization emphasized incremental progress. Whenever HRC leaders spoke about gay marriage, they pointedly shied away from making the case for gay marriage, preferring instead to stress the need to protect homosexual families. In August 2003, Birch went on *Fox News Sunday* to comment on President George W. Bush's opposition to gay marriage. When asked by host Brit Hume to comment on "whether it has to be the right to gay marriage, or whether something less than that would satisfactory to the organizations and the people you represent," Birch stressed the need for federal laws that would protect gay families. "What laws can we pass at the federal level or at the state level that would allow couples to have stability and to bring more assurance that more children in America, the children in gay families are being taken care of?"[19] A year later, in 2004, when gay marriage was defeated at the polls in many states, the HRC embraced a truce on gay marriage. Its leaders called for adopting a "new, more moderate strategy with less emphasis on legitimizing same-sex marriages and more on strengthening personal relationships."[20]

The traditional resistance to gay marriage by the gay rights establishment meant that in the United States, in contrast to most national experiences in Western Europe and Latin America, the campaign for gay marriage would emerge from the right rather than from the left. Indeed, the first explicit demands for gay marriage in the post-Stonewall era emerged from the intellectual movement known as the "new gay conservatism," which enjoyed a significant moment in the 1980s.[21] Gay conservatives "repudiated the gay movement's affiliation with the left"; they also sought to "rescue homosexuality from its association with gender deviance—with effeminate men and mannish women" while rejecting "the sexual license of the Gay Liberation movement" and urging gays "to restrain their erotic behavior."[22] Among the factors pushing these views was the onset of the HIV/AIDS pandemic, which dramatically transformed gay politics in the United States.

---

[18] Ellen McCarthy, "A Generation of LGBTQ Advocates Hopes the Clock Isn't Ticking Backward," *The Washington Post*, May 20, 2022. Available at https://www.washingtonpost.com/lifestyle/2022/05/20/lgbtq-progress/.

[19] Transcript: Elizabeth Birch on *Fox News Sunday*, August 3, 2003. Available at https://www.foxnews.com/story/transcript-elizabeth-birch-on-fox-news-sunday.

[20] Stephen M. Engel, *Fragmented Citizens: The Changing Landscape of Gay and Lesbian Rights* (New York: New York University Press, 2016), 192.

[21] Paul Robinson, *Queer Wars: The New Gay Right and Its Critics* (Chicago: University of Chicago Press, 2006).

[22] Ibid., 2.

96 Framing Equality

Like never before, AIDS radicalized the gay community, a counterreaction to the lethargic pace at which the Reagan administration confronted the onset of the AIDS pandemic. The most vivid example of this radicalization was the AIDS Coalition to Unleash Power (ACT UP), a protest organization founded in 1987 by the activist-writer Larry Kramer that became famous for civil disobedience acts such as staging funerals for people who had died of AIDS in front of the White House and interrupting Sunday mass at New York's St. Patrick's Cathedral.[23] But the pandemic also created a new sensibility among gay males that gave way to demands for state recognition of same-sex relationships, including marriage. Such demands were sent into overdrive by the wave of anti-gay discrimination unleashed by the pandemic.[24]

According to Eskridge, AIDS worked to "scare gay and bisexual men into safer sex with fewer sexual partners. Commitment to another partner became a more attractive norm for those infected by the virus that leads to AIDS as well as for those who are not infected. The need of people with AIDS for physical as well as emotional support brought many couples together and cemented more relationships than it tore apart."[25] AIDS also accelerated demands for legal protections for gay people and state recognition of same-sex unions by unleashing a wave of discrimination of its own in housing, the workplace, and healthcare. Seemingly suddenly, gay people, especially young gay males, who were disproportionately affected by the epidemic in its early years, found themselves fired from their jobs, kicked out of their homes, and unable to deed their pensions and assets to their romantic partners or even visit them in hospital.

By far, the most influential gay conservative making the case for gay marriage was journalist Andrew Sullivan. His 1989 *New Republic* essay "Here Comes the Groom" made what came to be known as the "conservative case" for gay marriage by emphasizing how gay marriage would facilitate the incorporation of homosexuals into mainstream society.[26] As he wrote, "Legalizing gay marriage would offer homosexuals the same deal society now offers heterosexuals: general social approval and specific legal advantages in exchange for a deeper and harder-to-extract-yourself from commitment to

---

[23] For a comprehensive look at ACT UP and its legacy, see Sarah Schulman, *Let the Record Show: A Political History of ACT UP New York* (New York: Farrar, Straus and Giroux, 2021) and Omar G. Encarnación, "Kramer vs. America: How Activists Shaped the Response to the 1980s AIDS Crisis," *Times Literary Supplement*, June 11, 2021.

[24] These demands were often expressed in the gay media, in papers like *New York Native*, a biweekly newspaper for gays published in New York City beginning in 1980. The paper's archive is found at the New York Public Library and available at https://archives.nypl.org/mss/2187.

[25] Eskridge, *The Case for Same-Sex Marriage*, 58.

[26] Andrew Sullivan, "Here Comes the Groom: A (Conservative) Case for Gay Marriage," *The New Republic*, August 28, 1989.

The United States   97

another human being. Like straight marriage, it would foster social cohesion, emotional security, and economic prudence."[27]

Not everyone was on board with the new sensibility ushered in by the AIDS pandemic. Indeed, by the late 1980s, before there were any viable legal and political pathways to the legalization of gay marriage on the horizon, there was already a gay marriage dissident movement afoot among gay activists. This movement debuted at the Second National March on Washington for Lesbian and Gay Rights, held on October 11, 1987, at the time the largest demonstration for gay and lesbian rights in American history. One of the marquee events of the march was "The Wedding." It featured two thousand same-sex couples pledging their vows in a mass wedding in front of the Internal Revenue Service building.[28] The Wedding was also, according to one account, "the most controversial event of the march," because "despite its campy-in-your-face-quality" it "promoted traditional relationships and patriarchal family forms that are inconsistent with, even opposed to, the gay lifestyle and signaled a dangerous redirection of the movement to achieve domestic partnership laws and policies designed to provide some recognition to same-sex couples by employers and local and state governments."[29]

By the late 1980s, opposition to gay marriage within the gay community had triggered a full-blown ideological civil war. Reflecting on the intensity of the conflict, which often seemed as fierce as the fight against conservatives, Bernstein and Taylor wrote, "Social movements generally face the most visible opposition from their opponents, but the battle for same-sex marriage is an exception. Rarely has a social movement goal so central to a movement's political agenda been so fraught. At the same time that anti-gay forces fight to preserve marriage for one man and one woman, lesbian and gay activists argue with passion about the viability and the social consequences of same-sex marriage."[30] Even members of the same organization were divided on gay marriage. This was most famously the case with Lambda Legal. In 1989, Lambda Legal's top leaders, Executive Director Tom Stoddard and Legal Director Paula Ettelbrick, took to the pages of *Out/Look* magazine and engaged in "the most famous articulation of the LGBT community's hopes and fears associated with same-sex marriage."[31] Their juxtaposition of

---

[27] Ibid.

[28] See "The Wedding, Histories of the National Mall." Available at http://mallhistory.org/items/show/532; Karen M. Dunak, "The Secret History of Gay Marriage," *Salon*, September 8, 2013. Available at https://www.salon.com/2013/09/08/the_secret_history_of_gay_marriage/.

[29] Bernstein and Taylor, "Marital Discord," 3.

[30] Ibid., Introduction.

[31] Carlos A. Ball, "Symposium: Updating the LGBT Intracommunity Debate over Same-Sex Marriage," *Rutgers Law Review* 61 (3), 2009, 493.

98 Framing Equality

opposite views on gay marriage endures as a testament to how divisive (but also insightful) the gay marriage debate became within the American gay community.

Stoddard's essay "Why Gay People Should Seek the Right to Marry" opened with a confession: that he was not a fan of the institution of marriage, given that it had been "oppressive especially (although not entirely) to women."[32] Despite that troubled history, Stoddard argued that gay marriage would lead "ultimately to a world free from discrimination against lesbians and gay men." In his view, alternatives to marriage, such as domestic partnerships and bans on anti-gay discrimination, only allowed for partial equality. In an essay provocatively titled "Since When Is Marriage a Path to Liberation?", Ettelbrick argued that marriage ran contrary to two primary goals of the gay and lesbian movement: the affirmation of gay identity and culture and the validation of many forms of relationships.[33] In doing so, gay marriage was antithetical to everything that the gay community stood for. As she put it, "Being queer is more than setting up house, sleeping with a person of the same gender, and seeking state approval for doing so. It is an identity, a culture with many variations. Being queer means pushing the parameters of sex, sexuality, and family, and in the process transforming the very fabric of society."

Resistance to gay marriage within the gay community persisted through the legalization of gay marriage nationwide in 2015, with gay activists attacking gay marriage from a variety of perspectives. On one end were organizations that while not technically against gay marriage were critical of all the political resources going into the gay marriage campaign and what this meant for the broader struggle for LGBTQ rights. Queers for Economic Justice, an organization formed in New York City in 2002, drew a lot of attention with the manifesto "Beyond Marriage." It argued for a broader vision for gay rights activism, including "homelessness and housing, economic justice, immigration, drug laws and public health, marriage and other family forms, and welfare."[34] On the other end were groups that were outright hostile to gay marriage. In 2009, critics of the gay marriage campaign launched Against Equality, an online community of noted academics and political commentators that argued that gay marriage was a direct threat to gay families by allowing the state to dictate which gay families were legitimate and which ones were not. "Marriage will never set us free," wrote Craig Willse and Dean Spade in 2013, noting that marriage is "a tool of social control to regulate sexuality and the family formation by establishing a favored form and rewarding it with

[32] Thomas Stoddard, "Why Gay People Should Seek the Right to Marry," *Out/Look* 6 (1989).

[33] Paula Ettelbrick, "Since When Is Marriage a Path to Liberation?" *Out/Look* 6 (1989).

[34] Queers for Economic Justice records, #7802. Division of Rare and Manuscript Collections, Cornell University Library.

certain benefits and obligations. Those left outside of what is recognized by the state risked being stigmatized and worse."[35]

In an interview for this book, Jonathan Rauch, a social policy analyst at Brookings, reflected on how the attempt by the "gay left" to revive the criticism of marriage in the gay liberation era affected the fortunes of the gay marriage campaign. "The gay left was suspicious and, in some cases, hostile to the marriage movement, primarily because they saw marriage as the kind of stultifying bourgeois institution we needed to be liberated from (the same regarding military service) and because same-sex marriage was grassroots-driven and threatened their ideological hold on the movement. However, the grassroots soon showed they would not rest until marriage was accomplished, and the gay left had to come on board." He added, "They could not very well oppose equality in this important sphere of life, and marriage was a practical necessity for gay couples."[36] The negative impressions about gay marriage coming from the gay left also gave license to social conservatives opposed to gay marriage to freely express their views without fearing being labeled as bigots. According to Rauch, "The gay left's liberationist arguments were a problem—recycled by the right as proof that we were trying to destroy marriage."[37]

While the gay marriage debate that pitted "assimilationists" and "liberationists" raged for at least two decades, the dynamics of the debate shifted dramatically in favor of gay marriage with *Baehr v. Lewin*. This 1993 decision by the Hawaiian Supreme Court found that prohibiting same-sex marriage was a violation of the state's constitution. As the first-ever win for gay marriage in an American court, or any other court in the entire world, this ruling provided a massive boost for the pro-gay marriage side. In particular, the ruling flew in the face of the "unanimous judgment" by the national leadership of the gay legal community that "it was premature to pursue constitutional litigation challenging state laws that denied same-sex couples access to marriage."[38] Indeed, "gay advocacy groups showed little interest in taking the case, viewing it as hopeless."[39] This attitude explains why no gay attorney would touch the case and why no gay organization offered any legal assistance. Eventually, the

---

[35] Craig Willse and Dean Spade, "Marriage Will Never Set Us Free," *Organizing Upgrade: Engaging Left Organizers in Strategic Dialogue*, September 6, 2013. Available at https://convergencemag.com/articles/marriage-will-never-set-us-free/.

[36] Author's e-mail correspondence with Mr. Rauch (June 21, 2022).

[37] Ibid.

[38] Michael Sant'Ambrogio and Sylvia A. Law, "Baehr v. Lewin and the Long Road to Marriage Equality," New York University School of Law, Public Law & Legal Theory Research Paper Series, Working Paper No. 11–37, June 2011, 707.

[39] John F. Kowal, "The Improbable Victory of Marriage Equality," The Brennan Center for Justice, September 29, 2015. Available at https://www.brennancenter.org/our-work/analysis-opinion/improbable-victory-marriage-equality.

100   Framing Equality

case fell into the hands of a straight local attorney named Daniel Foley, who had no experience with gay rights litigation.

But even in Hawaii, one of the nation's most liberal states, the prospect of legalized gay marriage set off a powerful political backlash, which underscored the view among gay rights groups of the risk of pursuing gay marriage, primarily through the courts. Sensing that the advent of gay marriage was imminent, Hawaii's state lawmakers quickly moved to organize a referendum to amend the state's constitution to grant the state legislature the authority to ban same-sex marriage. A comfortable margin eventually approved the amendment. As a consolation prize, the state legislature enacted a "reciprocal beneficiaries" law that provided limited benefits to same-sex couples. By the time the Hawaiian Supreme Court revisited the issue of gay marriage, in 1999, the Court had no choice but to declare that there was no right to a same-sex marriage in the state's constitution.

Reflecting on the backlash triggered by the decision in Hawaii, former HRC executive director Elizabeth Birch, who spent her teenage years in Hawaii, highlighted how this backlash was brought about by "a lot of grandstanding" and "naïveté" on the part of gay marriage activists.[40] "No one read Hawaii correctly when it came to what it would take to actually change public opinion in the state sufficiently to ever have a chance for a successful result in the state legislature. Anyone can file a suit. That has little to do with changing the soil in a setting to allow for actual marriage equality statute or and/or State Supreme Court decision to manifest." She added that: "In the end, the HRC spent about $1.7 million running a ground and media campaign in Hawaii . . . a huge investment of time, employees on the ground, communication, and marketing. We got slaughtered because the groundwork would take years."

Baehr's negative consequences extended beyond Hawaii. As noted by legal historian Michael Klarman, one of the principal consequences of the backlash over the decision in Hawaii was to undermine the logical evolution of gay rights in the United States, at least as these rights progressed in other countries, whereby the end of anti-gay discrimination opened the way for a broader set of rights, such as gay marriage.[41] A more immediate impact of the Hawaii decision, however, was to nationalize the conflict over gay marriage. As argued by legal scholar Jane Schacter, the local battle in Hawaii "quickly went national, as organized groups associated with traditional values joined the fray to preserve traditional marriage," and the state of Utah wasted no time in passing a law restricting marriage for same-sex couples.[42]

---

[40] Author's e-mail correspondence with Ms. Birch (July 14, 2022).

[41] Klarman, *From the Closet to the Altar*.

[42] Schacter, "Courts and the Politics of Backlash," 1185.

Not surprisingly, as recalled by Jeff Trammell, a veteran gay rights activist with close ties to the Democratic establishment (he was one of the founders of the Stonewall Democrats) and a former advisor on LGBTQ issues to presidential candidates Al Gore and John Kerry, "the situation in Hawaii brought considerable consternation among gay rights activists."[43] Organizations like the HRC and Lambda Legal were less than thrilled about developments in Hawaii. They feared a costly and potentially counterproductive legal fight. They were also of the view that a legal battle for marriage rights would prevent gay activists from prevailing on other more urgent and arguably winnable fights—such as enacting federal legislation banning anti-gay discrimination, fighting the HIV/AIDS epidemic, repealing sodomy laws in those states that still had those laws in their books, and protecting parental rights for same-sex couples.

Nonetheless, the Hawaii decision brought elation to gay marriage activists such as Evan Wolfson, who is broadly recognized as the "architect of the marriage equality movement."[44] For Wolfson, a former Lambda Legal lawyer who served as legal counsel in *Baehr*, the Hawaii ruling signaled that it was time for gay activists to stop bickering and seize the legal momentum created by the Hawaiian decision. Acting as a peacemaker between the warring sides of the gay marriage civil war, Wolfson wrote in 1994, "We should end, or at least suspend the intra-community debate over whether to seek gay marriage. The ship has sailed."[45]

Framing the Case for Gay Marriage

At the core of Wolfson's thinking for making gay marriage the law of the land across the United States was his belief that gay marriage was a right protected under the US Constitution's Fourteenth Amendment of equality under the law. This belief eventually became the foundational legal reasoning for litigating gay marriage up to the US Supreme Court. Wolfson first articulated his novel and provocative argument about same-sex marriage in his 1983 Harvard Law School thesis, a seventy-seven-page document that historian Josh Zeitz has characterized as "a founding document of the marriage equality movement."[46] Not surprisingly, in the Hawaii decision Wolfson saw validation for his ideas. As he noted in an interview for this book, "The Hawaii

[43] Author's online interview with Mr. Trammell (May 31, 2022).

[44] Chris Kompanek, "Evan Wolfson, Architect of the Marriage Equality Movement," *Financial Times*, June 26, 2015. Available at https://www.ft.com/content/8450a034-159b-11e5-be54-00144feabdc0.

[45] Evan Wolfson, "Crossing the Threshold: Equal Marriage and Rights for Lesbians and Gay Men and the Intra-Community Critique," *New York University Review of Law and Social Change* 21 (1994): 611.

[46] Josh M. Zeitz, "The Making of the Marriage Equality Revolution," Politico, April 28, 2015. Available at https://www.politico.com/magazine/story/2015/04/gay-marriage-revolution-evan-wolfson-

102 Framing Equality

decision showed a route to victory in the US Constitution's 14th Amendment and its guarantee of equal protection under the law." He added that in the text of this amendment, he saw "freedom from government intrusion; and freedom of autonomy—which includes the right to marry."[47]

In embracing the Fourteenth Amendment as a legal tool for legalizing gay marriage, Wolfson was following in the footsteps of Homophile leaders such as Frank Kameny, a co-founder of the Mattachine Society of Washington, DC, who is often recognized as the father of the contemporary gay rights movement. He is also the most famous victim of the Lavender Scare, the midcentury witch-hunt of homosexuals triggered by President Dwight Eisenhower's Executive Order 10450 of 1953 that banned homosexuals from serving in the federal government.[48] Directly inspired by the African American civil rights movement, Kameny embraced the idea of homosexuals as a minority deserving of constitutional protection, not unlike African Americans. He also coined the phrase "gay is good" after the black power movement slogan "black is beautiful." According to historian Nathaniel Frank, as a movement slogan, the phrase "gay is good" embodied Kameny's belief that "homosexuality was not to be merely tolerated and confined to the shadows but should be celebrated as a moral good."[49]

Wolfson was also embracing a tradition by ordinary gay and lesbian couples of going to court to demand the right to marry. The best-known example of this tradition is that of Jack Baker and Michael McConnell of Hennepin County, Minnesota. In 1970, they became "the first same-sex couple known to apply for a marriage license."[50] When the license was denied, the couple appealed to the Minnesota Supreme Court, which did not dignify the couple's appeal by asking a single question. In declining the appeal, the justices cited the Bible. "The institution of marriage as a union of man and woman, uniquely involving the procreation and rearing of children within a family, is as old as the Book of Genesis." The couple appealed to the US Supreme Court, which dismissed the case with a single sentence: "The appeal is dismissed for want of a substantial federal question." It was more

---

117412/. See, also, Wolfson's *Why Marriage Matters: America, Equality, and Gay People's Right to Marry* (New York: Simon and Schuster, 2005).

[47] Author's interview with Mr. Wolfson (New York, September 21, 2018).

[48] Kameny famously appealed his firing from the US Map Survey all the way to the US Supreme Court, which declined to review his case. He argued that discrimination against gay people was un-American because it violated American principles of equality under the law. See Eric Cervini, *The Deviant's War: The Homosexual v. the United States of America* (New York: Farrar, Straus and Giroux, 2020).

[49] Frank, *Awakening*, 28.

[50] This section borrows from Erik Eckholm, "The Same-Sex Couple That Got a Marriage License in 1971," *The New York Times*, May 16, 2015. Available at https://www.nytimes.com/2015/05/17/us/the-same-sex-couple-who-got-a-marriage-license-in-1971.html.

The United States   103

than apparent that for the Court, the idea that homosexual couples had a constitutional right to marriage was nothing short of preposterous.[51]

Wolfson's arguments got a big boost from *Goodridge v. Department of Public Health*, a 2003 ruling from the Supreme Court of the Commonwealth of Massachusetts that determined that preventing homosexual couples from marriage was a violation of the state's constitution. *Goodridge* cited *Lawrence v. Texas*, a 2003 ruling from the US Supreme Court that struck down all remaining sodomy laws still in the books in the United States, as a rationale for legalizing same-sex marriage in Massachusetts, when noting, "Our obligation is to define the liberty of all, not to mandate our moral code." *Lawrence* ended the distinction of the United States as the last major Western democracy with laws criminalizing gay sex. At the time of the ruling, ten states—Alabama, Florida, Idaho, Louisiana, Mississippi, North Carolina, South Carolina, Michigan, Utah, and Virginia—still banned consensual sodomy (defined as oral and anal sex) regardless of the sex of those involved, and four—Texas, Kansas, Oklahoma, and Missouri—prohibited sodomy acts by same-sex couples.

In 2003, with the help of a $2.5 million challenge grant from the Evelyn & Walter Hass Jr. Fund, Wolfson created Freedom to Marry to advocate for gay marriage nationwide.[52] The organization's core mission was devising a national messaging strategy for the budding gay marriage campaign. Early on, Freedom to Marry settled on a framing strategy that the organization called "an informational approach," also known as "rights and benefits." It highlighted the very unequal, unfair, and discriminatory manner in which American marriage law treated gay and lesbian couples by denying them some one thousand marriage rights and benefits. These rights and benefits included many things that most heterosexual couples took for granted—such as adoption rights, tax benefits, inheritance rights, paying a visit to a spouse in the hospital, time off from work to take care of a sick spouse, and even the ability to make healthcare decisions about a spouse in case of illness or an accident.

Freedom to Marry television and print advertisements amplified the rights and benefits messaging. They usually featured lawyers, legal scholars, and

---

[51] The couple remained undeterred in their desire to marry. McConnell adopted Baker to ensure inheritance and other legal protections. Baker also changed his first name to the gender-neutral Pat (though he continued to be known as Jack), and they relocated to another county, Blue Earth County, where an unsuspecting clerk issued the couple the first US marriage license to a same-sex couple, on September 3, 1971. All of this exposure brought about serious consequences. In addition to losing his legal appeals, McConnell was fired from his job at the University of Minnesota Library. He filed a suit in federal court to get his job back, but lost.

[52] On the history of Freedom to Marry, see Solomon, *Winning Marriage*.

104 Framing Equality

retired judges testifying about the discriminatory nature of existing marriage laws and the consequences of constitutional amendments to ban gay marriage. A case in point is an ad from 2004 intended to oppose an amendment to the Oregon Constitution banning gay marriage. It featured a retired state Supreme Court justice wearing a suit and seated in a law library alongside an American flag intoning, "The Oregon Constitution is supposed to protect everyone, but that will change if constitutional amendment 36 passes."[53]

According to Holly Pruett, a marketing consultant for Freedom to Marry, the rights and benefits messaging had multiple purposes, starting with "countering the claim by social conservatives that gay and lesbian couples were asking for special rights."[54] She added that it "reflected the effort to fact-check claims about 'special rights' and to create greater awareness of the legal vulnerability experienced by LGBTQ people when it came to unemployment, housing, medical care, and the rest."[55] Last, but not least, the rights and benefits messaging responded to the contention that gay marriage would hinder religious freedom. As noted by Amy Mello, field director for Freedom to Marry in California, "We wanted to stress that we were not asking people to change their religious views only, but only to accept that gay and lesbian couples were entitled to the rights and benefits of marriage accorded to any straight couple seeking to marry."[56]

The legalistic nature of the rights and benefits messaging stood in striking contrast to the traditional morality championed by Sullivan and other gay conservatives. Sullivan's argument that gay marriage would help mainstream homosexuality struck a chord with some in the gay community. William Eskridge's *The Case for Same-Sex Marriage* argued about the civilizing potential of gay marriage to transform male homosexuality away from a life of promiscuity. As he noted, "It should not have required the AIDS epidemic to alert us to the problem of sexual promiscuity and the advantages of committed relationships."[57] He added, "To the extent to which males in our culture have been more sexually adventurous (more in need of civilizing), same-sex marriage could be a particularly useful commitment device for gay and bisexual men."[58] Jonathan Rauch's *Why Marriage Is Good for Gays, Good for Straights, and Good for America* contended that rather than hastening

---

[53] These campaign ads can be viewed at the Freedom to Marry Collection at Yale University's Sterling Library. Available at https://archives.yale.edu/repositories/12/archival_objects/3180005.
[54] Author's online interview with Holly Pruett (June 22, 2022).
[55] Ibid.
[56] Author's online interview with Amy Mello (June 23, 2022).
[57] Eskridge, *The Case for Same-Sex Marriage*, 9.
[58] Ibid.

the social decline of marriage, same-sex marriage would shore up traditional values.[59]

But Sullivan's moral framing bombed with conservatives, whom he felt would be natural allies for his cause. William J. Bennett, Reagan's secretary of education and the author of many books on morality and virtues, mocked Sullivan's ideas by noting that gay marriage would be "the most revolutionary change ever made" to the institution of marriage. He added, "Society would have to accept that marriage is an arbitrary social construct that can be and should be pried apart from its cultural, biological, and religious underpinnings and redefined by anyone laying claim to it."[60] Conservatives also ridiculed the notion that marriage would work to domesticate homosexuals by noting that "gay activists who argue that same-sex civil marriage will domesticate gay men are, in all likelihood, clinging to a foolish hope. This foolish hope does not justify yet another effort to meddle with marriage."[61]

Harsher still was the reaction from some in the gay community. Sullivan recalled in 2015 that "he was picketed and heckled by gay groups who called him an assimilationist. . . . We were regarded as patriarchal, heterosexist, right-wing scum."[62] His advocacy ran head-on against the self-described "queer activists" who gave a new lease on life to gay liberation ideology. Queer activists challenged "mainstreaming" and saw gay marriage as an existential threat to the gay community. Mattilda Bernstein Sycamore captured this sentiment when noting, "Gay marriage advocates brush aside generations of queer efforts to create new ways of loving, lusting for, and caring for one another, in favor of a 1950s model of white-picket fence, 'we're-just-like-you' normalcy."[63] Prominent among queer activists was Queer Nation. This organization made its debut during New York's 1990 Gay Pride Parade passing out an "inflammatory manifesto" bearing the title "I Hate Straights."[64] Queer Nation rejected "the very categories of sex, gender, and sexual orientation that

---

[59] Jonathan Rauch, *Gay Marriage: Why It Is Good for Gays, Good for Straights, and Good for America* (New York: Holt, 2005).

[60] William J. Bennett, *The Broken Hearth: Reversing the Moral Collapse of the American Family* (New York: Doubleday, 2001), 111–112.

[61] "Ten Arguments from Social Science Against Same-Sex Marriage," The Witherspoon Institute. Available at https://www.frc.org/issuebrief/ten-arguments-from-social-science-against-same-sex-marriage.

[62] Molly Ball, "How Gay Marriage Became a Constitutional Right," *The Atlantic*, July 1, 2015. Available at https://www.theatlantic.com/politics/archive/2015/07/gay-marriage-supreme-court-politics-activism/397052/.

[63] Mattilda Bernstein Sycamore, "There's More to Life than Platinum: Challenging the Tyranny of Sweatshop-Produced Rainbow Flags and Participatory Patriarchy," in *That's Revolting: Queer Strategies for Resisting Assimilation*, ed. Mattilda Bernstein Sycamore (Berkeley, CA: Soft Skull Press, 2008), 3.

[64] Susan Stryker, "Queer Nation," glbtq, 2015. Available at http://www.glbtqarchive.com/ssh/queer_nation_S.pdf.

106   Framing Equality

were used by the mainstream LGBT movement as a basis from which to gain recognition and legal rights."[65]

By the early 2000s, with the rise of Freedom to Marry, and the historic legal wins of gay marriage in Hawaii and Massachusetts, the rights and benefits messaging had eclipsed the conservative case for marriage and sidelined the criticisms of gay marriage by the queer movement. Undoubtedly, the type of messaging promoted by Freedom to Marry benefited greatly from a situation in which a legal framing was, arguably, the only framing that a highly fractured gay activist community could rally around. A 2013 report by David Dodge, a researcher at Political Research Associates, titled "The Right's Marriage Message: Marketing Inequality at the Dawn of Marriage Equality," revealed the outsized role of the rights and benefits messaging in how gay marriage was marketed to the American public.[66]

Based on a review of television and radio advertisements used by gay rights groups during statewide ballot measure campaigns from 1998 to 2009, Dodge found two prominent messaging approaches. The first one, found in 61 percent of all pro-gay marriage advertising, had a "rights-based media messaging," which sought to convey to voters that LGBTQ families are denied fundamental rights and protections. The second one was "avoidance-based media messaging," which reflected an assumption that voters will not connect with or be persuaded by media that prominently features LGBTQ individuals and their stories.

From the start, the legal framing struggled to achieve its aims. As Freedom to Marry's Amy Mello noted, "The legal battle involved different issues in different states—what applied to Iowa did not necessarily apply to New Jersey."[67] She added that in some states, like New York, litigation was not part of the process of legalizing gay marriage, so a different messaging was needed there. In the case of New York, the state legislature legislated gay marriage in June 2011, and the drivers of the campaign were not national organizations like Freedom to Marry but local organizations, such as the now-disbanded Empire State Pride Agenda.

There was also the thorny issue of the implied comparison between the struggle for marriage by same-sex couples and the struggle for civil rights by African Americans. Although gay marriage activists went out of their way to say that marriage discrimination was not the same as racial discrimination,

---

[65] Bernstein and Taylor, "Marital Discord," 13.

[66] David Dodge, "Why Marriage Won: Rightwing Messaging and the 2012 Elections," Political Research Associates, December 13, 2012. Available at https://politicalresearch.org/2012/12/13/why-marriage-won-right-wing-messaging-and-2012-elections.

[67] Author's online interview with Ms. Mello (June 23, 2022).

The comparison was unavoidable, especially as some gay activists drew parallels between laws that once prohibited interracial marriage and those prohibiting gay marriage. Naturally, many in the African American community felt that the gay marriage campaign was riding on the coattails of the civil rights movement. As reported by National Public Radio, "The campaign for same-sex marriage has often been compared to the black civil rights movement of the 1960s. And that comparison has irritated many African-Americans." The report quoted Washington, DC, Reverend Patrick Walker as saying, "I don't like folding the civil rights and gay rights movements together.... White LGBT folks have always the option, no matter how painful, to keep their sexual orientation private and escape discrimination."[68]

Ultimately, however, the messaging itself was the problem. Above all, the modesty of the informational approach to marriage discrimination did not make for a persuasive framing of gay marriage. For one thing, there was very little in this approach to make the general public understand why marriage mattered to gay and lesbian couples. It left many Americans asking themselves, if marriage rights and benefits for same-sex couples could be achieved through civil unions, then what was the rationale for undertaking the reinterpretation of marriage? As noted by Giulia Mariani and Tània Verge in their discussion of the rights and benefits messaging, "While these discursive strategies contributed to persuading judges and lawmakers to grant some legal rights to same-sex couples through civil unions, they failed to make them see the need for displacing the traditional institution of marriage."[69]

The informational approach also made for an impersonal campaign, a point conveyed in several analyses that concluded that a rights-based discourse was not going to be enough to increase public support for gay marriage. Aiming at Freedom to Marry's messaging strategy, Kevin Mumford wrote, "I feel alternately disappointed and angered at the narrowness of the vision that the movement and its leaders feel compelled to offer us.... What becomes clear along the way is that Wolfson understands marriage like a lawyer, both as a contract and as a matter not only of obligations but also

---

[68] Karen Grigsby Bates, "African Americans Question Comparing Gay Rights Movement to Civil Rights," July 2, 2015. Available at https://www.npr.org/2015/07/02/419554758/african-americans-question-comparing-gay-rights-movement-to-civil-rights. It should be noted that many notable civil rights leaders have made an analogy between the gay rights movement and the civil rights movement, most notably the late John Lewis, a civil rights icon. He's quoted by NPR as having said, "I fought too hard and too long against discrimination based on race and color not to stand up and speak up against discrimination against our gay and lesbian brothers and sisters. I see the right to marriage as a civil rights issue."

[69] Giulia Mariani and Tània Verge, "Discursive Strategies and Sequenced Institutional Change: The Case of Marriage Equality in the United States," *Political Studies* 71, no. 2 (2021): 468.

privileges."[70] According to Ronald Shaiko, "The current state of the gay and lesbian movement as it relates to the issue of gay marriage is not very healthy. For the most part, GLBT organizations are on the defensive and have little in the way of a proactive agenda to counter the efforts of religious conservatives and family values groups across the country. Unless and until movement activists and leaders are willing to engage their opponents in a spirited debate about the place of gays and lesbians in our society, they are destined, at least for the next few decades, to remain second-class citizens."[71]

Many critics were also dismayed by the lack of engagement with moral issues in the campaign's framing.[72] Gay marriage activists at Freedom to Marry generally ceded the moral ground to the opposition. In an article titled "Gay Is Good: The Moral Case for Marriage Equality and More," legal scholar Chai Feldblum pointedly criticized the legal framing of the campaign for failing to emphasize morality. In words that in no small measure proved to be prescient, she wrote, "The struggle for marriage equality in this country is ripe for an intervention. If the effort continues along in the manner in which it has been headed, gay couples may or may not succeed in gaining access to civil marriage. But even if gay couples succeed in 'getting marriage,' the gay rights movement may have missed a critical opportunity—a chance to make a positive moral case for gay sex and gay couples. In other words, it will have missed the opportunity to argue that 'gay is good.'"[73]

In a similar vein, legal scholar Carlos Ball decried the lack of explicit incorporation of morality in the framing of the gay marriage campaign, something he felt was necessary to combat negative portrayals of the gay community. He contended that the struggle for "societal acceptance" of same-sex relationships requires a "frontal attack" on the "deeply held view of many Americans regarding the immorality of homosexuality." He added that it is "impossible" to "grapple with the issue by simply asking for equality and state neutrality and protection against discrimination."[74] Elsewhere, Ball attributed the reluctance of the American marriage equality movement "to defend the moral goodness of homosexuality in public policy debates on gay rights" to "the movement's historic focus on privacy and the right to be left alone" and

---

[70] Kevin J. Mumford, "The Miscegenation Analogy Revisited: Same-Sex Marriage as a Civil Rights Story," *American Quarterly* 57, no. 2 (June 2005): 524.

[71] Ronald G. Shaiko, "Same-Sex Marriage, GLBT Organizations, and the Lack of Spirited Political Engagement," in *The Politics of Same-Sex Marriage*, eds. Craig A. Rimmerman and Clyde Wilcox (Chicago: University of Chicago Press, 2007), 95.

[72] See, especially, Gordon A. Babst, Emily R. Gill, and Jason Pierceson, eds., *Moral Argument, Religion, and Same-Sex. Marriage: Advancing the Common Good* (Lexington Books, 2009).

[73] Chai R. Feldblum, "Gay Is Good: The Moral Case for Marriage Equality and More," *The Yale Journal of Law and Feminism* 17 (2005): 139.

[74] Carlos A. Ball, "Moral Foundations for a Discourse on Same-Sex Marriage: Looking beyond Political Liberalism," *Georgetown Law Journal* 85, no. 6 (1997): 1927, 1942.

The United States **109**

"the success of the Christian right in setting the terms of the moral debates involving gay rights."[75]

Interestingly, even opponents of gay marriage were critical of the rights and benefits messaging for anchoring the gay marriage campaign on a very technical understanding of marriage. Writing in 2004, President Maggie Gallagher, head of the National Organization for Marriage (NOM), observed:[76]

> Advocates of same-sex marriage advance two mostly implicit theories about the relationship between law and marriage. The first one is that marriage law consists of a package of benefits we give to reward and facilitate those who undertake marriage responsibility. The second (related) theory is that marriage itself is a product of the laws that produce and define it. Marriage is a legal construct, like a corporation, with no intrinsic purpose or function at all. In this view, marriage does not refer to any larger reality outside the law. Marriage is whatever the law defines it as.

A different but related criticism of the gay marriage campaign was the lack of historical context, especially the absence of references to how the exclusion of gays and lesbians from the institution of marriage fit into a long trend in American history of animus toward homosexuals. Unlike their counterparts abroad, there was no effort by American gay marriage activists to leverage the United States' dark history of discrimination and violence directed at the gay community.[77] In an interview for this book, Charles Francis, the president of the Mattachine Society of Washington, DC, faulted the gay marriage campaign for lacking a historical understanding of how "the denial of the right to marry to gay and lesbian couples was rooted in a deeply-seated animus towards homosexuals in the practices of the American government, especially federal authorities and institutions."[78] He noted that his organization did its best to bring this dark history to light in its amicus brief to the US Supreme Court during the deliberation of *Obergefell*. It said, "For decades, this animus was one of the basic assumptions of American life. It was so persistent, so prevalent, and so instrumental to the way that we structured our institutions, treated our fellow citizens, and organized our lives that, in retrospect, it is often overlooked."[79]

---

[75] Carlos Ball, "The Proper Role of Morality in State Policies on Sexual Orientation and Intimate Relationships," *New York University Review of Law & Social Change* 34 (2010): 83.

[76] Maggie Gallagher, "(How) Will Gay Marriage Weaken Marriage as a Social Institution: A Reply to Andrew Koppelman," *University of St. Thomas Las Journal* 2 (Fall 2004): 35.

[77] The United States has not officially apologized for this history or made efforts to make amends for it. See Encarnación, *The Case for Gay Reparations*.

[78] Author's interview with Charles Francis (Washington, DC: August 30, 2019).

[79] Mattachine Society of Washington, DC, *Amicus Brief in Support of Marriage Equality*. Available at https://mattachinesocietywashingtondc.org/legal-documents/amicus-marriage-equality/. The briefing was written by the legal firm of McDermott Will & Emery.

110   Framing Equality

It took the trauma of Proposition 8 to force a reckoning with the rights and benefits messaging. Organized by ProtectMarriage.com, a cluster of religious organizations and family values activists, Proposition 8 was a marriage referendum triggered by a ruling from the Supreme Court of California that legalized gay marriage. On November 4, 2008, in the same election that elected Barack Obama the first African American president of the United States, Californians voted on adding the following words to the state's constitution: "Only marriage between a man and a woman is recognized as legal in California."[80] After a fiercely contested campaign in which both sides spent a combined $80 million, Proposition 8 was approved by a narrow margin: 52 percent in favor and 48 percent against it. Polls had predicted a win for the gay marriage movement, a reflection of California's liberal political bent and the massive level of resources invested to fight the amendment. All of this led the pro-gay marriage side to assume that victory was a foregone conclusion. According to Freedom to Marry's Amy Mello, "Proposition 8 was at the time the largest grassroots volunteer campaign in American history."[81] She added, "We were so convinced of a win in California that many of our volunteers had left the state before the final vote for Nevada and other states to work for the Obama campaign."

Freedom to Marry's Proposition 8 post-mortem was brutal in its assessment of what went wrong with the attempt to save gay marriage in the nation's largest state. A fight that many thought was winnable was lost, and some twenty thousand gay marriages were thrown into legal limbo. The post-mortem highlighted a litany of errors and missed opportunities, including taking African American and Latino support for granted, underestimating the opposition's capacity to fight back, and, especially, ineffective messaging strategies. "We knew that before marriage went on the ballot again, we had some serious challenges to address—our messaging, chief among them. . . . We were not making the case to conflicted voters in a persuasive way, and they were crucial to winning at the ballot box. Moreover, we were vulnerable to opposition attacks that raised fears that marriage for gay couples would be dangerous to children."[82]

No one who had followed the gay marriage campaign could claim to be surprised by the findings. For years, many observers of the campaign in the media had been sounding the alarm about the messaging problem. Indeed,

---

[80] On Proposition 8, see Jo Becker, *Forcing the Spring: Inside the Fight for Marriage Equality* (New York: Penguin Books, 2015).

[81] Author's online interview with Ms. Mello (June 23, 2022).

[82] "Messaging, Messengers and Public Support," Freedom to Marry. Available at http://www.freedom tomarry.org/pages/Messaging-Messengers-and-Public-Support.

the messaging problem was symptomatic of a movement that seemed to be in perpetual disarray. Molly Ball, who chronicled the ups and downs of the struggle for gay marriage for *The Atlantic*, noted in an interview for this book that "disagreement and organization was a hallmark of the movement." There was "no central strategy or consistent messaging almost since its inception. Instead, multiple groups tried different approaches, hoping that something would stick."[83] Ball further contended that the messaging problem was aggravated by the fact that national gay leaders were not always in control of the messaging because of the decentralized nature of the American gay rights movement. As seen previously, ordinary gays and lesbians began to demand marriage rights decades before gay activists made gay marriage a priority. Reflecting on this development, Ball observed, "Ordinary gay people got ahead of the activists on marriage equality." She added that this reflects something characteristic of American social movements: "Grassroots activists are often at odds or out of sync with what the national leaders are up to."[84]

In 2015, in the blog *Open Democracy*, Freedom to Marry communications director Kevin Nix acknowledged the ineffectiveness of the rights and benefits messaging. "For decades, the gay rights movement emphasized the countless rights and benefits that came with marriage. But that legal frame, including the word rights, did not work. It was sterile, materialistic, and unpersuasive."[85] According to Nix, new and extensive public opinion data was the primary factor for abandoning the rights and benefits message. It suggested that some people who wanted to support LGBT people were not convinced that gay couples deserved marriage since they were of the view that domestic partnerships and civil unions could already provide those benefits. Furthermore, the new polling data revealed that the emphasis on rights and benefits conveyed that gay couples wanted marriage for "political reasons" rather than for the reason they had gotten married, which was to affirm their love and commitment. Even people who had been married multiple times told the pollsters that love and commitment rather than rights and benefits were their primary reasons for getting married.

The 2012 presidential election, which featured gay marriage votes in Washington, Maine, Maryland, and Minnesota, was the start of the last stretch of the marriage equality campaign. Several factors were pointing to a change in fortunes for the campaign. By 2012, support for gay marriage was

---

[83] Author's online interview with Ms. Ball (July 25, 2022).

[84] Ibid.

[85] Kevin Nix, "It's All in the Frame: Winning Marriage Equality," Open Democracy, September 8, 2015. Available at https://www.opendemocracy.net/en/openglobalrights-openpage/its-all-in-frame-winning-marriage-equality-in-america/.

112 Framing Equality

approaching 50 percent of the American public, an almost ten-point increase since 2008.[86] This increase reflected a convergence of factors, starting with the realization that gay marriage in states like Massachusetts was not causing the doomsday scenarios predicted by conservatives. Ahead of the 2015 decision that decided the issue of gay marriage, the opposite side submitted a document to the US Supreme Court that cited "scientific reasons" for why gay marriage was harmful. Among them was that gay marriage would increase abortions, create a spike in early deaths by homosexuals, and disadvantage children, based on the assumption that "same-sex marriage will hurt underprivileged women and children" since redefining marriage would create a new era "where men and women are viewed as interchangeable."[87]

By 2012, the gay civil war over gay marriage had also lessened significantly. This meant that gay activists were beginning to rally around a common cause. Curiously, this newfound unity was an unintended consequence of the gay marriage backlash that had been afoot since the Hawaiian Supreme Court decision on gay marriage in the mid-1990s. The backlash to this decision prompted gay activists who had been very critical of gay marriage to want to join the struggle. As noted by journalist Sasha Issenberg, "All of a sudden, some gay-rights activists who had been principled opponents of seeking marriage decide that, because their opponents want to deny them that right, they feel basically obliged to fight for it."[88] The backlash also managed to turn off many Americans, further boosting the gay marriage campaign. According to Chauncey, "The intensity of the backlash against marriage equality eventually produced its own backlash. Many heterosexuals sought to distance themselves from the antigay animus it expressed."[89]

More important, however, in lifting the fortunes of the marriage equality movement was a shift in messaging signaled by "Marriage Matters," a multimillion-dollar public relations campaign financed by grants from some of America's leading philanthropists, including Jeff Bezos, Bill and Melinda Gates, Michael Bloomberg, and Paul Singer. This media campaign broke new ground in how gay marriage was marketed in America. Up until then, gay marriage supporters had argued for upholding the legal principles of nondiscrimination and equal treatment. They also pointed out the unfairness

---

[86] See https://www.pewresearch.org/religion/fact-sheet/changing-attitudes-on-gay-marriage/.

[87] Pema Levy, "The Science of How Gay Marriage Will Destroy America," *Mother Jones*, April 27, 2015. Available at https://www.motherjones.com/kevin-drum/2015/04/opponents-same-sex-marriage-claim-science-their-side/.

[88] Issac Chotiner, "Why the Marriage-Equality Movement Succeeded," *The New Yorker*, June 10, 2021. Available at https://www.newyorker.com/news/q-and-a/sasha-issenberg-on-the-fight-for-marriage-equality.

[89] George Chauncey, "The Long Road to Marriage Equality," *The New York Times*, June 26, 2013. Available at https://www.nytimes.com/2013/06/27/opinion/the-long-road-to-marriage-equality.html.

that gay couples were denied the same rights and benefits that were available to heterosexual couples. In contrast, the new messaging, generally referred to as "love and commitment," used storytelling to connect with ordinary Americans and persuade them to support gay marriage by featuring heterosexual and homosexual couples talking about the importance of marriage in their domestic lives, how long they had been together, and what they wished for their children and grandchildren. In essence, this meant the end of the erasure of gay people from the gay marriage campaign. The new messaging also stressed the so-called golden rule—treating others as you would like to be treated.

Freedom to Marry also tweaked the delivery of the messaging. According to the organization's leaders, "We cracked the code on message, and then focused our work on message delivery. The messenger mattered, too. Gay and lesbian couples across the country humanized and dramatized their stories in the press, in television ads, and on social media. Couples from all walks of life swung open the window for all of America to get to know them." The new campaign also recruited new messengers—"family members, labor and business leaders, military personnel, clergy, President Obama—to get out on the stump and be vocal. These heterosexual validators gave undecided folks and soft opponents permission to 'evolve' their thinking, at their own pace, toward the freedom to marry."[90]

The new framing is rightly credited with winning gay marriage referendums in Maine, Minnesota, Maryland, and Washington. These wins broke the momentum of the anti-gay marriage movement and provided a boost for forthcoming legal battles. According to a 2012 report by Political Research Associates, a significant reason why gay activists began to turn the tide in 2012 was "due to how both sides waged their media campaigns."[91] It noted that before 2012, "opponents of LGBTQ rights such as the National Organization for Marriage (NOM) and Focus on the Family traditionally ran extremely effective media campaigns with the help of rightwing spin-masters. Pro-LGBTQ media campaigns, on the other hand, largely failed to connect with important middle-of-the-road voters." After 2012, this dynamic "flipped," with opponents of gay marriage running surprisingly ineffective campaigns compared to previous years, while pro-LGBTQ advocates did a much better job winning over hearts and minds of voters with their ads. More revealing, the report notes that in 2012 "pro-LGBTQ advocates largely abandoned the rights-based and avoidance-based media messaging in favor of one that

[90] Evan Wolfson and Kevin Nix, "The Chief Engine of Change: Conversation," *Stanford Social Innovation Review*, February 12, 2015.
[91] Dodge, "Why Marriage Won.".

114   Framing Equality

was strongly pro-LGBTQ. The bulk of advertisements stressed how LGBTQ couples and their families are affected–on an emotional level–due to their inability to marry."

The Political Research Associates report also noted that while a rights-based messaging had saturated much of the public's thinking about same-sex marriage, this did not work to build support for gay marriage; if anything, the opposite was the case. That finding connected with why Freedom to Marry moved away from the "rights and benefits" messaging. A 2010 Freedom to Marry study cited by Political Research Associates found that when heterosexuals were asked why they thought LGBTQ couples would want to get married, 42 percent responded for "rights" and "benefits." However, when asked why couples like you would want to get married, 72 percent of respondents said to "publicly acknowledge their love and commitment." The study concluded that "in essence, pro-LGBTQ advocates have been communicating to voters that LGBTQ people want to get married for different reasons than their heterosexual peers. As a result, voters are confused why other forms of relationship recognition that provide legal protections, such as civil unions and domestic partnership, aren't enough."

Fueling the Conservative Backlash

Despite its shortcomings, the legal framing of the gay marriage campaign was compelling enough to make gay marriage the law of the land across the United States. On June 26, 2015, the US Supreme Court's decision in *Obergefell* ruled that Americans had a constitutional right to same-sex marriage. At the time of the ruling, thirty-six states, the District of Columbia, and Guam had already allowed same-sex marriage by statute, court mandate, or a popular referendum. In one single stroke, the Court struck down all the barriers to same-sex marriage erected across the United States since the 1990s. These barriers included, most notably, dozens of bans on gay marriage erected between 1998 and 2012. To the delight of gay rights activists, Justice Anthony Kennedy, the principal author of the decision, noted, "No union is more profound than marriage, for it embodies the highest ideals of love, fidelity, devotion, sacrifice, and family. In forming a marital union, two people become something greater than once they were."[92] President Obama and First Lady Michelle Obama marked the occasion by illuminating the White House with the rainbow flag colors, a symbol of gay pride.

---

[92] "Supreme Court Ruling Makes Same-Sex Marriage a Right Nationwide," *The New York Times*, June 26, 2015. Available at https://www.nytimes.com/2015/06/27/us/supreme-court-same-sex-marriage.html.

But the triumph at the Supreme Court did not come without significant costs for the gay community. As I argue next, the legalistic rights and benefits messaging not only failed to change hearts and minds at a critical time when most Americans were becoming aware of gay marriage, but it also left the gay marriage campaign ill-equipped to cope with the massive legal and political backlash unleashed by the Christian right. Without an effective messaging strategy that could move hearts and minds and that could counter the opposition's framing of gay marriage as a threat to the family and religious freedom, the opposition was unrestrained in its ability to attack the gay community. In sum, the failure to craft a more ambitious and compelling messaging limited the transformative capacity of gay marriage while at the same time helping enable a robust gay marriage backlash whose legacy endures to this day.

Although conservative opposition to gay marriage in the United States dates to such moral panics as Anita Bryant's 1977 Save Our Children campaign, it was not until 1996, with the creation of the National Campaign to Protect Marriage, that conservative opposition to marriage equality began to coalesce.[93] It responded to the fear that Hawaii's Supreme Court decision in favor of gay marriage would force other states into recognizing gay marriage performed in that state. Fronting what came to be known as the "defense of marriage" movement was a coterie of evangelical leaders, red-state lawmakers, and family values organizations. That this coalition of actors came together so swiftly did not surprise students of the Christian right. As noted by Schacter, the advent of gay marriage was "something of a perfect storm for the Religious Right—the controversy combines in a single issue several of that movement's foundational commitments—commitments to normative heterosexuality, to traditional gender roles, to combating perceived judicial activism, and to the idea that marriage is an institution under widespread social siege and in need of defense."[94]

The Defense of Marriage Act, or DOMA, enacted by the US Congress in 1996, at the height of the moral panic over gay marriage in the United States, was the Christian right's first salvo in its fight against gay marriage. It was also the legal linchpin of a national gay marriage backlash. DOMA barred federal recognition of gay marriage and freed other states from the responsibility of recognizing gay marriages performed in other states. Less known is that the law was a vicious attack on gay parenting. It dictated that a nonbiological parent could not have a legal relationship with a child of the biological parent in a same-sex couple. The law also denied medical leave for same-sex couples to care for their partners or nonbiological children. It also mandated that

---

[93] Chapter 1 offers a broad discussion of this period of American gay rights history.
[94] Schacter, "Courts and the Politics of Backlash," 1214.

116 Framing Equality

same-sex couples could not adopt children, and during divorce proceedings, they could not petition for custody, visitation rights, or child support.[95]

The gay marriage campaign's response to DOMA, especially the law's claim that gay parents were incapable of providing good parenting to their children, mirrored the decision by gay rights activists not to engage with the Christian right in discussions of morality, including who is fit and unfit to be a parent. According to Feldblum, "DOMA opponents mostly eschewed substantive arguments completely and simply charged that supporters of the legislation wanted to create a wedge issue during an election year."[96] This tame response, in her view, reflected the tendency among gay marriage advocates to respond to conservative moral rhetoric "by invoking a counter moral rhetoric of equality and rights: marriage is a 'right' that should be made available to same-sex couples on the same grounds as it is made available to opposite-sex couples." She added that gay marriage advocates "never argue that gay couples embody a moral good identical to straight couples, and rarely argue that same-sex parents are as optimal as different-sex parents."[97]

Emboldened by DOMA, the defense of marriage movement set its eyes on enacting a gay marriage ban in the constitution of every state using a popular vote. That effort reached a crescendo during the 2004 presidential election, which dealt a massive blow to the gay marriage movement. According to Klarman, in 2004 the gay marriage movement experienced "as resounding a defeat as any social movement is likely to experience in American history."[98] That year, more than twenty million Americans voted in eleven state referendums on whether or not to ban gay marriage, with the opposition to gay marriage prevailing in all of them with an overall margin of two to one.[99] In the view of some, this support for the campaign against gay marriage was the deciding factor in determining the winner of the 2004 elections. According to *Washington Post* columnist Dan Balz, gay marriage was the deciding factor in determining the winner of the 2004 elections. "In 2004, Republicans used ballot initiatives barring same-sex marriage to spur turnout among conservative voters. That strategy is thought to have helped then-President George W. Bush win reelection."[100]

---

[95] See Defense of Marriage Act (DOMA), Cornell Law School, Legal Information Institute. Available at https://www.law.cornell.edu/wex/defense_of_marriage_act.

[96] Feldblum, "Gay Is Good," 141–142.

[97] Ibid., 141–142.

[98] Klarman, *From the Closet to the Altar*, 113.

[99] "Voters Pass All 11 Bans on Gay Marriage," *NBC News*, November 1, 2004. Available at https://www.nbcnews.com/id/wbna6383353.

[100] Dan Balz, "Parties Scramble to Come to Terms with Opinion Shift on Same-Sex Marriage," *The Washington Post*, March 26, 2013. Available at https://www.washingtonpost.com/politics/parties-scramble-to-

The United States   **117**

There was nothing accidental about why so many gay referendums were part of the 2004 electoral campaign. The intention was to capitalize on the unpopularity of the *Lawrence* and *Goodridge* decisions, which came down within months of each other. Within one month after the *Lawrence* decision was announced, according to Gallup, support for legalizing gay sex had plummeted a dramatic twelve points, to only 48 percent, down from 60 percent.[101] At the same time, public support for gay marriage fell in the months following *Lawrence* from about 38 percent to 30 percent. Sensing the unpopularity of court rulings on homosexuality and gay marriage, Bush's reelection campaign, headed by campaign manager Ken Mehlman (today an openly gay man) and chief political strategist Karl Rove, decided to make gay marriage a wedge issue in the electoral campaign.

According to Trammell, although today Mehlman and Rowe talk about "the Republican effort to advance LGBT rights, in 2004 they were cynically invested in using gay marriage to increase turnout among Evangelicals."[102] Mehlman and Rowe also persuaded Bush, who before 2004 had taken no official position on gay marriage, to endorse an amendment to the US Constitution banning gay marriage. When justifying the amendment, Bush noted that this was the only way to protect "the most fundamental institution in civilization."[103] First proposed in May 2002, the Federal Marriage Amendment (FMA) stated, "Marriage in the United States shall consist only of the union of a man and a woman. Neither this Constitution nor the constitution of any State, nor state or federal law, shall be construed to require that marital status or the legal incidents thereof be conferred upon unmarried couples or groups."

Aside from boosting Bush's reelection campaign, the FMA was intended to freeze the momentum of the gay marriage movement. According to Patrick Sammon, the former president of the Log Cabin Republicans, an organization that supports LGBTQ equality and conservative values, "The social conservatives might have been more successful with the FMA, at least from the standpoint of getting more support from Democratic legislators, if they had worded the amendment differently, not as an outright ban but rather by

---

come-to-terms-with-opinion-shift-on-same-sex-marriage/2013/03/26/. This argument that the 2004 election was decided by gay marriage is not universally shared. For a contrarian's perspective, see Daniel A. Smith, Matthew DeSantis, and Jason Kassel, "Same Sex-Marriage Ballot Measures and the 2004 Presidential Election," *State and Local Government Review* 38, no. 2 (2006): 78–91.

[101] "Gay and Lesbian Rights," Gallup. Available at https://news.gallup.com/poll/1651/gay-lesbian-rights.aspx.

[102] Author's zoom interview with Mr. Trammell (May 31, 2022).

[103] David Stout, "Bush Backs Ban in Constitution on Gay Marriage," *The New York Times*, February 24, 2004. Available at https://www.nytimes.com/2004/02/24/politics/bush-backs-ban-in-constitution-on-gay-marriage.html.

118 Framing Equality

stipulating that gay marriage could not be imposed by the courts but only by the legislature or the voters. But that wording was unacceptable to social conservatives because it would have eventually allowed marriage equality to move forward at the state or federal level. Their strategy was to stop gay marriage on its track once and for all—no matter how future generations evolved on the issue."[104]

Given the high threshold for success, it is not surprising that FMA failed to get off the ground.[105] But this failure was compensated by the success of the effort to ban gay marriage on a state-by-state basis. Between 1998 and 2012, thirty-one states banned gay marriage in their state constitutions. Remarking on this extraordinary feat, *The Atlantic* noted, "Prior to November (2012), gay marriage had been placed on 31 state ballots—and voted down 31 times. Even in blue states like California (2008) and Maine (2009), defeat was universal. To opponents of gay marriage, that perfect record had become a powerful talking point—proof that American voters stood firmly against any redefinition of the fundamental societal institution."[106] Some bans also prohibited any private arrangement between two people of the same sex resembling marriage. Virginia's Marshall-Newman Amendment, ratified on November 7, 2006, noted, "This Commonwealth and its political subdivisions shall not create or recognize a legal status for relationships of unmarried individuals that intends to approximate the design, qualities, significance, or effects of marriage . . . nor shall this Commonwealth or its political subdivisions create or recognize another union, partnership, or other legal status to which is assigned the rights, benefits, obligations, qualities, or effects of marriage."[107]

For the Christian right, banning gay marriage seemed like an all-around winning proposition. The strategy resonated with the strong moral lens through which Americans have traditionally viewed homosexuality. As recently as 2004, 57 percent of Americans told the General Values Survey that same-sex relations "are always wrong." In the 1980s, this further peaked at 78 percent.[108] According to Gallup, although in 2019 the percentage of Americans answering the question "Do you think gay and lesbian relations between consenting adults should or should not be legal?" stood at 73 percent, as

---

[104] Author's online interview with Mr. Sammon, June 17, 2021.

[105] Any successful amendment to the US Constitution requires approval by a two-thirds majority in both the US House of Representatives and the US Senate.

[106] Molly Ball, "The Marriage Plot: Inside This Year's Epic Campaign for Gay Equality," *The Atlantic*, December 11, 2012. Available at https://www.theatlantic.com/politics/archive/2012/12/the-marriage-plot-inside-this-years-epic-campaign-for-gay-equality/265865/.

[107] Constitution of Virginia. Available at https://law.lis.virginia.gov/constitution/article1/section15-A/.

[108] Nathaniel Persily, "Gay Marriage, Public Opinion and the Courts," Working Paper, University of Pennsylvania Law School, 2006, 11.

The United States **119**

recently as 2006 it was 49 percent and 32 percent in 1987.[109] Banning gay marriage was in keeping with a long tradition of "gay bans" in American history—running from colonial-era anti-sodomy laws to President Dwight Eisenhower's midcentury executive order banning gays and lesbians from employment in the federal government.

According to Amy L. Stone's *Gay Rights at the Ballot Box*, "Between 1974 and 2009, the Christian right placed 146 anti-gay ballot measures on the ballot, using direct democracy to successfully fight LGBT legislative gains on both the state and local level."[110] The popularity of the use of referendums by the Christian right reflected the almost unique advantages for blocking gay rights that putting gay marriage to a popular vote posed relative to pursuing a gay marriage ban through the legislature or the courts. As noted by Stone, "The Religious Right is far more successful at the ballot box, where it can rely on voters' homophobia, than in the legislative or judicial arenas. Thus, the anti-gay Right has strategically engaged in constant attempts to derail LGBT rights not just through the use of referendums to rescind local gay-rights laws, but also with initiatives that attempt to ban same-sex marriage, fire gay and lesbian teachers, and eliminate the potential for future LGBT rights legislation."[111]

By embracing the strategy of banning gay marriage using a popular vote, the anti-gay marriage movement was also banking on ensuring the long-term success of their efforts, knowing that removing a gay marriage ban from any constitution is a herculean endeavor. Anti-gay marriage activists were also hoping to put the gay movement on the defensive and, more specifically, against the side of democracy by promoting gay marriage referenda as the ultimate expression of the popular will. "Let the people decide" became a mantra for many in the anti-gay marriage movement.[112] Putting gay marriage on the ballot box also forced the marriage equality movement to spend money and resources that they would rather spend on educating the public about homophobia, fighting the AIDS epidemic, and protecting LGBTQ youth.

To accompany the campaign to ban gay marriage nationwide, opponents of gay marriage employed several messaging strategies. Most of these strategies went unchallenged by the gay marriage campaign because of concerns that confronting them might distract from the messaging about the discriminatory nature of existing marriage laws. When speaking of limiting

---

[109] "Gay and Lesbian Rights," Gallup. Available at https://news.gallup.com/poll/1651/gay-lesbian-rights.aspx.

[110] Amy L. Stone, *Gay Rights at the Ballot Box* (University of Minnesota Press, 2012), Introduction.

[111] Ibid.

[112] "Gay Marriage: Let the People Decide," *The Weekly Standard*, November 18, 2014.

marriage to heterosexual couples, the Family Research Council (FRC), a leading "family values" organization, avoided the phrase "gay marriage ban." Instead, they spoke about "defending marriage." To justify banning gay marriage, the FRC also employed such pithy phrases as "sex makes babies, society needs babies, and children need mothers and fathers."[113]

More broadly, to justify banning gay marriage, the anti-gay marriage movement advanced two main messages: "social consequences" and "conflicting rights." While the first message emphasized the dangers that gay marriage posed for society, the second one suggested that gay rights and religious freedom were mutually exclusive. According to one study from 2013 of conservative advertising against gay marriage, 75 percent of all ads stressed the message that gay marriage would weaken traditional marriage, followed by the claims that gay marriage would harm kids, advance "the gay agenda," and create victims of gay marriage by restricting religious freedom.[114]

By the early 2000s, as the gay marriage campaign was beginning to gain traction, the attacks on gay marriage had grown darker and eerily reminiscent of the moral crusades against homosexuality of the 1970s, with claims linking gay marriage to criminality and deviance. Former Republican senator and presidential candidate Rick Santorum, a devout Catholic, famously compared gay marriage to bestiality when noting in a 2003 interview that "in every society, the definition of marriage has not ever to my knowledge included homosexuality. That's not to pick on homosexuality. It's not, you know, man on child, man on dog, or whatever the case may be."[115] In her book *The Abolition of Marriage*, NOM president Maggie Gallagher equated same-sex marriage to polygamy, arguing, "For all its ugly defects, [polygamy] is an attempt to secure stable mother-father families for children . . . [and] there is no principled reason why you don't have polygamy if you have gay marriage."[116]

Although today a ghost of its former self, during its heyday NOM was "the leading national anti-LGBT organization."[117] Between 2007, the year of its creation, to 2010, its budget mushroomed from $500,000 to $9 million.[118] NOM was also the engine behind the mobilization of Americans against gay

---

[113] John Corvino and Maggie Gallagher, *Debating Same-Sex Marriage* (New York: Oxford University Press, 2012), 94.

[114] Dodge, "Why Marriage Won."

[115] The transcript of the original interview is available at https://usatoday30.usatoday.com/news/washington/2003-04-23-santorum-excerpt_x.htm.

[116] Cited in "Profiles on the Right: National Organization for Marriage (NOM)," Political Research Associates, November 11, 2013.

[117] "How NOM Became a Vehicle to Hide Anti-LGBT Donors," *The Huffington Post*, March 30, 2012. Available at https://www.huffpost.com/entry/nom-donors_b_1391428.

[118] Ibid.

The United States **121**

marriage. Between 2013 and 2017, the group organized the March for Marriage in Washington, DC, named after the March for Life, the annual protest march that pro-abortion forces began organizing after the *Roe v. Wade* decision was announced in 1973. NOM was also the mastermind behind the messaging of the campaign against gay marriage.

In typical backlash fashion, NOM promoted the retrograde messaging that children need a mom and a dad and that gay marriage implies that a married mom and dad are dispensable. NOM also stressed the view that being against gay marriage is not anti-gay; it is just pro-marriage, a message intended to reassure people of faith that they were not homophobes. "Gay marriage advocates believe there isn't any difference between two men in a sexual union and a husband and wife, and those of us who see this difference are blinded by hatred and prejudice. They delegitimize opponents, brand us as haters, and then try to strip us of our rights," said Gallagher in 2010.[119]

But it was NOM's media tactics that gave the organization the notoriety of having established "a new standard for odious political advertising."[120] According to the online magazine *Slate*, "The tactics used by Proposition 8 campaigners were not merely homophobic. They were laser-focused to exploit Californians' deepest and most irrational fears about gay people, indoctrinating an entire state with cruelly anti-gay propaganda."[121] Especially notable was a media campaign depicting gay marriage as a threat to children, a powerful weapon for stoking fears about LGBTQ people. One notorious TV ad of the campaign in favor of Proposition 8 featured "upset and baffled first graders, who'd been taken to San Francisco's city hall where they were forced to watch their teacher's lesbian wedding."[122]

A more notorious NOM ad was "Gathering Storm," a 60-second video clip released in 2009 and part of a $1.5 million campaign that targeted five states where gay marriage was being debated. It warned Americans about the looming threat that gay marriage posed to parental rights and religious freedom. Set against a backdrop of menacing clouds and violent lightning, the video featured actors pretending to be ordinary Americans expressing

---

[119] Maggie Gallagher, "The Core Civil Right to Vote for Marriage," *Townhall*, June, 16, 2010. Available at https://townhall.com/columnists/maggiegallagher/2010/06/16/the-core-civil-right-to-vote-for-marriage-n788582.

[120] Michael Hiltzik, "A Reminder That the Prop 8 Campaign Brendan Eich Supported Was Odious," *Los Angeles Times*, April 7, 2014. Available at https://www.latimes.com/business/hiltzik/la-fi-mh-prop-8-campaign-20140407-story.html.

[121] Mark Joseph Stern, "Just a Reminder: The Campaign for Prop 8 Was Unprecedentedly Cruel," *Slate*, April 4, 2014. Available at https://slate.com/human-interest/2014/04/brendan-eich-supported-prop-8-which-was-worse-than-you-remember.html.

[122] Lillian Faderman, *The Gay Revolution: The Story of the Struggle* (New York: Simon and Schuster, 2015), 608.

122   Framing Equality

concerns about gay marriage. "The winds are strong," says a white man. "I am afraid," chimes a young black woman. Most worried, however, is a parent from Massachusetts (where gay marriage was already legal) complaining of being unable to prevent the government from teaching her children that same-sex marriage is appropriate. Although the ad was widely parodied in the national press (*New York Times* columnist Frank Rich called it "an Internet camp classic"), NOM credited this media attention with helping them spread their message.[123]

The gay marriage campaign's response to NOM's attacks reveals a lot about how the decision to stick to a purely legalistic messaging through 2012, before the love and commitment messaging was introduced, resulted in losing winnable fights, such as Proposition 8. The response also says much about why the campaign struggled to make headway in advancing support for gay marriage among the general public. Most notably, media efforts to fight Proposition 8 for the most part excluded visual representation of gay couples and their children, based on the belief that making gay people the face of the campaign would distract from the messaging about discrimination and potentially even risk offending people's sensibilities.

In her account of the many messaging problems that bedeviled the fight against Proposition 8, historian Lilian Faderman reported, "The feeble organized effort led by Equality for All/No on 8 was replete with bad choices. They grappled for a while with whether to tell honest stories about gay and lesbian lives, or to de-gay the campaign. The de-gaying side won."[124] She added, "One of No on 8's worst decisions was to keep kids out of the campaign. No children of same-sex couples talking about how the right to marry would help their families. Not even a response to TV ads about how same-sex marriage would harm children."

More puzzling is that pro-gay marriage media efforts avoided references to gay marriage itself. Rauch recalled that one advertisement against Proposition 8 "never uses the phrase gay marriage or even the word gay."[125] The absence of references to gay marriage and gay couples, according to Rauch, was rooted in the desire for a messaging "that appeals to the largest possible number of swing voters while causing a minimum of political backlash." But, as he argues, this came at a considerable cost. "Whatever the tactical considerations, the absence of gay couples and gay marriage from California's

[123] Frank Rich, "The Bigots' Last Hurrah," *The New York Times*, April 18, 2009. Available at https://www.nytimes.com/2009/04/19/opinion/19Rich.html.

[124] Faderman, *The Gay Revolution*, 607–608.

[125] Jonathan Rauch, "Campaigns for and against Same-Sex Marriage," The Brookings Institution, October 26, 2008. Available at https://www.brookings.edu/opinions/campaigns-for-and-against-same-sex-marriage/.

gay marriage debate makes for an oddly hollow discussion. It leaves voters of good conscience to conjure in their own minds the ads that are not being aired: Ads that show how gay marriage directly affects the couples and communities that need it most." He cites a series of ads that could have been run by the campaign, such as one "showing a gay teenager celebrating his parents' 20th anniversary and dreaming of his own someday."

In the post-*Obergefell* era, anti-gay marriage activists have pursued a variety of short- and long-term objectives. In the short term, the priority has been to weaken gay marriage. This strategy has taken several forms. The most apparent is victimization. Soon after the *Obergefell* decision came down, some conservatives began to view themselves as victims of the marriage equality movement. The most famous of these "victims" was Kim Davis, a Kentucky county clerk from Rowan County who became a national figure after she was sent to jail for refusing to sign a marriage certificate for a same-sex couple. In justifying her defiant behavior, Davis claimed that "granting marriage licenses to gay and lesbian couples is a violation of God's definition of marriage and an infringement of my personal beliefs as an Apostolic Christian."[126]

A sense of victimization also drove the religious freedom movement. In recent years, social conservatives have embraced "religious freedom restoration acts," or RFRAs. These laws are fueled by the sense that gay marriage impinges upon the civil rights of Christians and their adherence to the traditional definition of marriage. Within three years of the *Obergefell* decision, at least eight states had enacted new laws that "permit people to infringe on the rights of LGBT individuals and their families to the extent they believe that discriminating against them is necessary to uphold their own religious or moral beliefs."[127] RFRAs vary in scope, but most permit people and businesses to refuse to participate in a same-sex wedding ceremony or to provide goods and services related to such ceremonies. Others would permit child welfare agencies and physical and mental health providers to refuse service to LGBT people.

Social conservatives have also sought to freeze LGBTQ equality by blocking most LGBTQ legislation that makes it to the US Congress. In 2015, a Republican-controlled Congress declined to consider an initiative by the Obama administration to add sexual orientation to the 1964 Civil Rights Act. This initiative was intended to remedy for the failure of Congress to enact a

---

[126] "Kim Davis, Kentucky Clerk, Held in Contempt and Ordered to Jail," *NBC News*, September 3, 2015. Available at http://www.nbcnews.com/news/us-news/kentucky-clerk-kim-davis-held-contempt-court-n421126.

[127] "All We Want Is Equality: Religious Exemptions and Discrimination against LGBT People in the United States," Human Rights Campaign, February 19, 2018. Available at https://www.hrw.org/report/2018/02/19/all-we-want-equality/religious-exemptions-and-discrimination-against-lgbt-people#.

124 Framing Equality

federal ban on anti-gay discrimination, dating back to 1974, with the introduction of the Equality Law. That proposed law did not even get a vote in the House of Representatives. It took another intervention by the US Supreme Court, in 2020, with its ruling of *Bostock v. Clayton County, Georgia*, to affirm that the prohibition of sex discrimination in the 1964 Civil Rights Act applied to discrimination based on sexual orientation and gender identity.

In the long term, the main objective of social conservatives is to overturn *Obergefell*. Anti-gay marriage activists have been inspired by the success of the anti-abortion movement in overturning *Roe v. Wade*, the 1973 US Supreme Court decision that legalized abortion. In 2022, with its decision of *Dobbs v. Jackson Women's Health Organization*, the Court struck down abortion's constitutional protection. Borrowing a page from the pro-life playbook, the anti-gay marriage movement has sought to cast *Obergefell* as an illegitimate ruling. Just like the pro-life movement has argued that there's no right to an abortion under the US Constitution, anti-gay marriage activists contend that there's nothing in the US Constitution related to gay marriage.

Only time will tell whether the anti-gay marriage movement will succeed in undoing gay marriage. At present, there are reasons for being both hopeful and concerned. On the optimistic side, in December 2022, the US Congress repealed DOMA. The law had remained on the books despite being wholly eviscerated by the US Supreme Court in 2015. In a testament to how much of the Republican Party's social agenda remains under the control of the Christian right and how much animosity toward gay marriage remains among the party's leadership, thirty-six Republican senators voted against DOMA's repeal. At the same time that it repealed DOMA, Congress enacted the Respect for Marriage Act. This law calls for all states to recognize same-sex unions regardless of where that union took place. It did not, however, codify *Obergefell* into law by requiring every state to license same-sex marriages as they are currently obligated. As put by the American Civil Liberties Union (ACLU), "The Respect for Marriage Act would not require any state to allow same-sex couples to marry."[128] If the US Supreme Court were to change its mind on gay marriage, as it did with abortion, some thirty-five gay marriage bans would automatically be reactivated.[129]

However, a deep sense of cognitive dissonance mars the contemporary picture of LGBTQ rights. According to Gallup, the percentage of Americans

[128] American Civil Liberties Union, "Here's What You Need to Know about the Respect for Marriage Act," July 21, 2022. Available at https://www.aclu.org/news/lgbtq-rights/what-you-need-to-know-about-the-respect-for-marriage-act.

[129] Elaine S. Povich, "Without Obergefell, Most States Would Have Same-Sex Marriage Bans," Pew Research Center, July 7, 2022. Available at https://www.pewtrusts.org/en/research-and-analysis/blogs/stateline/2022/07/07/without-obergefell-most-states-would-have-same-sex-marriage-bans.

expressing support for "gay marriage" reached a record 71 percent in 2023. That is a 20-percent point increase since 2015.[130] At the same time, LGBTQ Americans are being targeted in ways not seen since the 1970s. According to an HRC report, the years of the first Trump administration (2017 through 2021) were "the most virulently anti-LGBTQ" in decades.[131] Trump appointed judges known for their animus toward gay people, banned transgender service members from the military, and proposed a change to the Affordable Care Act to remove protections for LGBTQ people.

Upon returning to office in 2025, one of Trump's first actions was an executive order stating: "It is the policy of the United States to recognize two sexes, male and female."[132] This order was in keeping with the hundreds of anti-LGBTQ bills that have been introduced in Republican-controlled state legislatures in recent years. According to the ACLU, in 2023 alone, the number of anti-LGBTQ laws introduced across the United States amounted to 491, with several dozen signed into law, including bans on drag shows, gender-affirming care for minors and adults, participation of transgender athletes in sports, and the teaching of sexual orientation and gender identity from kindergarten through the third grade, including Florida's "Don't Say Gay" law.[133] When defending these bans, conservative leaders and lawmakers have cited concerns about "grooming," a homophobic slur that exploits people's worst fears about gays and children.

Even gay marriage, despite its popularity with Americans, has recently come under attack. In 2020, Justices Samuel Alito and Clarence Thomas argued that when the US Supreme Court legalized gay marriage it "invented a right not based in the text of the Constitution" that depicts people of goodwill as "bigots."[134] Shortly thereafter, in 2022, after the US Supreme Court revoked the right to legalized abortion, Alito and Thomas argued that the Court should also reconsider other decisions involving privacy, due process, and equal protection rights, including gay marriage and contraceptives.

---

[130] Justin McCarthy, "U.S. Same-Sex Marriage Support Holds at 71% High," Gallup, June 5, 2023. Available at https://news.gallup.com/poll/506636/sex-marriage-support-holds-high.aspx.

[131] "The Real List of Trump's Unprecedented Steps for the LGBTQ Community," The Human Rights Campaign, June 11, 2020. Available at https://www.hrc.org/news/the-list-of-trumps-unprecedented-steps-for-the-lgbtq-community.

[132] "Defending Women from Gender Ideology Extremism and Restoring Biological Truth to the Federal Government," The White House, January, 20, 2025. Available at https://www.whitehouse.gov/presidential-actions/2025/01/defending-women-from-gender-ideology-extremism-and-restoring-biological-truth-to-the-federal-government/.

[133] "Mapping Attacks on LGBTQ Rights in U.S. State Legislatures in 2024," American Civil Liberties Union, May 31, 2024.

[134] Adam Liptak, "Justices Thomas and Alito Question Same-Sex Marriage Precedent," The New York Times, October 5, 2020. Available at https://www.nytimes.com/2020/10/05/us/politics/thomas-alito-same-sex-marriage.html.

126 Framing Equality

Arguments like this one give hope to the Christian right and conservatives in general that someday the court will see fit to overturn *Obergefell* and return the decision about who regulates marriage to the individual states.

In response to this onslaught of anti-gay attacks, in 2023 the HRC declared a "state of emergency for LGBTQ people." The declaration, the first of its kind in the organization's forty-three-year history, was unsparing in its description of the threat level: "The multiplying threats facing millions in our community are not just perceived—they are real, tangible, and dangerous. In many cases, they are resulting in violence against LGBTQ+ people, forcing families to uproot their lives as they flee their homes in search of safer states, and triggering a tidal wave of increased homophobia and transphobia that puts the safety of each one of us at risk."[135]

A Troubled Legacy

Understandably, many gay rights activists are concerned about the present state of LGBTQ rights in the United States, including Wolfson. I interviewed him in May 2022, just days after the US Supreme Court's decision to strike down the right to legal abortion was leaked to the press.[136] He noted that while he was worried about the future of gay marriage, he was heartened by its popularity among Americans and by the support for gay marriage that Freedom to Marry managed to achieve in significant sectors of American society, including business corporations and faith communities. He added that he was more concerned about attacks on women, people of color, transgender people, and immigrants than he was about gay marriage being reversed by the courts. Most of all, however, he was concerned about American democracy. He added that it was incumbent on the gay rights movement to be engaged in the protection of American democratic institutions. "There are no gay rights without democratic freedoms."

I asked Wolfson to address the criticism that the messaging of Freedom to Marry put too much emphasis on rights and benefits at the expense of promoting the humanity and dignity of gay and lesbian couples. He noted that, in hindsight, he wishes that "the shift in messaging from rights and benefits to love and commitment had occurred sooner. To some extent, the emphasis on civil rights and legal equality got in the way of personal stories about why gay and lesbian couples valued marriage in their relationships. That is,

---

[135] Human Rights Campaign, National State of Emergency for LGBTQ+ Americans. Available at https://www.hrc.org/campaigns/national-state-of-emergency-for-lgbtq-americans.
[136] Author's interview with Mr. Wolfson (New York, May 17, 2022).

perhaps, the only regret I have." But he quickly amended that comment by saying that "there was a logical progression in the messaging of emphasizing first the discrimination that gay and lesbian couples faced before making the case that gay couples desired marriage for the same reasons as heterosexual couples."

In response to whether a more ambitious and idealistic framing might have made a difference in the legacy for LGBTQ equality, he responded that transforming American society was never the intention of Freedom to Marry. "We stressed a message about equality under the law and how gay marriage would serve to integrate gays and lesbians into existing norms. Our goal was never to create a social revolution by reinventing marriage; we only wanted to join an existing institution. We did not have to convince everyone; we just had to convince enough people. And when we achieved our goal, we closed shop."

Wolfson also reflected on the unique messaging challenges of the American gay marriage campaign, noting that the diversity of the gay rights community in the United States made keeping everyone on the same message an uphill struggle. He qualified that statement by adding that the American gay rights community "has always been pluralistic in its points of view, which is a sign of its strength." He also noted that the leaders of national LGBT rights organizations, especially the HRC and the National Gay and Lesbian Task Force, "were disproportionally against same-sex marriage," noting that for these organizations "same-sex marriage was the wrong fight at the wrong time." He also said that the campaign could have done without the attacks from the gay left. "We could have used less of that."

Lastly, we discussed the backlash. He noted that the backlash was going to happen regardless of the framing, given the longstanding animosity of the Christian right toward the LGBTQ community. "The backlash was inevitable," he noted, adding that a strong opposition to gay rights by the Christian right and family values organizations preceded the gay marriage campaign by decades. He also warned about making a causal connection between the legal framing of the gay marriage campaign and the persistence of any political backlash.

Indeed, it is important to note that much of the current backlash does not stem from an overreliance on a legal or rights-based strategy to advance gay marriage but rather from resistance to the transgender rights movement. Indeed, most anti-gay laws recently enacted in the United States target gender identity rather than sexual orientation. These laws reflect the opposition of most Americans to the medicalization of gender nonconformity, especially of minors, and to the belief that gender identity is the real basis for a person's

128 Framing Equality

sex.[137] But as I have argued in this chapter, the current backlash is not unrelated to the modesty of the legal framing of the gay marriage campaign. Above all, the framing of the campaign helped enable the current backlash by not making a more ambitious, persuasive, and imaginative case for gay marriage.

As seen in this chapter, the gay marriage campaign did not ask Americans to do more than accept a change in the legal landscape of the institution of marriage to allow for the admission of gay and lesbian couples. Nor did the campaign confront the dehumanizing attacks on homosexuals. Perhaps this was too much to ask or to wish for. After all, transforming society was never the objective of gay marriage activists in the United States. But when looking at how gay marriage activists in other countries framed gay marriage around human rights principles, such as dignity, or as a means for expanding citizenship, it is hard to avoid the impression that the American campaign, for all of its legal accomplishments and epoch-making moments, was a big missed opportunity to do more to advance LGBTQ equality.

---

[137] According to a 2022 Pew survey, most Americans "favor protecting trans people from discrimination, but fewer support policies related to medical care for gender transitions." It further notes that 60 percent of Americans say a person's gender is determined by their sex assigned at birth, up from 56 percent in 2021 and 54 percent in 2017. See Kim Parker, Juliana Menasce Horowitz, and Anna Brown, "Americans Complex Views on Gender Identity and Transgender Issues," Pew Research Center, June 28, 2022. Available at https://www.pewresearch.org/social-trends/2022/06/28/americans-complex-views-on-gender-identity-and-transgender-issues/.

Chapter 4
Brazil

A Political Framing

On December 29, 2018, just before the inauguration of Jair Bolsonaro as Brazil's new president, the *New York Times* made note of an unusual story coming out of South America's largest democracy: a dramatic spike in the number of same-sex couples seeking to marry. The headline captured the situation: "Gay Couples Rush to Wed Before Brazil's New President Takes Office."[1] The Brazilian government officially recorded the phenomenon. According to Brazil's statistics agency IBGE, "Same-sex marriage rose 62 percent in 2018, and a fifth of the 9,529 gay weddings took place in December."[2] Many (maybe most) of those couples rushing to the altar were acting on the advice of the Brazilian Bar Association, which cautioned that under the incoming administration all gay rights were at risk. The warning was well-founded. As discussed shortly, during his congressional career, Bolsonaro's homophobia was rarely disguised. He went out of his way to advertise it. As a presidential candidate, he made it very clear that if given the chance, he would act to roll back many of the gay rights protections that Brazil's LGBTQ community had achieved since the country made a successful transition to democracy in 1985, including same-sex marriage.

Concerns about gay marriage were also driven by lingering resentment among Bolsonaro supporters over how it became legal in Brazil. As in the United States, it was the courts, rather than the legislature, that legalized same-sex marriage. On May 5, 2011, Brazil's Federal Supreme Court ruled that it was a violation of the Brazilian Constitution for the state to treat homosexual and heterosexual families differently. Overnight, gay and lesbian couples in Brazil found themselves with access to all the rights and benefits of marriage available to heterosexual couples—including adoption,

---

[1] Shasta Darlington, "Gay Couples Rush to Wed before Brazil's New President Takes Office," *The New York Times*, December 29, 2018. Available at https://www.nytimes.com/2018/12/29/world/americas/brazil-bolsonaro-gay-marriage.html.

[2] Fabio Teixeira, "Gay Marriage Soared ahead of Bolsonaro Presidency in Brazil," *Reuters*, December 5, 2019. Available at https://www.reuters.com/article/us-brazil-lgbt-marriage/gay-marriage-soared-ahead-of-bolsonaro-presidency-in-brazil-idUSKBN1Y92RO/.

Framing Equality. Omar G. Encarnación, Oxford University Press. © Oxford University Press (2025).
DOI: 10.1093/9780190880330.003.0005

130   Framing Equality

welfare benefits, healthcare protections, inheritance and tax rights, hospital and prison visitation privileges, and even surrogacy and in-vitro fertilization. Decided unanimously (one justice abstained, having already stated his position that the Brazilian Constitution did not prohibit gay civil unions), the ruling stunned gay rights activists. Recalling the news of the ruling in an interview for this book, Gustavo Bernardes, the head of the LGBT Office of the Secretariat of Human Rights under the Dilma Rousseff administration, noted that the "speed and firmness of the ruling was wholly unexpected by the LGBT movement; so much so that few gay activists bothered to travel to Brasília to follow the proceedings."[3]

But the ruling created as many headaches as it sought to solve. It was not altogether clear what precisely the Court had authorized when it called for complete parity between heterosexual and homosexual unions. While some notary publics concluded that the Court had legalized gay marriage and began issuing marriage licenses to same-sex couples, others were of the view that the Court had only authorized same-sex civil unions with identical benefits to marriage. Complicating matters, on October 25, 2011, the Superior Court of Justice, the highest court in Brazil for deciding non-constitutional issues related to federal law, ruled in favor of a request for a marriage license by a lesbian couple. But that ruling, which struck down two lower courts' rulings against the women, only applied to the case under review. Underscoring the seeming arbitrariness of the decisions reached by different courts across Brazil, the magazine *Veja* ran a story that declared, "For every couple, a different decision."[4]

To clear up the confusion, the judiciary was compelled to intervene again. This time, it was the National Council of Justice, a fifteen-member panel created in 2004 to oversee the judicial system headed by the chief justice of the Federal Supreme Court. On May 14, 2013, the Council unambiguously decided in favor of gay marriage by ordering all notary publics to issue a marriage license to any same-sex couple that asked for one, noting that this was the mandate of the Federal Supreme Court's 2011 decision. The Council's intervention made Brazil the third country in Latin America to legalize gay marriage, after Argentina and Uruguay, and, at the time, the largest country in the entire world with gay marriage on its books.[5]

The back-to-back decisions by the judiciary leading to the legalization of gay marriage triggered a political firestorm with all the characteristics of a

---

[3] Author's electronic communication with Mr. Bernardes (June 21, 2018).

[4] "Casamento gay: para cada casal, uma sentença," *Veja*, June 28, 2012. Available at https://veja.abril.com.br/brasil/casamento-gay-para-cada-casal-uma-sentenca/.

[5] Uruguay also legalized gay marriage in 2013, by an act of the Uruguayan Congress on April 2, 2013. The law went into effect on August 5, 2013.

quintessential backlash, including attacks on the courts and gay activists. But neither the intensity nor the outcome of the backlash matched that of the United States. These are striking developments, considering that in Brazil, as in the United States, the courts had the final say on gay marriage and evangelical leaders led the fight against gay marriage. There were no attempts in Brazil to put gay marriage to a popular referendum to ban it either at the federal or state level. Nor did the Brazilian Congress see fit to enact national legislation that would encumber gay marriage, such as the Defense of Marriage Act, the 1996 law passed by the US Congress that barred federal recognition of gay marriage. Brazil, for the most part, was also spared the post-gay marriage assault on the LGBTQ community experienced by the United States, including a ban on transgender people serving in the military enacted by the Trump administration in 2017 and state laws banning gender-affirming care and discussion of homosexuality in schools. Ironically, Brazilian gay activists achieved their most significant victory under Bolsonaro: a landmark decision from the Federal Supreme Court criminalizing homophobia. Making homophobia a crime has been the top goal of the gay rights movement since its formation back in the 1970s.

As discussed in this chapter, numerous factors conspired to make the war over gay marriage less toxic in Brazil than in the United States, including a notable history of tolerance toward homosexuality and the difficulties of getting legislation of any kind enacted in the Brazilian Congress. Ultimately, however, the Brazilian experience closely mirrors the framing strategies of gay rights activists. According to our typology of gay marriage framing approaches, Brazil is a paradigm of "political framing." This framing freely mixes legal and moral arguments to justify gay marriage. It is also distinguished by a pragmatic and even cautious discourse about gay marriage. It upholds the view that the state has the legal and moral obligation to protect the rights and welfare of gay and lesbian couples but that this protection does not require the label of marriage. Despite having Latin America's largest and most politically connected gay rights movement, for decades Brazilian gay activists campaigned exclusively for same-sex civil unions. They also studiously avoided the term "marriage" to put some rhetorical distance between themselves and the institution of marriage. Indeed, gay activists were so careful around the term marriage that some scholars concluded that there was no interest in gay marriage in Brazil.[6]

---

[6] See, especially, Jordi Díez, *The Politics of Gay Marriage in Latin America: Argentina, Chile, and Mexico* (New York: Cambridge University Press, 2016), 254.

132 Framing Equality

It was only in 2011, the year that the Federal Supreme Court legalized same-sex civil unions, that calls for gay marriage began to be heard in Brazil. At that point, the rhetoric about gay marriage acquired a strong moral grounding. Brazilian gay activists began to demand "the same rights with the same name," the slogan from the Spanish gay marriage campaign. They also cast gay marriage as a means for affirming human rights and extending full citizenship to gay and lesbian couples. These moral appeals resonated broadly, especially with the courts, which at the time were becoming increasingly concerned about the human rights situation in Brazil. They also resonated across Brazilian civil society, including the Catholic Church, a reflection of the peculiarities of Brazilian Catholicism. Unlike its counterpart in Spain, the Brazilian National Conference of Bishops has a history of promoting human rights for minority groups, including homosexuals. Primarily influenced by the social progressivism of Liberation Theology, this history did not make the Catholic Church an ally of the gay community in its fight for marriage rights. But it undercut the evangelical opposition to gay marriage. For the most part, the Brazilian Catholic Church sat out the war over gay marriage and LGBTQ rights in general.

While successful at mitigating backlash, the political framing had its drawbacks. Messaging was never a priority for the Brazilian gay rights movement. It was seen as secondary to lobbying politicians, state officials, and the courts. For its part, deliberately delaying making the case for gay marriage undermined building support for gay marriage among the general public and the capacity of gay marriage to bolster LGBTQ equality. Brazil never had the robust societal debate about gay marriage afforded by the moral framing in Spain or even by the legal framing in the United States. In sum, the political framing was effective in preventing backlash but much less so in bolstering LGBTQ equality.

The political framing of the gay marriage campaign in Brazil has deep roots in domestic politics. Mixing legal claims and moral appeals to advance LGBTQ equality dates to the mid-1980s, when gay rights activists used human rights principles to shape the debate surrounding Brazil's new democratic constitution and the fight against HIV/AIDS. The pragmatic discourse around gay marriage reflected concerns that marriage demands might trigger backlash and compromise bigger policy priorities, such as the criminalization of homophobia. It also mirrored the recognition in the Brazilian Constitution of "stable unions," a category of relationships that entitles unmarried couples to all the rights and benefits of marriage. A less apparent factor was the incorporation of the gay rights movement into the *Partido dos Trabalhadores* (PT), or Workers' Party, around the time of the transition to democracy in the mid-1980s and into the bureaucracies of the state itself under the Lula and Rousseff administrations. This incorporation afforded political visibility and access to the national legislature and state agencies to gay rights activists. But it also encouraged them to moderate their demands, since they had to negotiate and reconcile their priorities with the political agenda of the PT, including appealing to the evangelical population. Not surprisingly, since its emergence in the late 1970s, the Brazilian gay rights movement has behaved more like political insiders than outside agitators.

Gay Politics before Gay Marriage

Brazil's first gay rights organization–*Somos: Grupo de Afirmação Homossex-ual* (We Are: Homosexual Affirmation Group)—was created in 1978 during the period known as *abertura*, or opening, a policy of political liberalization begun by President Ernesto Geisel in 1973.[7] It opened the way for the country's return to democracy by 1985 after two decades of military dictatorship. Somos's emergence also suggested the relative tolerance of military rule in Brazil. According to Luiz Mott, Brazil's best-known gay rights activist and the founder of *Grupo Gay da Bahia* (GGB), the oldest gay rights group in Latin America still in existence, "The generals were relatively tolerant of pornography, transvestism, and flamboyant homosexuality, deeming it all part of Brazilian culture."[8] To underscore this claim, Mott points out that his organization, GGB, was the first gay rights group in Latin America to secure legality from the government in 1980. Following this breakthrough, the unofficial slogan of the still-nascent Brazilian gay rights movement became "It is legal to be homosexual."[9]

None of this is to say that the military dictatorship was a friend of the gay community. Under the old regime, the police were in the habit of rounding up gays, lesbians, transsexuals, and prostitutes in São Paulo and Rio de Janeiro as part of moralist crusades intended to clean up downtown areas.[10] As anthropologist Edward MacRae wrote about gay rights politics in Brazil during the 1970s and 1980s, "The methods were the same as always—lightning

[7] On the early history of the gay rights movement in Brazil, see and James N. Green, "The Emergence of the Brazilian Gay Liberation Movement, 1977–1981," *Latin American Perspectives* 21, no. 1 (Winter 1994); 38–55.

[8] Author's electronic correspondence with Mr. Mott (June 21, 2013).

[9] Omar G. Encarnación, *Out in the Periphery: Latin America's Gay Rights Revolution* (New York: Oxford University Press, 2916), 165.

[10] On the history of homosexuality in Brazil, see James N. Green, *Beyond Carnival: Male Homosexuality in Twentieth-Century Brazil* (Chicago: University of Chicago Press, 1999).

134 Framing Equality

strikes at meeting sites, illegal imprisonment for the investigation of criminal or political antecedents, even in the case of people whose documents were in order, and the use of an extreme brutality, especially with prostitutes and transvestites."[11] The military regime also banned gay carnival balls and censored plays about homosexuality. Such bans were legal under the 1968 Institutional Act No. 5. It overruled the Brazilian Constitution and suspended habeas corpus and judicial review.

Somos drew inspiration from the struggle for equality by Afro-Brazilians, which first appeared in the 1930s, when it was known as the Brazilian Black Front, broadly recognized as the first civil rights organization in Brazil.[12] The name Somos honored the memory of the magazine of Argentina's *Frente de Liberación Homosexual* (FLH), a gay rights organization that brought European-style gay liberation politics to Latin America. Before being extinguished by the military coup that put an end to democracy in Argentina in 1976, the FLH became Latin America's premier gay rights organization. After 1976, several FLH leaders migrated to Brazil, including the writer Néstor Perlongher. This migration ensured a significant role for the FLH in influencing gay activism in Brazil. Somos was also influenced by a cluster of US gay rights activists working in Brazil in the 1970s, including historian James Green, then a graduate student, and Winston Leyland, editor of the San Francisco tabloid *Gay Sunshine*.[13]

Eventually, Somos incorporated other gay organizations to become the *Movimento Homossexual Brasileiro*, or MHB. These developments were enabled by the support that the group received from the PT, an emerging revolutionary force in Brazilian politics. During the 1980s, the PT gave Brazilian gay activists a level of recognition, visibility, and resources that was the envy of most gay rights movements in Latin America and, frankly, most of the world. The PT's first platform unambiguously supported the gay rights movement. "We will not accept that homosexuality be treated as a disease or a matter for the police, and we will defend respect for homosexuals, calling them to the greater mission of constructing a new society."[14]

---

[11] Edward MacRae, "Homosexual Identities in Transitional Brazilian Politics," in *The Making of Social Movements in Latin America: Identity, Strategy, and Democracy*, eds. Arturo Escobar and Sonia Alvarez (Boulder: Westview Press, 1992), 191.

[12] See Michael G. Hanchard, *Orpheus and Power: The Movimento Negro of Rio de Janeiro and São Paulo, Brazil, 1945–1988* (Princeton: Princeton University Press, 1994).

[13] See James N. Green, "Desire and Revolution: Socialists and the Brazilian Gay Liberation Movement in the 1970s," in *Human Rights and Transnational Solidarity in Cold War Latin America*, ed. Jessica Stites Mor (Madison: University of Wisconsin Press, 2013).

[14] Partido dos Trabalhadores, *Resoluções de Encontros e Congressos: Resoluções de Encontros e Congressos, 1979–1998* (São Paulo: Fundação Perseu Abramo / Diretório Nacional do PT, 1998), 111.

Brazil   135

The PT also stood out among other political parties in Brazil and elsewhere for its opposition to the classification of homosexuality as an illness by the World Health Organization (paragraph 302.0). While other contenders wavered on the issue, the PT was resolute. "Paragraph 302.0 is a violation of human rights. The discrimination contained in this paragraph is a shameful conceit, as the sexuality of the individual is a universal right," declared a PT representative in a forum on gay rights hosted by *Folha de S. Paulo* in 1982.[15] Lastly, the PT facilitated intra-group collaboration between gay activists and other social movements, such as feminist organizations, environmentalists, the trade unions, and the Afro-Brazilian movement, since the party functioned as an umbrella for most of Brazil's progressive social movements. This was part of the party's strategy to marshal the energy of Brazilian civil society to pursue an ambitious democratization agenda that prominently featured sexual rights.[16]

PT legislators assisted gay activists in participating in the National Constitutional Assembly, a body organized in 1985 to draft a new constitution.[17] A priority for gay activists was a ban on discrimination based on sexual orientation. But opposition from evangelical leaders thwarted this plan. The fallout for gay activists was heartbreaking. Gay activists learned that their power in the new democracy was limited. In accounting for the defeat, João Antonio Mascarenhas, the leading proponent of the proposed constitutional ban on discrimination based on sexual orientation and the president of the Rio-based gay rights organization *Triângulo Rosa*, observed that gay activists were unable to overcome "opposition to the rights of sexual minorities in the federal legislature" posed by "conservatism, machismo, homophobia, and religion."[18] Echoing Mascarenhas, Mott recalled the success of evangelical leaders "in painting the constitutional initiative as special or privileged rights for gays and a potential barrier to religious freedom."[19]

But the debate about sexual orientation triggered by the drafting of the new constitution was not for naught. Although gay activists failed in their attempt to write an explicit ban on anti-gay discrimination in the constitution, they

---

[15] Luiz Mott, "Partidos Políticos e a homossexualidade," unpublished manuscript made available to the author on June 21, 2013.

[16] See Margaret Keck, *Democratization and the Workers' Party in Brazil* (New Haven: Yale University Press, 1995).

[17] For a broader discussion of this important chapter in Brazilian gay rights history, see Gustavo Gomes da Costa Santos and Bruno Leonardo Ribeiro de Melo, "The Opposition to LGBT Rights in the Brazilian National Congress (1986–2018): Actors, Dynamics of Action and Recent Developments," *Journal of the Brazilian Sociological Society* 4, no. 1 (Jan–Jun 2018): 80–108.

[18] Juan Pedro Pereira Marsiaj, *Political Parties, Culture, and Democratization: The Gay, Lesbian, and Trasvesti Movement in the Struggle for Inclusion in Brazil*, paper presented at the Annual Meeting of the American Political Science Association, September 1–4, 2005, 9.

[19] Electronic communication with Mr. Mott (June 21, 2013).

136 Framing Equality

succeeded in incorporating a ban on "any form of discrimination" (found in Article 3) that some contend applies to sexual orientation and gender identity.[20] Gay activists and their political allies also successfully introduced a ban on anti-gay discrimination in the constitutions of several Brazilian states and cities, starting with the constitutions of the states of Mato Grosso and Sergipe. Last but not least, the debate over a ban on anti-gay discrimination is broadly reflected in the privileged place that the new constitution grants to human rights principles, especially dignity. Particularly notable is a stipulation in the constitution that universal healthcare is a human right. All of this reflected a shift among Brazilian gay activists away from gay liberation and Marxism and toward human rights as the gay activist community's main philosophical framework.

Brazilian gay rights activists made the most of the human rights stipulations built into the new constitution to confront the HIV/AIDS pandemic, which made Brazil the biggest hotspot for the pandemic outside of Africa.[21] They stressed the claim that access to medical treatment for all people living with AIDS was a human right. This rhetorical strategy, which took hold in São Paulo, home to Brazil's leading human rights organizations, inspired the Brazilian National AIDS Program, or PNDA. Crafted by gay activists, politicians, economists, and bureaucrats in the early 1990s and funded at the unprecedented level of $250 million by the Brazilian government and the World Bank, the policy guaranteed free and universal access to antiretroviral therapy through the national healthcare system. In doing so, the law contravened the advice of the World Bank and the US government, which recommended that developing countries emphasize affordable prevention over costly treatment. For those already infected with the virus, this recommendation essentially amounted to a death sentence. But it is hard to argue with the PNDA's success in stopping what some have called the "Africanization" of AIDS in Brazil.[22] By the early 2000s, the rate of Brazilians living with AIDS was roughly half what the World Bank had predicted, with an estimated 1.2 million HIV cases averted.

---

[20] Some constitutional scholars have argued that the objective of banning anti-gay discrimination in the 1988 constitution was in fact accomplished. They point to Article 3 of the constitution, which states, "The fundamental objectives of the Federal Republic of Brazil" include "to promote the well-being of all, without prejudice as to origin, race, sex, color, age and any other form of discrimination." For more on this debate, see José Afonso da Silva, *Curso de Direito Constitucional Positivo*, 25th ed. (São Paulo: Saraiva, 2005).

[21] See, especially, Tim Frasca, *AIDS in Latin America* (New York: Palgrave, 2005) and Jane Galvão, "Brazil and Access to HIV/AIDS Drugs: A Question of Human Rights and Public Health," *American Journal of Public Health* 95, no. 7 (July 1995): 1110–1116.

[22] João Biehl, "The Activist State: Global Pharmaceuticals, AIDS and Citizenship in Brazil," *Social Text* 22, no. 2 (Fall 2004): 105.

Gay activists such as Mott also used human rights approaches to publicize anti-gay violence in Brazil by working with international organizations. Through this work, Mott sought to amplify the victimization and suffering of LGBTQ people in Brazil. A case in point is the propensity of gay activists in Brazil to refer to their country as the home of a "homocaust" in connection to the wave of gay killings that for decades has tarred the country's reputation as tolerant toward LGBTQ people.[23] According to the data from Mott's organization (GGB), in 2023 "a total of 257 deaths were reported among LGBTQIA+ individuals in Brazil."[24] Since 2008, according to GGB, violent attacks on the gay community in Brazil have climbed steadily and average about one killing per day.[25]

By the 1990s, and in no small measure due to the struggle against HIV/AIDS, which dramatically mobilized gay activists in Brazil, the Brazilian gay rights movement had become the largest and most resourceful in all of Latin America.[26] Among the key developments of the era was the emergence, in 1995, of the *Associação Brasileira de Gays, Lésbicas, Bissexuais, Travestis e Transexuais* (ABGLT), a national network of some three hundred LGBT groups that claims the title of Latin America's largest gay rights organization. Among its founders was Toni Reis, an activist from the southern state of Paraná. Reis spent time in Europe during the late 1980s and early 1990s, where he became active with gay rights organizations and realized "how far behind we were in Brazil."[27] Under Reis's leadership, the new organization rapidly became the official voice of the Brazilian gay rights community.

Invigorated gay rights activists demonstrated their strength at the seventeenth annual meeting of the International Lesbian and Gay Association (ILGA), held in Rio de Janeiro in 1995. This was the ILGA's first gathering in a South American country. Befitting the occasion, Brazil's gay community organized its first-ever gay pride parade. Held on the fashionable and very prominent Atlantic Avenue, the parade left little doubt about the diversity,

---

[23] See, especially, Luiz Mott, *Epidemic of Hate: Violations of the Human Rights Violations of Gay Men, Lesbians, and Transvestites in Brazil* (San Francisco: International Gay and Lesbian Human Rights Commission, 1996).

[24] "Brazil: Violent Deaths of LGBTQIA+ Individuals Reach 257 in 2023," Agencia Brasil, January 27, 2025. Available at https://agenciabrasil.ebc.com.br/en/direitos-humanos/noticia/2024-01/violent-deaths-lgbtqia-individuals-reach-257-2023.

[25] The roots of anti-gay violence in Brazil are varied and complex. For a broader discussion of this issue, see Wallace Góes Mendes Cosme Marcelo Furtado Passos da Silva, "Homicide of Lesbians, Gays, Bisexuals, Travestis, Transexuals, and Transgender People (LGBT) in Brazil: A Spatial Analysis," ABRASCO, May 8, 2020. Available at https://www.scielosp.org/article/csc/2020.v25n5/1709-1722/en/.

[26] See, especially, Rafael de la Dehesa, *Queering the Public Sphere in Mexico and Brazil: Emergent Sexual Rights Movements in Emerging Democracies* (Durham: Duke University Press, 2010).

[27] Author's electronic correspondence with Mr. Reis (February 20, 2015).

138 Framing Equality

vibrancy, and growing political influence of Brazil's LGBTQ community. "The movement had come of age," reported Green in his effusive review of ILGA's Rio gathering.[28] A highlight of the gathering was a speech by PT congresswoman and future mayor of São Paulo Marta Suplicy, in which she pledged to team up with gay activists to introduce same-sex civil union legislation in the Brazilian Congress.

Brazil's pursuit of same-sex civil unions reflected a majority consensus among gay activists that civil unions were a preferable option to marriage. This consensus, according to Rita Colaço, a scholar of sex and gender in Brazil, reflected cultural factors such as "the negative views about the institution of marriage among the generation of activists that led the gay movement in the democratic era."[29] She added, "This was a generation of gay activists influenced by anarchism, the beat movement, and the counterculture. What was most important to them was to ensure the right to a life free of discrimination, especially in the face of alarming numbers of homicides, torture, and police extorsion practiced against homosexuals in the country." Colaço's views are echoed by João Silvério Trevisan, one of the founders of *Somos* and the MHB: "In 1995, the homosexual leaders were not very fond of the idea of marriage. We deemed it a heterosexual and bourgeois institution."[30]

Boosting the case for civil unions (while at the same time weakening the case for gay marriage) were the peculiarities of Brazilian family law, especially how favorably it viewed unmarried cohabitation. Many gay activists were of the view that same-sex unions qualified as "stable unions," a status recognized under the Brazilian Constitution. It also stipulates that the state should facilitate the conversion of stable unions into marriage. According to the legal scholar Adilson José Moreira, these peculiarities about the Brazilian Constitution were a reflection of the "social acceptance of domestic cohabitation" in Brazil by both homosexual and heterosexual couples.[31] This acceptance mirrors the complicated history of the institution of marriage in Brazil. According to Moreira, this history included "the maintenance of religious marriage as a privilege reserved almost exclusively to wealthy families during the colonial period, social disapproval of interracial relationships, prohibition of divorce for most of Brazilian history, the marginal economic

---

[28] James N. Green, "More Love and More Desire: The Building of the Brazilian Gay Movement," in *The Politics of Sexuality in Latin America*, eds. Javier Corrales and Mario Pecheny (Pittsburgh: University of Pittsburgh Press, 2010), 71.

[29] Author's interview with Ms. Colaço (May 9, 2018).

[30] Author's interview with Mr. Trevisan (June 14, 2018).

[31] Adilson José Moreira, "We Are a Family!: Legal Recognition of Same-Sex Unions in Brazil," *American Journal of Comparative Law* 60, no. 4 (2012): 1010.

status of extensive portions of the population, and the absence of state officials in more remote geographic areas."[32]

However, more pressing political realities encouraged the prioritization of civil unions. Veteran gay rights activists like Mott were concerned that a campaign for gay marriage or civil unions would distract from what they believed was a vastly more important priority: enacting a law or a constitutional amendment criminalizing homophobia, which they thought was the root cause of anti-gay violence. The model for this law was a provision in the 1988 constitution banning racism. These activists were also doubtful that the PT was capable of delivering something as ambitious as gay marriage, considering that the party had to reconcile its commitments to the gay community against other party priorities, such as addressing social and economic inequality, combating racism, and advancing reproductive rights. The party also had to accommodate other liberal constituencies that were not on board with gay rights. For example, the members of the so-called Catholic Left, a pivotal force in the emergence of the PT as a viable political institution in the 1980s in the state of São Paulo, were uncomfortable with homosexuality and balked at making gay rights a priority for the party.

More importantly, for some gay activists, especially the ABGLT, which was closely affiliated with the PT, keeping gay marriage demands at bay was seen as politically advantageous for both the gay movement and the PT. For these pragmatic gay activists, any progress toward gay marriage had to be incremental and geared toward making gay rights advances palatable to conservatives. As PT representative José Genoino explained to the newspaper *O Globo* in 2010 when describing his party's proposal for a national same-sex civil unions law, "The current project provides for civil unions among gay couples, but excludes from the text terms considered controversial such as 'matrimony' and 'adoption.'" According to Genoino, this was the strategy adopted by legislators and gay rights activists "to prevent further rejection of the bill by his fellow lawmakers and the Catholic church."[33]

Undoubtedly, the failure of the civil unions bill in the Brazilian Congress strengthened pragmatic arguments in favor of civil unions and against gay marriage. Despite the support of the center-right administration of Fernando Henrique Cardoso (1995–2002) and the subsequent PT administrations of Luiz Inácio Lula da Silva and Dilma Rousseff (2002–2016), the civil unions bill failed to get support from the majority of the legislators. Not even the

---

[32] Ibid., 1004–1006.

[33] Amauri Arrais, "Argentine Gay Marriage Law Should Influence Brazil, Activists Say," *O Globo*, July 15, 2010.

willingness of gay activists to make the bill as noncontroversial as possible made a difference. This dispiriting outcome pointedly suggested that if civil unions were an uphill battle, gay marriage was a near impossibility. As recently as 2011, the ABGLT and other gay rights activists affiliated with the PT made this argument repeatedly as they continued to make the case for a same-sex civil unions law and to insist on an incremental approach to the legalization of gay marriage.

The most serious attempt by the Brazilian congress to legislate a same-sex civil unions law came in 1994 with the introduction of a bill by PT Congresswoman Suplicy. In 1996, the Registered Civil Partnership Bill was renamed in the face of charges from conservatives that the original bill required a constitutional amendment since the reference in the Brazilian Constitution to stable unions dealt with the union of one man and one woman. To make the bill more palatable to conservative legislators, the revised bill also excluded joint child adoption by same-sex couples. But the bill stalled in the Chamber of Deputies. It was withdrawn twice by Congresswoman Suplicy, and it was never put to a vote.

Some gay rights activists blamed the PT for the failure of the civil union's bill, accusing party leaders of not providing leadership on the issue and of throwing the gay rights movement under the bus whenever the movement's demands became inconvenient. According to Trevisan, "Suplicy wanted to demonstrate modern parliamentary leadership, but it was more like a marketing thing to advance her career."[34] Lula and Rousseff have also been the target of harsh criticism by the activists. Trevisan noted that, as president, Lula back-peddled his support for same-sex civil unions for fear of upsetting the evangelical movement, and that during her 2010 presidential run, and again during her 2014 re-election campaign, Rousseff caved to pressures from the evangelicals by drawing a clear line against same-sex marriage. Carlos Tufvesson, a gay rights activist and former LGBT coordinator of the city of Rio de Janeiro, noted in an interview for this book that "many LGBT militants once proclaimed the PT the LGBT Party of the World, but, in reality, the party never was that not even in Brazil."[35]

But it is also the case that gay leaders were often hesitant to put pressure on the PT for fear of jeopardizing their hard-won positions of influence within the party, an unintended consequence of the incorporation of gay activists into the PT. Gustavo Bernardes, the former general coordinator for LGBT issues in the Secretariat of Human Rights under the Rousseff administration,

---

[34] Author's interview with Mr. Trevisan (June 14, 2018).
[35] Author's interview with Mr. Tufvesson (May 9, 2018).

noted in an interview, "I believe that the failure of the PT to enact a national civil unions law through Congress can be linked to the dependency of the LGBT Movement on government resources. Brazil has no culture of self-financing or private financing of civil society organizations. Dependency creates complacency."[36] A related factor was the failure of gay rights activists to build support for the civil unions law beyond the National Congress, either because they believed that support from the PT would be sufficient to secure the law or because they thought that Brazilians were culturally predisposed to support gay rights.[37]

The Evangelical Opposition

All of this said, the main obstacle to legalizing same-sex civil unions in Brazil was religious opposition.[38] A Brazilian National Conference of Bishops statement labeled the bill the product of "a hedonistic and consumerist culture, with increasing moral permissiveness." The Conference also appealed to the legislators "not to approve bills that would decriminalize abortion, guarantee human sterilization, and recognize same-sex civil unions." But the stiffest opposition came from the evangelical movement. Aside from depicting the bill as "an attempt of half a dozen homosexual advocates to impose on the Brazilian nation a behavior that would injure their moral convictions," evangelical leaders essentially blackmailed the Cardoso administration by threatening to "oppose the fiscal adjustment, which was a priority for the government at the time." In sum, "the bill was used as a 'currency' between members of the evangelical caucus and executive power. This strategy became the *modus operandi* of opponents to LGBT rights, especially for the members of the Evangelical caucus."

The evangelical movement's capacity to derail the civil unions bill reflected a changing religious landscape. Similar to the rise of the Moral Majority in the United States in the early 1980s, the Brazilian evangelical movement has recently gone from "the political sidelines to the center."[39] Enabling this political journey is the explosive growth of Brazil's evangelical population in

[36] Author's interview with Mr. Bernardes (April 17, 2018).

[37] On this point, see Omar G. Encarnación, "A Latin American Puzzle: Gay Rights Landscapes in Argentina and Brazil," *Human Rights Quarterly* 40 (2018): 194–218.

[38] The quotes from this paragraph come from Santos and Melo, "The Opposition to LGBT Rights in the Brazilian National Congress (1986–2018)," 86–87.

[39] Dom Phillips and Nick Miroff, "In Brazil's Political Crisis, a Powerful New Voice: Evangelical Christians," *The Washington Post*, May 26, 2016. Available at https://www.washingtonpost.com/world/the_americas/in-brazils-political-crisis-a-powerful-new-force-evangelical-christians/2016/05/26/5c8b9bdc-1c7d-11e6-82c2-a7dcb313287d_story.html.

142 Framing Equality

the twentieth century.[40] Although as recently as the 1970s the percentage of Brazilians that professed a Protestant affiliation was negligible (at the time more than 90 percent of Brazilians claimed a Catholic affiliation), in recent decades that percentage has grown to approximately 25 percent, with the bulk of them claiming to be evangelical or charismatic.[41] This growth has been accompanied by the rise of vast evangelical ministries that control large media empires—newspapers, radio and television stations, and elaborate internet operations.[42]

Brazilian evangelical leaders have skillfully weaponized their resources to engineer a moral panic about gay rights, and gay marriage in particular, that bears striking similarities to the American experience. Perhaps no one has been more relentless and effective in attacking the gay community than Silas Malafaia, the leader of the Pentecostal church *Assembleia de Deus Vitória em Cristo* (Assembly of God Victory in Christ), a branch of the Assemblies of God organization in Brazil. His pointed verbal attacks on the Brazilian gay rights movement have made news all over the world, including a lengthy profile in the *New York Times*.[43] In it, Malafaia declared himself "public enemy No. 1 of the gay movement in Brazil." The profile makes reference to a notorious interview with journalist Marília Gabriela that made headlines all over Brazil (and that prompted the *New York Times* profile) in which Malafaia noted, "Nobody is born gay; homosexuality is a behavior. . . . There is no homosexual chromosome; there is only male and female." He added that, when it comes to homosexuality, his attitude is to love the sinner but not the sin. "I love homosexuals like I love criminals and murderers."[44]

A key factor animating the evangelicals' entry into the political fray in Brazil is a growing sense of moral decline. In particular, many evangelicals point to the long rule of the PT between 2003 and 2016 as the root cause of this

---

[40] On the growing role of evangelicals in politics in Brazil, see Gary Reich and Pedro dos Santos, "The Rise (and Frequent Fall) or Evangelical Politicians: Organization, Theology, and Church Politics," *Latin American Politics & Society* 55, no. 4 (Winter 2013); 1–22; Felipe Pena, "Religion: Evangelism in Brazil," *Americas Quarterly*, Summer 2012. Available at https://www.americasquarterly.org/fulltextarticle/religion-evangelicalism-in-brazil/; Carlos Ribeiro Caldas, "O papel da Igreja Universal Brasileira Do Reino de Deus na globalização do neopentecostal atual," *Ciências da Religião: História e Sociedade* 8, no. 2 (2010): 107–121; David Stoll, *Is Latin América Turning Protestant? The Politics of Evangelical Growth* (Berkeley: University of California Press, 1991); and David Martin, *Tongues of Fire: The Explosion of Protestantism in Latin America* (New York: Wiley Blackwell, 1993).

[41] "Brazil's Changing Religious Landscape," Pew Research Center, June 18, 2013. Available at https://www.pewforum.org/2013/07/18/brazils-changing-religious-landscape/.

[42] See Omar G. Encarnación, "Amid Crisis in Brazil, the Evangelical Bloc Emerges as a Political Power," *The Nation*, August 18, 2017. Available at https://www.thenation.com/article/amid-crisis-in-brazil-the-evangelical-bloc-emerges-as-a-political-power/.

[43] Simon Romero, "Evangelical Leader Rises in Brazil's Culture Wars," *The New York Times*, November 25, 2011. Available at https://www.nytimes.com/2011/11/26/world/americas/silas-malafaia-tv-evangelist-rises-in-brazils-culture-wars.html.

[44] Author's translation of the transcript of the interview provided by *Correio 24 Horas*.

Brazil   **143**

decline. Indeed, evangelical leaders blame the PT for putting Brazil "on a path to moral ruin" by having legalized gay marriage, giving Brazil one of Latin America's highest abortion rates (even though the procedure remains illegal), and making pornography ubiquitous.[45] Such accusations go hand in hand with the evangelicals' long-standing view of Lula, a Catholic, as "satanic" and "demonic," an image that Lula tried hard to shake by bringing evangelicals into his inner sanctum while in office between 2003 and 2010.[46]

When attacking the demands by gay rights activists for a same-sex civil unions law and gay marriage, Brazilian evangelical ministries generally employ a retrograde discourse that emphasizes the view that gay rights are a direct threat to the family and religious freedom. The source material for this discourse is the same one that inspired gay rights opponents in the United States: Reverend Louis P. Sheldon's *The Agenda: The Homosexual Plan to Change America*, an inflammatory book that argued that gay activists were transforming "the business community, public schools, and the media," to promote their lifestyle among America's children, and that explained how readers could "restore the moral fabric of the nation."[47] The book was translated into Portuguese by a Brazilian Pentecostal church and distributed to the legislators in Brasília.

In recent years, American evangelical influence in Brazil has grown more direct, which some have attributed to the defeat of the Christian right in the United States on a host of social issues, including gay marriage. As reported by *Reuters*, having lost the fight against same-sex marriage at home, "leading U.S. Evangelical Christians are joining in the culture wars in Latin America as cheerleaders for opponents of gay legal partnerships, abortion, and pornography."[48] In doing so, American evangelical missions are partaking in something akin to a colonial enterprise in Latin America, and especially in Brazil, by seeking to replace the Catholic Church as the leading force in shaping culture wars—from guns to abortion to gay marriage.

Among the veterans of America's culture wars active in Brazil is Exodus International, a leader of the "ex-gay movement." The group has had a presence in Brazil since the 1990s, exporting "conversion therapy," a psychological treatment intended to eradicate same-sex attraction through

---

[45] Phillips and Miroff, *The Washington Post*, "In Brazil's Political Crisis, a Powerful New Voice."

[46] Jandira Queiroz, "Pentecostal with History of Hate Speech Selected as President of Brazil's Human Rights Body," *Religion Dispatches*, March 12, 2013. Available at http://religiondispatches.org/pentecostal-with-history-of-hate-speech-selected-as-president-of-brazils-human-rights-body/.

[47] Louis P. Sheldon, *The Agenda: The Homosexual Plan to Change America* (Charisma House, 2005). The quoted passages come from the online flyer promoting the book.

[48] U.S. Evangelicals Cheer on Latin American Culture Wars," *Reuters*, August 10, 2014. Available at https://www.reuters.com/article/us-usa-latam-evangelical.

144 Framing Equality

biblical teachings.[49] A more recent arrival is the American Center for Law and Justice through its Brazilian subsidary, the Brazilian Center for Law and Justice, or BCLJ.[50] The ACLJ is famous for drafting the Defense of Marriage Act and for championing a constitutional amendment to ban gay marriage. The political agenda and tactics of the BCLJ mirror those of its American counterpart. Jandira Queiroz, an observer of religion and politics in Brazil who has reported extensively on the expansion of American anti-gay activists in Latin America, notes that through its Brazilian branch, the ACLJ is using some of the same tactics that the organization developed in the United States: "wooing government officials and facilitating access to them, building alliances with key evangelical powerbrokers, and hiring local staff to serve as its face."

Despite the striking similarities in strategies, Brazil's anti-gay rights movement is not a clone of its American counterpart. Evangelical anti-gay rights activism in Brazil has been infused with aspects of the local political culture, especially the propensity of conservative Brazilians to take to the streets to protest. This explains the impressive capacity of evangelical leaders to mobilize the public against gay rights, something demonstrated every year in São Paulo. Just days ahead of the city's famed gay pride parade—the world's largest gay pride parade (drawing upwards to three million people every year), evangelical leaders organize the *Marcha para Jesus* or March for Jesus, an event notorious for its over-the-top denunciations of atheism, abortion, and homosexuality. The march's 2016 edition, which drew some three hundred and fifty thousand people, was described by the website *The Christian Herald World* as "the world's largest Christian event."[51]

Another key difference is the straightforward way religious leaders influence policy in Brazil. There's nothing in Brazil analogous to the 1954 Johnson Amendment, which limits how religious organizations can influence politics in the United States. Many evangelical caucus members, which traditionally comprise about 15 percent of the Chamber of Deputies, are evangelical pastors. These religious authorities are elected into office under the Brazilian Republican Party, widely known as the political branch of the Universal

---

[49] Jandira Queiroz, Fernando D'elio, and David Maas, *The Ex-Gay Movement in Latin America: Therapy and Ministry in the Exodus Movement* (Boston, MA: Political Research Associates, 2013).

[50] See, especially, Jandira Queiroz, "Christian Evangelical Right Sets Up American Foothold in Brazil," January 26, 2013. Available at http://oblogdeeoblogda.me/2013/01/26/christian-evangelical-right-sets-up-american-style-foothold-in-brazil/. "Anti-Gay Legal Group Targets Home of the World's Largest Pride Parade," Political Research Associates, January 26, 2013. Available at http://www.politicalresearch.org/2013/01/26/aclj-new-brazil-home/#sthash.n0M6k9VD.dpbs.

[51] "March for Jesus 2016: Brazil's Christians Celebrate Freedom in Christ in World Largest Religious Event," *The Gospel Herald World*, March 29, 2016. Available at http://www.gospelherald.com/articles/64391/20160529/march-for-jesus-2016-brazils-christians-celebrate-freedom-in-christ-in-worlds-largest-christian-event.htm.

Church of the Kingdom of God, and the Social Christian Party, a party known for its opposition to gay rights and abortion. Acting in concert with other conservative forces in the Brazilian Congress, especially the so-called BBB bloc (shorthand for beef, Bible, and bullets), evangelical pastors can stop almost any bill they object to in the Chamber of Deputies.

Emboldened by their success in defeating the civil unions law, the evangelical movement set its sights on other priorities of the gay rights community that arrived with the coming of the Lula administration, in 2003. In 2004, evangelical leaders doomed "Brazil without Homophobia," an education program implemented by the Lula administration with collaboration from gay rights organizations and human rights activists to curb violence against the LGBTQ population. The program was undermined by evangelical leaders from the outset. Some provisions that required congressional approval, such as a demand for the government to gather statistics on anti-gay violence, were never approved by Congress. In 2011, evangelical leaders forced Rousseff to veto "Schools without Homophobia," a policy proposal intended to promote LGBTQ tolerance known by the pejorative name of "the gay kit." She almost had no choice, having signed during her presidential campaign in 2010 "an open letter in which she committed herself not to pursue reform in the moral policy arena," such as abortion and gay marriage.[52]

Framing the Case for Stable Unions and Gay Marriage

By 2010, facing seemingly insurmountable obstacles in the Brazilian Congress to secure a same-sex civil unions law and almost any LGBTQ legislation, gay activists shifted their focus to the courts. This shift in strategy was a telling example of "venue shopping," or the attempt by activists to find the best possible policy-making setting to advance their goals.[53] By the late 1990s, a convergence of factors actively encouraged this shift. The most prominent was the remaking of the judiciary that was taking place under the Lula and Rousseff administrations. It was marked by the arrival of a cluster of new justices, including Joaquim Barbosa, the first Afro-Brazilian to be appointed to the Federal Court, by Lula in 2003. In 2012, Barbosa was elevated to the role of chief justice. These new justices were especially willing to assert themselves on gay rights and other issues impacting Brazil's marginalized communities, such as affirmative action for Afro-Brazilians and Indigenous peoples, by

[52] Díez, The Politics of Gay Marriage in Latin America: Argentina, Chile, and Mexico, 254.
[53] Sarah B. Pralle, "Venue Shopping, Political Strategy, and Policy Change: The Institutionalization of Canadian Forest Advocacy," Journal of Public Policy 23, no. 3 (2003): 233–260.

146   Framing Equality

exploiting a constitutional stipulation that allows the Court to impose remedies on communities and people claiming discrimination in the event of lack of action by the legislators.

Gay activists were also taking inspiration from the success that some same-sex couples were having in securing marriage rights from the courts. In 1998, for instance, the State Supreme Court of Rio de Grande do Sul became "one of the first tribunals to challenge the characterization of stable union as an inherently heterosexual institution" when it recognized the rights of a surviving partner to receive part of the property accumulated during the years that he lived with the deceased companion.[54] In August 2010, the Federal Supreme Court ruled in favor of a gay couple from the state of Paraná (formed by a British citizen and a Brazilian, Toni Reis, the president of ABGLT) that the couple could adopt any child, regardless of age and gender.

Developments from abroad also created a sense of urgency. In December 2009, Mexico City became the first locality in Latin America to allow gay marriage after the Mexico City Council enacted an ordinance making this possible. The Mexican Supreme Court later upheld the ordinance. A more seismic jolt came on July 15, 2010, when Argentina enacted Latin America's first national gay marriage law. That law was a carbon copy of the law passed by Spain in 2005, which granted identical benefits to homosexual couples as those already available to heterosexual couples. It also did not carve out any conscience exemptions. In both cases (Spain and Argentina), this parity in marriage law was achieved by amending the Civil Code with the removal of all references to the gender of those entering into the union. These foreign developments had a significant impact on Brazil, which historically has seen itself as the vanguard of gay rights in Latin America (if not the entire Iberian-Latin world), including having the distinction of being the first Latin American country to have legalized gay rights organizations. At a minimum, developments in Mexico and Argentina created the perception that Brazil was being left behind in advancing LGBTQ rights.

The shift in venue from the legislature to the courts in the struggle for state recognition of same-sex relations compelled gay activists to consider a messaging strategy. Before 2010, there was not much need to focus on messaging because the main task at hand was to cobble the necessary votes in Congress to pass the civil unions bill. As they approached the courts, gay activists displayed all the qualities that make Brazil such a compelling case of political framing. For starters, gay activists freely mixed legal arguments and moral appeals. They embraced the legal argument that gay unions qualified

---

[54] Moreira, "We are a Family!" 1028.

as stable unions as understood by the Brazilian Constitution. As noted previously, stable unions, which have virtually identical rights to marriage and can be converted into marriage, recognize a long history of domestic cohabitation in Brazilian history. Accordingly, gay activists argued that denying the status of stable unions to same-sex couples was a violation of the Brazilian Constitution. But gay activists also began casting demands for state recognition of same-sex couples in language that pointedly made the case that the state had a legal and moral obligation to respect the dignity of same-sex unions.

Behind the revamped rhetoric about same-sex relationships was a new generation of gay activists deeply influenced by developments in Argentina. The gay rights movement in that country was reinvented in the post-authoritarian era to capitalize upon the influence of human rights on Argentine politics in the last decades. This influence can be seen most tellingly in Argentina's success during the 1980s in putting the old military regime on trial on charges of human rights abuses. Making Argentina's experience relevant to Brazil was helped by the arrival in Brazil after 2010 of some of the architects of Argentina's gay marriage campaign. The most notable among them was Bruno Bimbi, a chief strategist with FALGBT, the organization that led the fight for gay marriage in Argentina. Bimbi was also connected to the activists who spearheaded Spain's successful gay marriage campaign in 2005.

Gay activists also displayed a keen sense of political pragmatism. They insisted that their goal was not marriage but rather the recognition of same-sex couples as stable unions. In fact, at the heart of the case in front of the Federal Supreme Court was not the constitutionality of gay marriage but rather the conception of the family in the Brazilian Constitution. According to Paulo Iotti, an attorney with the São Paulo-based advocacy group Lawyers for Sexual and Gender Diversity and a member of the legal team that argued the case for stable unions before the Federal Supreme Court, the case rested on the view that the definition of stable unions incorporated into the Civil Code, which was limited to heterosexual couples, contravened the interest expressed in the Brazilian Constitution of protecting the diversity of family arrangements. The case had nothing to do with the institution of marriage and whether gay couples were allowed into it.[55]

To show the dismal failure of existing laws to protect gay and lesbian families in Brazil, the testimony offered to the Federal Supreme Court by Iotti and his colleagues highlighted the struggles and humiliations that gay and lesbian families encountered because of their inability to have their relationships recognized by the state. It was not uncommon for some notary publics

---

[55] Author's interview with Mr. Iotti (New York City, January 17, 2020).

148   Framing Equality

to decline to grant a document acknowledging that a same-sex couple lived together. If they agreed to issue such a document, that document did not have much legal weight and was, in fact, likely to be disregarded by the courts in a separation dispute and/or custody battle. The testimony also showed that most same-sex couples living together were forced to structure their relationships like a business partnership whose primary purpose was to protect assets and property instead of preserving a loving relationship based on trust and respect.

Iotti also noted in an interview for this book that when framing the case for stable unions for same-sex couples, gay activists and their allies in the government relied heavily upon legal theories that recognized the morality and dignity of homosexual relationships. One such theory was "homo-affection." Promoted by Maria Berenice Dias, a former judge from Rio Grande do Sul and a noted legal theorist and the president of the sexual and gender diversity section of the Brazilian Bar Association, this theory argues that same-sex coupling is rooted not only in sex but also in affection (much like heterosexual coupling), and therefore deserving of constitutional protection as a family unit.[56] The theory also makes a broader argument about homosexuals that draws on human rights principles by affirming the dignity of homosexual people and the moral equivalence between homosexual and heterosexual couples.[57]

Lastly, the stable unions litigation broadly demonstrated the propensity and skill of Brazilian gay activists to work through the political system to achieve their goals. It was brought to the Federal Supreme Court by federal prosecutors concerned with the plight of gay and lesbian couples who approached the courts. Pointing to the prominent role of public prosecutors in advancing gay rights in Brazil, Moreira wrote, "Through a series of lawsuits aimed at protecting minorities, federal prosecutors successfully sought to promote greater inclusion of same-sex couples."[58] More to the point, the 2011 stable unions ruling originated in a case filed by Sérgio Cabral, the governor of Rio de Janeiro. He availed himself of the provision in the Brazilian Constitution that allows selected public officials to petition the Federal Supreme Court to rule on any issue deemed of utmost importance to the country. Cabral had grown frustrated by his inability to provide marital benefits to same-sex couples in Rio de Janeiro. Prosecutor General of the Republic Roberto

---

[56] See Maria Berenice Dias, *União Homossexual: O Preconceito & a Justiça*, 2nd ed. (Porto Alegre: Editora Livraria do Advogado, 2001).

[57] See Paulo Iotti, *Manual da Homoafetividade. Da Possibilidade Jurídica do Casamento Civil, da União Estável e da Adoção por Casais Homoafetivos* (São Paulo: Spessoto, 2019).

[58] Moreira, "We are a Family!" 1006–1007.

Gurgel supported him. Cabral and Gurgel believed the Brazilian Constitution protects same-sex unions under the sable unions clause.

When the Federal Supreme Court began to debate the recognition of gay relationships as stable unions, the Rousseff administration intervened to emphasize how critical this recognition was for advancing human rights in Brazil. Gustavo Bernardes, head of the office of LGBT affairs of the Secretariat of Human Rights, and Maria Do Rosário, the minister for human rights, met with Chief Justice Cezar Peluso to stress the importance of the case to the government and the gay community. In an interview for this book, Bernardes noted that "both the brief filed by the Human Rights Secretariat with the Supreme Court and the meeting with the chief justice stressed that the case for stable unions for homosexual couples was anchored on the legitimacy of gay rights under universal human rights principles and in keeping with the Courts' responsibility to uphold the dignity of gay families."[59]

Gay activists also mobilized the extensive human rights apparatus within the Brazilian state. Since the transition to democracy in 1985, Brazil has built an impressive human rights apparatus within the state's bureaucratic structures, including the office of the presidency. In 1997, the Cardoso administration created the National Human Rights Secretariat within the Ministry of Justice, focusing on LGBT issues since its inception. Under the Lula administration, the Secretariat was elevated to the president's office. In 2011, the Rousseff administration gave human rights a massive boost by creating the Brazilian National Truth Commission to examine the human rights abuses of the military regime in place between 1964 and 1985. The Commission is part of a process of assisting Brazil to come to terms with the legacy of human rights abuse committed under the old military dictatorship.[60] It grew out of the Third National Plan for Human Rights, a policy platform enacted in 2009 that also called same-sex civil unions.

The National Truth Commission was the first body of its kind to include a section on "LGBT discrimination, repression and marginalization."[61] Unveiled in 2014, the Commission's report stated: "Although there was no formalized and coherent state policy to exterminate homosexuals, the state's ideology of national security clearly contained a homophobic perspective that represented homosexuality as harmful, dangerous, and contrary to the family. This view legitimized direct violence against LGBT people, violations of

---

[59] Author's electronic communication with Mr. Bernardes (June 21, 2018).

[60] See Rebecca J. Atencio, *Memory's Turn: Reckoning with Dictatorship in Brazil* (Madison: University of Wisconsin Press, 2014).

[61] Author's electronic correspondence with Mr. Green (December 29, 2020).

150 Framing Equality

their rights and of their way of living and socializing."[62] Although no prosecutions or reparations came out of the Commission, the Commission's work, as noted by James Green, who served as an advisor to the Commission, occasioned a "rethinking of how we understand discrimination and repression of LGBT people during the dictatorship and other authoritarian moments in Brazil and elsewhere."[63]

As seen later, the political framing outlined above shaped the legal decisions that led to legalizing gay marriage in Brazil and, perhaps most importantly, the public's reaction to these decisions. The first decision came on May 5, 2011, from the Federal Supreme Court. It ruled that nothing in the Brazilian Constitution prohibited the recognition of gay and lesbian couples as "stable unions." In the Court's view, "Stable unions simply represent one particular type of adult relationship that deserves legal protection, along with other forms of constitutionally protected family arrangements. Consequently, there is no conflict between the constitutional definition of stable unions and the recognition of same-sex couples as family entities."[64]

Activists from the country's leading gay rights organizations were elated with the decision, which they greeted as a long-sought vindication of their activism. "This is a historic moment for all Brazilians, not just homosexuals. This judgment will change everything for us in society—and for the better," said Marcelo Cerqueira of the *Grupo Gay da Bahia*.[65] In his response to the ruling, Toni Reis, the president of ABGLT, noted that the ruling "opened the way for a series of rights previously denied to same-sex couples in Brazil, such as joint adoption of children and inheritance."[66] And, true to form, when noting what was next for the gay rights movement, Reis pointedly did not mention gay marriage. He noted that future priorities were legislation to curb anti-gay violence and an education campaign to battle homophobia.

But gay marriage was foremost in the minds of activists working outside of the network of established gay rights organizations. Key among them was Congressman Jean Wyllys, Brazil's best-known gay activist and most famous human rights advocate. He was also the most prominent Brazilian gay activist embracing a moral discourse about gay marriage. In 2010, he successfully

---

[62] "Brazil's Truth Commission: Abuse Rife Under Military Rule," BBC, December 10, 2014. Available at https://www.bbc.com/news/world-latin-america-30410741.

[63] Author's electronic correspondence with Mr. Green (December 29, 2020).

[64] Moreira, "We are a Family!" 1004.

[65] "Brazil's Supreme Court Approves Gay Civil Unions," *Associated Press*, June 5, 2011. Available at https://www.france24.com/en/20110506-supreme-court-recognises-gay-civil-unions-homosexual-rights-brazil.

[66] Toni Reis, "Where Next for Brazil's Gay Rights?" *The Guardian*, May 11, 2011. Available at https://www.theguardian.com/commentisfree/cifamerica/2011/may/11/brazil-gay-rights-same-sex-unions-legalised.

parlayed his celebrity as the first openly gay participant in the television show *Big Brother Brasil* (in 2005) to win a seat in the Brazilian Congress under the Freedom and Socialism Party. From his congressional perch, Wyllys became a fearless critic of the evangelical movement's opposition to gay rights. He famously accused neo-Pentecostal preacher Silas Malafaia of having blood on his hands for demonizing gay people. He has credited his gay marriage activism to having fallen as a teen under the influence of priests affiliated with the Brazilian Catholic Left, a political movement which, as explained shortly, did much to usher in human rights within the Brazilian Catholic Church and Brazil as a whole.

On March 31, 2011, Wyllys became the most prominent Brazilian gay activist demanding gay marriage with the creation of a "Gay Marriage Front." This declaration suggested Wyllys' independence from the gay rights establishment and the absence of any political restrictions on his activism. He was not a PT congressman; instead, he was elected into office under the PSOL, a small left-wing party. In calling for the legalization of gay marriage, Wyllys was breaking with the consensus among gay rights activists in Brazil of avoiding gay marriage demands—not only because marriage was not officially a priority for them (the priority was the criminalization of homophobia and transphobia) but also because they feared that gay marriage demands would undermine the case for stable unions at the Federal Supreme Court. Not surprisingly, Brazil's leading gay rights organizations, such as ABGLT, were less than happy with Wyllys's gay marriage activism. As noted by Bimbi, who served as Wyllys's principal legislative assistant, although most gay organizations eventually came around to embrace gay marriage, "initially they claimed that gay marriage was something foreign brought to Brazil by the Argentines."[67]

In attendance at Wyllys's gay marriage declaration were 171 Brazilian lawmakers, most of them members of the LGBTQ caucus, and several notable foreign visitors, including Argentine National Deputy Vilma Ibarra, who played a prominent role in her country's gay marriage fight, and Pedro Zerolo, the architect of Spain's gay marriage campaign. Ibarra and Zerolo were known in their home countries for advancing the argument that gay marriage was a moral imperative intended to advance human rights and democratic citizenship, to make amends for a history of discrimination against the gay community, and to restore dignity to gay people. While in Brazil, Zerolo urged the Brazilian parliamentarians and Human Rights Secretary Maria Do Rosário to "stay the course" on marriage equality and to "make possible what

---

[67] Author's electronic communication with Mr. Bimbi (July 26, 2024).

152 Framing Equality

seems impossible." He added that he was proud that Spain, which legalized gay marriage in 2005, was "serving as a model for an increasing number of Latin American countries."[68]

The gay marriage campaign was boosted by the introduction of a gay marriage bill by Congressman Wyllys, in April 2012, roughly a year after the legalization of same-sex civil unions. It called for amending the Brazilian Constitution to guarantee civil marriage equality for all people, regardless of their sexual orientation. Wyllys contended that "the celebration of marriage is the social legitimation of conjugal relations. Thus, depriving homosexuals of this right is a symbolic exclusion that has a strong cultural and social impact—this is why gay marriage is so important."[69] More provocatively, perhaps, he argued that a "law would have a social and cultural impact that goes beyond the right to marry.... This would have an impact on the reduction of homophobia in the medium term, as has happened in other countries."

Wyllys analogized the exclusion of gays and lesbians from the institution of marriage to racial and gender discrimination. In an interview with the Spanish daily *El Mundo*, Wyllys noted, "It would be unacceptable today to bar interracial marriage; it makes no sense why the same would not be the case with homosexual unions. We are not demanding religious marriage but rather civil marriage."[70] Wyllys also made ample use of his reputation as the moral conscience of the Brazilian Congress. In speeches to Congress and media appearances, he contended that gay marriage would deepen citizenship, comparing gay marriage to the extension of the right to vote to women, in 1932, and the election of the country's first female president, in 2010.[71]

There was nothing accidental about Wyllys's conjoining of gay marriage and homophobia, which gay activists have long contended is the root of Brazil's epidemic of anti-gay violence. The campaign for civil unions and gay marriage in Brazil played out against an escalating wave of violence against LGBTQ people that, as noted already, gay activists began to chronicle with the democratic transition of the mid-1980s. Although the roots of this violence are varied—including the social conservatism that runs through Brazilian culture and the fact that Brazil is a highly violent society (according to one report, the country has "the highest absolute number of homicides in the

---

[68] "Gay Marriage Front in Brazil Attracts 171 Lawmakers," *On Top*, March 31, 2011. Available athttp://www.ontopmag.com/article/7973/Gay_Marriage_Front_In_Brazil_Attracts_171_Lawmakers.

[69] Jean Wyllys, "The Struggle for LGBT People in Brazil," Parliamentarians for Global Action, November 3, 2017.

[70] German Aranda, "El matrimonio homosexual, legal en Brasil sólo en la práctica," *El Mundo*, July 29, 2013. Available at https://www.elmundo.es/america/2013/07/30/brasil/1375147946.html.

[71] Jean Wyllys, "Why I Proposed Marriage Equality in Brazil," *The Advocate*, April 13, 2012. Available at https://www.advocate.com/politics/commentary/2012/04/13/oped-why-i-proposed-marriage-equality-brazil.

world")—it is the case that "in Brazil LGBTQ people are disproportionately harassed and victimized precisely because of who they are."[72]

According to Bimbi, although many in Brazil dismissed the gay marriage bill as "a publicity stunt," it was important for the gay marriage campaign "to create a parallel legislative path to legalizing gay marriage to the legal process already underway—if only to create a historical precedent."[73] Wyllys's gay marriage bill was also intended to pressure the judiciary into legalizing gay marriage. Behind the scenes, as recalled by Bimbi, gay activists were petitioning the National Council of Justice to clarify the stable unions ruling. In particular, gay activists objected to how the ruling unfairly burdened gay couples. While heterosexual couples had direct access to a marriage certificate, gay couples first had to register as stable unions and then petition that the union be converted to marriage. This additional complication for gay couples, Bruni said, "contravened the sentiment and the intent of the Federal Supreme Court ruling of 2011 that all couples needed to be treated equally."

To underscore the unfairness facing same-sex couples—not only the complication of securing a marriage certificate but also the fact that Brazilian states were interpreting the Federal Supreme Court's 2011 decision differently—gay marriage activists responded with a savvy social media campaign. It borrowed the slogans employed in the Spanish and Argentine gay marriage campaigns, especially "the same rights with the same names," and conceived new slogans tailored to the situation in Brazil, especially "love has no zip code." The campaign was boosted by pro-marriage publicity efforts featuring Brazil's leading celebrities and artists, including singers Caetano Veloso and Carlinhos Brown and actress Sonia Braga.

On May 14, 2013, the National Council of Justice legalized same-sex marriage in Brazil. The ruling was not a high-minded declaration of the constitutional right of same-sex couples to marry, as was the case in the United States. But it got the job done. The ruling noted that notary publics could not refuse to convert stable unions between couples of the same sex into marriage or to decline a request for a marriage license by a same-sex couple.[74] The overwhelming vote by the Council (fourteen to one) came with the comment that it was in accordance with the 2011 ruling of the Federal Supreme Court that it is a violation of the Brazilian Constitution to treat unions between

---

[72] Pedro Augusto P. Francisco and Robert Muggah, "Brazilian LGBTQ Community Faces Surging Violence, but They're Fighting Back," Open Democracy, December 9, 2023. Available at https://igarape.org.br/en/brazils-lgbtq-community-faces-surging-violence-but-theyre-fighting-back/.

[73] Author's electronic communication with Mr. Bimbi (July 26, 2024).

[74] "CNJ determina que cartorios registrem casamento civil de casais do mesmo-sexo," O Globo, May 5, 2013. Available at https://oglobo.globo.com/politica/cnj-determina-que-cartorios-registrem-casamento-civil-de-casais-do-mesmo-sexo-8383218.

154 Framing Equality

same-sex couples differently than heterosexual ones. Maria Cristina Peduzzi, the dissenting vote, argued that only the national congress had the mandate to legalize gay marriage.

Minimizing the Conservative Backlash

As in the United States, the coming of gay marriage via judicial fiat unleashed a furious backlash from conservative forces. The most vociferous opposition to the rulings from the Federal Supreme Court and the National Council of Justice that led to the legalization of gay marriage came from evangelical leaders. In keeping with their historic opposition to gay rights, these leaders denounced the rulings and tried their best to undo them. In June 2013, tel-evangelist Silas Malafaia held multiple rallies in Brasília, with some drawing as many as forty thousand followers.[75] The purpose of the mobilization was twofold. There was a clear desire to demonize gay rights, same-sex unions in particular: "Gay activism is moral garbage," Malafaia said to a cheering crowd in the Brazilian capital, adding that "Satan will not destroy our family values." But the protestors also intended to intimidate the legislators by telegraphing that "they should not ignore Brazil's fast-growing Evangelical churches if they wanted to stay in office."

Evangelical lawmakers attacked the rulings as an act of judicial activism that granted special rights to the gay community based on a misguided read-ing of the Brazilian Constitution. Conservative legal scholars, such as Nelson Nery Junior, a former appellate prosecutor for the state of São Paulo, backed the legislators. He argued that the recognition of same-sex marriage contra-vened Article 1514 of the Civil Code and the Federal Constitution, both of which recognize marriage to be the union of a man and a woman.[76] The National Association of Evangelical Jurists "tried to halt implementation of the National Council of Justice decision by appealing to a 'conscience clause' that would exclude officers who had religious objections to marrying two men or two women."[77]

Evangelical lawmakers also entertained legislative proposals to protect and defend the traditional family. But, in contrast to the American experience,

[75] This section draws from "Evangelicals in Brazil Rise in Power with Consequences for Catholics, Gays," *Reuters*, June 9, 2013. Available at https://www.reuters.com/article/us-brazil-evangelicals-idUS BRE95805120130609.

[76] Nelson Nery Jr., "Prefacio," in *Jurisdição Constitucional e Direitos Fundamentais* 20, ed. George Abboud (Editora Revista Dos Tribunais, 2011).

[77] Luiz Carlos Teixeira Coelho Filho, "Inclusivity the Brazilian Way: Same-Sex Marriage in the Episco-pal Church of Brazil," *Journal of Anglican Studies* 18 (2020): 13.

none of these proposals bore any fruit—at least from the standpoint of generating legislation. Indeed, as suggested by an extensive study of opposition to LGBTQ rights in the Brazilian Congress from 1986 to 2018 by sociologists Gustavo Gomes da Costa Santos and Bruno Leonardo Ribeiro de Melo, most bills introduced in Congress by opponents of gay rights have been "legislative decrees, which are approved only by the National Congress." The study also noted that "most of the anti-LGBT rights bills have been archived, withdrawn, or rejected."[78]

The closest the evangelical movement came to changing the course of gay marriage was the now-defunct *Estatuto da Família* (Family Statute). This bill redefined the family for federal purposes as "the entity formed from the union between a man and a woman, through marriage or stable union, and the community formed by any of the parents and their children."[79] The bill was approved by a review committee of the Chamber of Deputies in October 2015, but it was never brought up for a vote in the full chamber. Telling, too, is that despite the popularity of the claim among evangelicals that gay marriage is a threat to religious freedom, there are no religious freedom restoration laws in Brazil. In the United States, these laws allow for discrimination against gay people if that discrimination is rooted in sincerely held religious views.

The absence of legal backlash in Brazil does not mean there was no political backlash. Most notably, the evangelical movement brought the Rousseff administration's gay rights agenda to a halt. According to Gustavo Bernardes, head of the office of LGBT affairs of the Human Rights Secretariat under the Rousseff administration, "The recognition of gay marriage (and before that, gay stable unions) was followed by hysteria on the part of the Evangelical movement" which resulted in freezing all LGBTQ bills.[80] More suggestive still, in 2013, in a retaliatory move against the gay community, evangelical leaders gained control of the Chamber of Deputies' Commission on Human Rights and Minorities. Usually, someone sympathetic toward the gay community and other minority communities has headed the commission, which has historically served as a platform for advocating for LGBTQ rights. But in March 2013, Marco Feliciano, a Pentecostal pastor with the Assemblies of God and a fierce opponent of homosexuality, managed to get himself elected chair of the commission as a result of the horse-trading of posts that is typical of Brazilian parliamentary rules.

[78] Santos and Melo, "The Opposition to LGBT Rights in the Brazilian National Congress," 104.
[79] "Câmara aprova Estatuto da Família formada a partir da união de homem e mulher," Câmara dos Diputados, August 10, 2015. Available at https://www.camara.leg.br/noticias/472681-camara-aprova-estatuto-da-familia-formada-a-partir-da-uniao-de-homem-e-mulher/.
[80] Electronic communication with Mr. Bernardes (June 21, 2018).

156 Framing Equality

An outspoken foe of the gay community, Feliciano has used his perch on the Human Rights Commission to wage a virtual war on the Brazilian LGBTQ community. In doing so, he opened space for hateful speech and actions against LGBTQ people. Among other outrageous things, he has declared that AIDS is "a gay cancer" and that Africa is a bastion of "paganism, occultism, penury." He also attributed diseases like Ebola and AIDS to the "first act of homosexuality in history."[81] He has also argued that feminism turns women gay. "When you stimulate a woman to have the same rights as men, she would want to work, her part of being a mother starts getting diminished. She will either not marry, or keep a marriage, or have a relationship with a person of the same sex, enjoying the pleasures of a childless union."[82] Efforts by other members of Congress, the media, and the public to remove Feliciano from his post at the Human Rights Commission, on grounds that he was making Brazil less liberal, proved futile. These efforts included an online petition that gathered almost half a million signatures.

As chair of the Human Rights Commission, Feliciano championed bills whose sole purpose was to project the image of social conservatives as defenders of the traditional family and Christian values, since the bills had virtually no chance of being enacted into law. One bill, introduced in 2011 by Eduardo Cunha (a former speaker of the house who was removed from this post in 2016 by the Federal Supreme Court on corruption charges), sought to create "Hetero Pride Day" to counter gay pride celebrations around the country. Another bill called for bringing back "reparative therapy," a therapy that Brazil outlawed in 1999. Introduced by Congressman João Campos, a member of the evangelical bloc, the bill would invalidate two provisions in the Federal Council of Psychology ordinance of 1999 banning reparative therapy.[83] The bill was greeted with alarm by the gay community and became a mobilizing force of the massive protest movement that rocked Brazil in 2013.

Yet another bill would have made it a crime "to satirize, ridicule or demean any religion during public manifestation of a social and cultural nature."[84] Law violators would be subject to hefty fines and prison terms to be determined by the military police. The bill was triggered by the provocative acts and images that are commonplace at gay pride parades around Brazil, many of

---

[81] "Religious Dispatches," March 12, 2013. Available at http://religiondispatches.org/pentecostal-with-history-of-hate-speech-selected-as-president-of-brazils-human-rights-body/.

[82] "Feminism Turns People Gay, Warns Brazil's Human Rights Boss," *Gay Star News*, March 21, 2013.

[83] "Brazilian Evangelical Lawmakers Push Gay Conversion Bill," Political Research Associates, June 28, 2013. Available at http://www.politicalresearch.org/2013/06/28/brazilian-evangelical-lawmakers-push-gay-conversion-therapy-bill/#sthash.WvQMUWIz.dpbs.

[84] "Projeto de lei que quer proibir sátiras à religião émesmo uma degraça," *Folha de S Paulo*, September 21, 2017. Available at http://f5.folha.uol.com.br/colunistas/tonygoes/2015/08/1671261-projeto-de-lei-que-quer-proibir-satiras-a-religiao-e-mesmo-uma-desgraca.shtml; accessed March 22, 2017.

Brazil **157**

which are famous for desecrating Christian symbols. One notorious example is the image of transwoman Viviany Beleboni at São Paulo's 2015 gay pride parade crucified seminude displaying a sign reading "Enough of Homophobia."[85] Such displays, in the eyes of conservative legislators pushing for the bill, represented instances of *Cristofobia* (or Christ-phobia) or "the practice of obscene and degrading acts which show prejudice against Catholics and Evangelicals." At a noisy demonstration in support of the bill on the floor of the Chamber of Deputies in June 2015, members of the *bancada evangélica* held pictures of gay pride rallies around Brazil that they believed were instances of Cristofobia.[86]

Bolsonaro's rise to power in 2018, which ushered in a wave of democratic threats, including attacks on the judiciary, the electoral system, and the press, breathed new life into the gay marriage backlash by strengthening homophobia "through the instantiation of a politics of disgust."[87] In Bolsonaro, the evangelical movement found someone willing to launch an all-out culture war on homosexuality and LGBTQ rights. During his three decades as a congressman from Rio de Janeiro, Bolsonaro made his dislike of homosexuals and disapproval of gay rights widely known. "Yes, I am homophobic and proud of it," he once proclaimed.[88] He also said that "he would rather his son die in an accident than be gay," that parents "should beat being gay out of their children," and that gay marriage was "a blow to family unity and family values."[89] He also claimed that "homosexual fundamentalists were brainwashing heterosexual children to become gays and lesbians to satisfy them sexually in the future."[90]

Unsurprisingly, Bolsonaro ran a homophobic presidential campaign against Fernando Haddad, a former mayor of São Paulo, running under the

[85] "Transexual que encenou crucificação na Parada Gay afirma ter sido agredida," *Folha de S Paulo*, September 8, 2015. Available at http://www1.folha.uol.com.br/cotidiano/2015/08/1666504-transexual-que-encenou-crucificacao-na-parada-gay-afirma-ter-sido-agredida.shtml.

[86] "Játivemos a Inquisição, diz leitor sobre discussão da cristofobia," *Folha de S Paulo*, June 14, 2015. Available at http://www1.folha.uol.com.br/paineldoleitor/2015/06/1641806-ja-tivemos-a-inquisicao-diz-leitor-sobre-discussao-da-cristofobia.shtml; accessed March 22, 2017.

[87] Rodrigo Borba, "Disgusting Politics: Circuits of Affects and the Making of Bolsonaro," *Social Semiotics* 31, no. 50 (2020): 15.

[88] Tom Phillips, "Brazil's fearful LGBT Community Prepares for a 'Proud Homophobe," *The Guardian*, September 27, 2018. Available at https://www.theguardian.com/world/2018/oct/27/dispatch-sao-paulo-jair-bolsonaro-victory-lgbt-community-fear.

[89] Zoe Sullivan, "LGBTQ Brazilians on Edge after Self-Described Homophobic Lawmaker Elected President," *NBC News*, October 29, 2018. Anthony Faiola and Marina Lopes, "LGBT Rights Threatened in Brazil under New Far-Right President," *The Washington Post*, February 18, 2019. Available at https://www.washingtonpost.com/world/the_americas/lgbt-rights-under-attack-in-brazil-under-new-far-right-president/2019/02/17/b24e1dcc-1b28-11e9-b8e6-567190c2fd08_story.html.

[90] Tom Phillips, "Brazil's Fearful LGBT Community Prepares for the Proud Homophobe," *The Guardian*, October 27, 2018. Available at https://www.theguardian.com/world/2018/oct/27/dispatch-sao-paulo-jair-bolsonaro-victory-lgbt-community-fear.

158 Framing Equality

PT banner. A meme that went viral falsely accused Haddad of supporting policies that would forcibly turn children gay and transgender. It showed a picture of Haddad with this quote attributed to him: "When they turn five, children will become the property of the state. It's up to us to decide if a boy will become a girl, and vice versa! It's the parents' job to respectfully comply with our decision! We know what's best for children."[91] This particular attack on Haddad mirrors a trend among Brazilian conservatives (which echoes developments in the United States) of trying to protect children from what they regard as ideological indoctrination on issues of gender identity.

Despite the intensity of Bolsonaro's homophobia, his impact on LGBTQ rights was nowhere near as meaningful as many had feared. One such worry was the notion that Bolsonaro would try "to undermine the meaning and practicalities of same-sex marriage incrementally through religious freedom laws, and finding ways to chip away at it."[92] Jorge Schwartz, a long-time observer of gay rights politics in Brazil (he was active with Somos in the 1970s), noted in an interview, "Although the evangelical movement remains deliriously homophobic, nothing has changed about homosexual rights in Brazil."[93] In an ironic twist of fate, under Bolsonaro Brazil experienced one of the biggest (perhaps the biggest) expansion of LGBTQ rights in the country's history. This expansion had significant implications for the deepening of LGBTQ equality.

In his inaugural speech, Bolsonaro spoke about the fight against "gender ideology," a phrase favored by rightwing politicians to telegraph their opposition to LGBTQ rights. While in office (2019–2022), Bolsonaro's attacks on gay rights focused on removing LGBTQ issues from federal agencies, especially the education and human rights ministries. Within hours of his inauguration, he banned LGBTQ issues from being deliberated by the Human Rights Ministry, part of a cluster of executive actions that targeted minority groups, including gays and indigenous peoples. He also appointed officials contemptuous of LGBTQ people and hostile to gay rights. According to the *Washington Post*, during her first day in office, Damares Alves, the evangelical pastor who served as Bolsonaro's minister of women and family, declared that "in the new Brazil girls wear pink, and boys wear blue. Girls will be princesses, and boys will be princes," she added. For his part, Bolsonaro's minister of

---

[91] "Top Pentecostal Leaders Supported the Far Right in Brazil's Presidential Campaign," *Vox*, October 8, 2018. Available at https://www.vox.com/mischiefs-of-faction/2018/10/8/17950304/pentecostals-bolsonaro-brazil.

[92] Tim Teeman, "LGBT Brazilians Fearful but Defiant as Bolsonaro Takes Office," *The Daily Beast*, January 4, 2019. Available at https://www.thedailybeast.com/lgbt-brazilians-fearful-but-defiant-as-bolsonaro-takes-power.

[93] Electronic communication with Mr. Schwartz (June 8, 2021).

education, Ricardo Vélez Rodríguez, "shut down a section of the ministry devoted to diversity and human rights."[94]

In 2018, just before Bolsonaro entered office, the Federal Supreme Court ruled that transgender people have the right to change their names legally without surgery or professional evaluation by self-declaring their gender identity. That decision set the stage for the Court's delivery of what is arguably the most important gay rights breakthrough in the country's history: the criminalization of homophobia. In a nine-to-one decision, the Court made homophobia and transphobia crimes similar to racism, meriting up to five years in prison. An incensed Bolsonaro accused the Court of "legislating from the bench" and suggested that "it was time to appoint an Evangelical Christian to the Supreme Court."[95] In 2020, the Federal Supreme Court allowed the broadcast of homosexual materials that religious people might find offensive, a ruling prompted by a *Netflix* film that depicted Jesus as a closeted homosexual. That same year, the Court lifted a ban on blood donations by gay males and ruled that municipalities could not ban sex educational materials that conservatives deemed "gender ideology."

Several factors worked to limit political and legal backlash in Brazil while at the same time allowing for the expansion of LGBTQ equality in the wake of the legalization of gay marriage. For starters, although evangelical leaders are skilled at blocking legislation, they are mostly incapable of generating legislation. Because of the highly fragmented nature of political representation in the Brazilian Congress—a reflection of Brazil's historic failure to produce coherent political parties—it is tough for this body to enact laws. At present, some thirty political parties are represented in the Brazilian Congress. This political fragmentation has forced administrations from the right and the left to operate under what Brazilian scholars call *presidencialismo de coalizão*, or coalition presidentialism. The practical outcome of this political phenomenon is that legislating almost anything involves forging complex alliances across multiple party coalitions.

Cultural factors also played a role. Although Brazilians are nowhere near as accepting of homosexuality as people outside Brazil tend to believe is the case, Brazilians have a well-earned reputation for celebrating freewheeling sexuality, sexual diversity, and gender nonconformity.[96] This reputation goes back to when the Europeans first focused on the country. "Beneath the Equator, sin does not exist," wrote the Dutch historian Caspar von Barlaeus in 1660 upon

---

[94] Faiola and Lopes, "LGBT Rights Threatened in Brazil under New Far-Right President."

[95] Ibid.

[96] On images of Brazil as a hyper-sexualized society, see Richard Guy Parker, *Bodies, Pleasures and Passion: Sexual Culture in Contemporary Brazil* (Boston, MA: Beacon Press, 1991).

returning to Europe from a visit to Brazil.[97] Such characterizations set Brazil apart from the rest of Latin America, where gender norms are usually rigidly upheld. These conceptions are attributed to the massive influx of enslaved Africans into Brazil, which is credited with taming Iberian machismo. In more recent times, images of "gay Brazil" have taken hold around the world— especially the hedonism of carnival in Rio de Janeiro, in many regards the very essence of Brazilian culture, and the extravaganza of São Paulo's gay pride march, the world's largest LGBT celebration. Both events are noted for their sexual debauchery.

Acceptance of homosexuality is also broadly displayed in the Brazilian media, especially in the popular telenovelas (TV soap operas). Analyzing the impact of telenovelas on the progression of gay rights in Brazil, Caufield noted, "In recent years, a few novelas broadcast by the powerful TV Globo network, such as *Senhora do Destino* (2006–07), and *Páginas da Vida* (2006–07), became platforms for arguments in favor of gay family rights. The novelas did not place same-sex couples in the steamy sex scenes that are the standard fare for heterosexual couples on the shows. Instead, gay couples have appeared as upstanding citizens, loyal family members, and responsible and loving parents: precisely the social roles that real-life LGBT individuals struggle to occupy in their appeals to the courts."[98] These portrayals reinforced the view of gay couples as stable unions, a long-standing socially accepted form of conjugal union in Brazil, even after civil marriage became available to the Brazilian population at large.[99]

There is also minimal appetite among Brazilians for policies that would marginalize/criminalize homosexuality. A 2016 survey by the International Lesbian, Gay, Bisexual, Trans, and Intersex Association puts Brazil at the top of all Latin American countries on the question of whether homosexuality should be a crime, with 60 percent strongly disagreeing with the question, followed by Argentina and Chile with 59 percent.[100] A 2022 survey from Datafolha revealed that roughly 80 percent of Brazilians believed that homosexuality should be accepted by society.[101] These findings echo the

[97] Richard Guy Parker, *Beneath the Equator: Cultures of Desire, Male Homosexuality, and Emerging Gay Communities in Brazil* (New York: Routledge, 1999), 1.

[98] Sueann Caufield, "The Recent Supreme Court Ruling on Same-Sex Unions in Brazil: A Historical Perspective," *International Institute Journal* 1, no. 2 (Fall 2011): 8.

[99] See, especially, Teresa Castro-Martin, "Consensual Unions in Latin America: Persistence of a Dual Nuptiality System," *Journal of Comparative Family Studies*, 33, no. 1 (January 2002): 35–55.

[100] Marilia Brocchetto, "The Perplexing Narrative about Being Gay in Latin America," *CNN*, March 3, 2017. Available at https://www.cnn.com/2017/02/26/americas/lgbt-rights-in-the-americas/index.html.

[101] "Datafolha: 8 em cada10 brasileiros acham que homossexualidade deve ser aceita," *Folha de S. Paulo*, June 4, 2022. Available at https://www1.folha.uol.com.br/poder/2022/06/datafolha-8-em-cada-10-brasileiros-acham-que-homossexualidade-deve-ser-aceita.shtml.

history of homosexuality in Brazil. The country has never erected any legal barriers to homosexuality, a reason behind the country's reputation as "the world's friendliest to homosexuals."[102] An overview of the history of LGBTQ rights in Brazil by Sueann Caufield noted, "The liberals who wrote the first legal codes after Brazil's independence from Portugal in 1822 were eager to move as far as possible from what they saw as barbaric punishment of moral offenses during the old regime. Sodomy was excluded from the 1830 criminal code without generating much debate."[103]

Ultimately, however, it was the political framing around gay marriage that did the most to blunt the backlash. For one thing, the rhetorical distancing that gay activists were able to put between themselves and the institution of marriage in discussions of the state's recognition of same-sex relationships, meant that evangelical leaders had no credibility when arguing that gay activists were out to destroy marriage. This argument, so common in the United States, was rarely heard in Brazil. Moreover, the pragmatic strategy of linking same-sex relationships to Brazil's history of recognizing unmarried cohabitation underscored the point that what was being demanded by gay activists was not extraordinary. Indeed, extending recognition of gay couples as stable unions was in keeping with Brazil's tradition of recognizing the value of nonconventional unions. Most Brazilians shared this recognition regardless of their gender.

Explaining how the pragmatism evident in the struggle for gay marriage by Brazilian gay rights activists helped minimize political backlash, Moreira wrote, "The social acceptance of domestic cohabitation as a legitimate form of adult relationship by both opposite and same-sex couples . . . explains why many gay and lesbian couples think that the institution of stable unions provides enough legal protection to their relationship. By adopting an incremental approach in a marriage system that has historically extended legal protection to unmarried couples, they have allowed the courts to gradually implement and further expand protection to same-sex relationships, thus avoiding much of the strong political backlash that usually results from granting them access to the institution of marriage."[104]

Just as important, if not more, in minimizing backlash was the resonance of the moral messaging linking gay unions to human rights. It gave gay rights a deep grounding in Brazilian legal and political institutions. According to Bernardes, "While the evangelicals in Congress were unmoved by the argument that extending marriage rights to homosexual couples was an extension

---

[102] Author's electronic correspondence with Mr. Mott (June 21, 2013).
[103] Caufield, "The Recent Supreme Court Ruling on Same-Sex Unions in Brazil," 8.
[104] Moreira, "We are a Family!" 1006.

162 Framing Equality

of human rights, this was not the case with the Federal Supreme Court."[105] Bernardes noted that the judiciary's receptivity to human rights was aided by Lula's remaking of the Federal Supreme Court as one the world's most sympathetic to human rights. That receptivity was signaled after Congress failed to pass bills to ban homophobia and approve same-sex civil unions. In 1998, Chief Justice José Celso Mello told *O Estado de São Paulo*, "It's of no use commemorating the fiftieth anniversary of the Universal Declaration of Human Rights if unjust practices which deny homosexuals their basic human rights continue to exist. The executive, legislative, and judicial bodies need to take note of these cruelties and acknowledge our need to confront the conditions of grave adversaries in which members of these extremely vulnerable groups are forced to exist."[106]

Indeed, the receptivity to moral appeals based on human rights signaled by the Federal Supreme Court was a significant factor in encouraging public prosecutors to bring gay rights cases to the Court in the first place. In its 2011 ruling on stable unions, the Federal Supreme Court broadly validated the plaintiffs' legal and moral arguments. "Stable unions simply represent one particular type of adult relationship that deserves legal protection, along with other forms of constitutionally protected family arrangements. Consequently, there is no conflict between the constitutional definition of stable unions and the recognition of same-sex couples as family entities."[107] But the ruling was also inspired by the 1948 Universal Declaration of Human Rights and its emphasis on the dignity of all individuals, as conveyed in the Brazilian Constitution. As noted by Moreira, "The principles of equality and human dignity authorize the inclusion of same-sex partners in the statutory definition of a cohabitant, since the Brazilian Constitution aims to promote emancipation."[108]

Just as revealing are some of the comments made by the justices following the ruling. Ellen Gracie wrote, "The recognition made by the court today responds to the rights of a group of people who have long been humiliated, whose rights have been ignored, whose dignity has been offended, whose identity was denied, and whose freedom was overwhelmed."[109] Gilmar Mendes noted, "Same-sex couples found themselves in a legal limbo, so the Court had an obligation to respond to protect the human rights of gay

[105] Electronic communication with Mr. Bernardes (June 21, 2018)

[106] Cited by Mott, "The Gay Movement in the Land of Carnival," unpublished manuscript provided to the author.

[107] Moreira, "We are a Family!" 1004.

[108] Ibid.

[109] "Brazil's Supreme Court Legalizes Same-Sex Unions," Amnesty International. Available at https://www.amnestyusa.org/updates/brazils-supreme-court-legalizes-same-sex-civil-unions/.

couples."[110] Carlos Ayres Britto, the author of the ruling, noted, "The freedom to pursue one's sexuality is part of an individual's freedom of expression."[111] He added, "Hopefully, legal recognition will pave the way to less violence for gays, lesbians, and transgender people in Brazil."

In the years since the legalization of gay marriage, the courts in Brazil have remained very receptive to moral arguments. This receptivity is a sign of the success of the gay rights movement in integrating the ethical arguments of the campaigns for same-sex civil unions and gay marriage, such as the need to extend dignity and respect to gay and lesbian couples, into the legal fabric of the Brazilian state. In justifying making homophobia a crime, in 2019, Justice Gilman Mendes said, "Sexual orientation and gender identity are essential to human beings, to the self-determination to decide their own life and seek happiness.[112]

Finally, the moral messaging resonated with many Brazilian Catholics, who remain the largest group of Catholics in the world—some 120 million people, or 60 percent of the Brazilian population. That this resonance would take place in Brazil should come as no surprise given the polling data that shows Brazilian Catholics holding a significant edge over Christian evangelicals in supporting issues like abortion and homosexuality.[113] But just as relevant is the history of progressivism within the Brazilian Catholic Church, which includes a long-standing tradition of championing human rights.[114] This tradition is usually associated with the popularity of Liberation Theology in Brazil. Born in Medellin, Colombia, at the 1968 Latin American Bishops' Conference, this movement emphasizes concern for those facing oppression.

Although the influence of Liberation Theology was felt all over Latin America, its legacy in Brazil was unique. A 2018 assessment of the movement noted, "The Brazilian church is the only church on the continent where liberation theology and its pastoral followers won decisive influence."[115] By 1970, the Brazilian National Conference of Bishops made public statements against state repression and rampant inequality. By 1973, it was engaged in a national

---

[110] "Supreme Court Unanimously Recognizes Legality of a Stable Union Involving Homosexuals," *Agencia Brasil*, May 5, 2011.

[111] "Brazil's Supreme Court Awards Gay Couples New Rights," *BBC*, March 6, 2011.

[112] "Brazil's Supreme Court Rules Homophobia a Crime," *Reuters*, June 13, 2019. Available at https://www.reuters.com/article/us-brazil-homophobia-idUSKCN1TF02N.

[113] In 2014, 51 percent of Brazilian Catholics approved of gay marriage versus 25 percent for Protestants. See "Religion in Latin America: Widespread Change in a Historically Catholic Region," Pew Research Center, November 13, 2014. Available at https://www.pewresearch.org/religion/2014/11/13/religion-in-latin-america/.

[114] See, especially, Amy Erica Smith, *Religion and Brazilian Democracy: Mobilizing the People of God*, Brazil (New York: Cambridge University Press, 2019), Chapter 6.

[115] Hugh McDonnell, "The Left Side of the Church," Jacobin, December 29, 2018. Available at https://jacobin.com/2018/12/church-liberation-theology-latin-america-left.

164 Framing Equality

campaign for human rights. By 1975, it was urging the military to return Brazil to civilian rule. Of special note is the official condemnation of the military government by the Conference in 1974.[116] That year, the Conference "excoriated the regime for allowing policemen to go unpunished for torture and killing, for presiding over unjust distribution of rural land, and for failing to protect the dwindling Indian population against the encroachment of white settlers."[117]

While in the rest of Latin America Liberation Theology remained focused on class issues, in Brazil it migrated toward sex and gender, including LGBTQ issues. In the 1980s, Brazilian clergy steeped in Liberation Theology developed what is known as the "theology of the body," including Rubem Alves, "one of the pioneers of Liberation Theology in Latin America."[118] Alves's work "provided LGBT Christians in Brazil a set of theological arguments that could link their struggles to the struggles of the poor, and ultimately, to Christ's redemptive sacrifice. Lesbian, gay, bisexual, and transgender bodies were also worthy of pleasure, since, by virtue of baptism, they were redeemed and will be resurrected. Therefore, religion should free them to love and be loved, without providing oppressive boundaries akin to those imposed by economic elites on the poor."[119] Consequently, no religious institution in Brazil is more identified with promoting progressive social change than the Brazilian Catholic Church.[120] And no other Catholic establishment has been more welcoming of homosexuals than the Brazilian Church.

As noted previously, the Catholic Left welcomed gay rights activists into the PT even though many of its leaders believed that homosexuality was a sin. There is also a robust Brazilian LGBTQ Roman Catholic movement, which is far from marginal to the official structures of the Catholic Church. As noted by one study, most groups that belong to the movement "are accompanied by clergy, which provide them with places to congregate, celebrating mass and taking communion."[121] Also noteworthy is the role of the Brazilian Catholic Church in nudging the Vatican into embracing a more tolerant view toward homosexuality in recent years.

---

[116] See John Burdick, *Legacies of Liberation: The Progressive Catholic Church in Brazil at the Start of a New Millennium* (New York: Routledge, 2004).

[117] "Brazil's Catholic Bishops Condemn Military Regime," *The New York Times*, November 20, 1976. Available at https://www.nytimes.com/1976/11/20/archives/brazils-catholic-bishops-condemn-military-regime-catholic-bishops.html.

[118] Coelho Filho, "Inclusivity the Brazilian Way," 14.

[119] Ibid., 15.

[120] See, Kevin Neuhouser, "The Radicalization of the Brazilian Catholic Church in Comparative Perspective," *American Sociological Review* 54 (1989): 233–244.

[121] Cris Serra, "Diversity as a Gift: LGBTQI+ Roman Catholic Organizations in Twenty-First-Century Brazil," *International Journal of Latin American Religions* 6 (2022): 270.

It was after visiting Brazil in 2013 that Pope Francis famously said "Who am I to judge?," when asked about gay people in the Catholic Church. The recent decisions allowing priests to bless same-sex couples and to baptize transgender people have been traced to lobbying from Brazilian bishops.[122]

Much of the foregoing explains the moderation that the Catholic Church in Brazil has displayed in the country's gay rights struggles. As recalled by Santos and Melo, "The National Conference of Bishops in Brazil was relatively distant from the debates about the proposal to include the term sexual orientation in the constitution." They attributed this to the fact that "at the time the most politically active sectors of the Catholic clergy in the national constitutional assembly were linked to liberation theology."[123] During the 1990s, when many Catholic leaders around the world were exploiting the HIV/AIDS epidemic to demonize the gay community, the Brazilian Catholic Church and gay activists joined forces with their participation in the National AIDS Program.[124] More recently, Brazilian Catholic leaders have spoken against anti-gay violence and homophobia and in favor of civil rights for LGBTQ people.

In 2014, in anticipation of São Paulo's pride march, the Archdiocese of São Paulo released a statement that put the Catholic Church squarely on the side of defending the human rights of the homosexual community. It noted, "We cannot remain silent in the face of the reality experienced by this population that is the target of prejudice and victim of systematic violation of their fundamental rights, such as health, education, work, housing, culture, among others. . . . [LGBTQ people] face unbearable daily verbal and physical violence, culminating in murders that are true hate crimes. . . . We are engaged in upholding human rights and do not agree with violence, regardless of the color and the sexual orientation of people."[125] In 2021, the National Conference of Bishops joined other major churches in Brazil in linking the backlash against gay rights as a cause of death among LGBTQ people. A statement released on Ash Wednesday, to coincide with the launch of a fundraising campaign (the Fraternity Campaign), read, "These homicides are caused by

---

[122] Naira Galarraga Gortázar, "The Brazilian Bishop Who Took the First Step toward the Catholic Church Embracing LGBTq+ People," *El País*, January 30, 2024. Available at https://english.elpais.com/international/2024-01-29/the-brazilian-bishop-who-took-the-first-step-toward-the-catholic-church-embracing-gays-and-transgender-people.html.

[123] Santos and Melo, "The Opposition to LGBT Rights in the Brazilian National Congress (1986–2018)," 84.

[124] Laura R. Murray, Jonathan García, Miguel Muñoz Laboy, and Richard G. Parker, "Strange Bedfellows: The Catholic Church and Brazilian National AIDS Program in the Response to HIV/AIDS in Brazil," *Social Science & Medicine* 72, no. 6, January 27, 2011: 945–952.

[125] "Brazilian Bishops Endorse Legal Equality, Promise to Accompany the LGBT Community," New Ways Ministry, May 24, 2014. Available at https://www.newwaysministry.org/2014/05/24/brazilian-bishops-endorse-legal-equality-promise-to-accompany-lgbt-community/.

hate speech, by religious fundamentalism, by (the) voices (of those) against recognizing the rights of the LGBTQI+ population."[126]

More surprising, perhaps, is that the Catholic clergy has criticized its own when they have attacked the homosexual community. In 2021, when state prosecutors launched an investigation of a Brazilian priest in the city of Tapurah, in Mato Grosso State, for a homily that included the Portuguese slur for "faggots," as a likely violation of the new ban on homophobia, Church officials sided with the state. Claudio Langroiva Pereira, a professor at the Pontifical Catholic University of São Paulo and a member of the Archdiocese of São Paulo's Justice and Peace Commission, noted, "The Mato Grosso State prosecutors launched that investigation because the Supreme Court has recently decided that acts of homophobia should be treated in a similar way that acts of racism, which are crimes according to Brazilian law. All citizens must be held responsible for their acts when their rhetoric harms fundamental human rights."[127]

Little wonder that the Brazilian National Conference of Bishops for the most part sat out the war over gay marriage. Officially, the Conference came out against gay marriage, but this opposition "lacked the virulence and willfulness of the Evangelical opposition."[128] In response to the legalization of gay marriage in 2013, the Conference noted, "Same-sex unions cannot be simply equated to marriage or family, which are based on matrimonial consent, in the spirit of complementarity and reciprocity between a man and a woman, open to the procreation and education of children . . . We join with all those who legitimately and democratically protest against the resolution."[129] But there was no attempt to mobilize Catholics against gay marriage or to pressure the politicians to oppose gay marriage, as was the case in Spain and Argentina. Nor, as was the case in the United States, did the hierarchy of the Catholic Church join evangelical groups in a coordinated campaign to oppose gay marriage.

More importantly, the pragmatic and cautious discourse about gay marriage adopted by gay activists appears seems to have brought the Church to the side of the activists. In a 2014 interview with *O Globo*, Leonardo Steiner, the secretary general of the Brazilian Conference of Bishops, said that while

---

[126] Jennifer Ann Thomas, "Brazil Churches Spark Controversy with LGBT+ Lent Campaign," *Reuters*, February 17, 2021. Available at https://www.reuters.com/article/us-brazil-lgbt-religion-trfn-idUSKBN2AH2NE.

[127] "Brazilian Priest Investigated over Anti-Gay Slurs in Homily," *Crux*, June 19, 2021. Available at https://cruxnow.com/church-in-the-americas/2021/06/brazilian-priest-investigated-over-anti-gay-slurs-in-homily/.

[128] Aranda, *El Mundo*, "El matrimonio homosexual, legal en Brasil sólo en la práctica."

[129] "Bishops Decry Gay Marriage Decision," ENCA, May 17, 2013. Available at https://www.enca.com/world/bishops-decry-gay-marriage-decision.

the Catholic Church is opposed to gay marriage, "there needs to be a dialogue on the rights attached to shared life between people of the same sex who decided to live together. They need legal support from society."[130] Steiner noted that the Church always evolves: "The Church isn't the same through the ages. It seeks answers for the present time, using the Gospel as the illuminating force for its action." When asked why the Church opposed gay marriage, Steiner said that it was up to Congress to decide the issue.

A Mixed Legacy

Having won the war over gay marriage with a political discourse designed to minimize conservative backlash, Brazilian gay activists now face the task of protecting gay marriage in a political climate that remains hostile to gay rights. Many gay rights activists would like to see the judicial decisions that led to the legalization of gay marriage by the Federal Supreme Court and the National Council of Justice codified into law. Aside from placing gay marriage on a firmer legal footing, a national gay marriage law would prompt the societal debate about gay marriage and LGBTQ rights more broadly that Brazil still lacks. As Bimbi noted, "A drawback of the very speedy way that the courts mandated same-sex marriage in Brazil is to have deprived the country of the social and cultural change that a public debate would have produced."[131]

Considering that the Brazilian congress remains under conservative control—to say nothing of the extreme ideological fragmentation of this body—gay activists are under no illusion that Congress will act on gay marriage anytime soon. Moreover, there still is a significant reservoir of opposition to gay marriage by right-wing legislators, who continue to see attacking gay marriage as an effective means for mobilizing conservative voters. In fact, in 2023, the Committee on Social Security, Social Assistance, Childhood, Adolescence, and Family of the Chamber of Deputies approved a bill (initially proposed in 2007) by far-right parties affiliated with former president Bolsonaro that would abolish gay marriage. According to its main sponsor, Deputy Francisco Eurico da Silva, an Evangelical pastor who acted as rapporteur for the bill, the courts "usurped responsibilities and powers that belong to Congress."[132]

---

[130] "Brazilian Bishop: Same-Sex Couples Need Legal Support," Catholic Culture, November 23, 2014. Available at https://www.catholicculture.org/news/headlines/index.cfm?storyid=21497.

[131] Author's electronic correspondence with Mr. Bimbi (September 11, 2024).

[132] "Brazil Far Right Moves to Ban Gay Marriage," EFE, October 10, 2023. Available at https://efe.com/en/latest-news/2023-10-10/brazil-rights-far-right-moves-to-ban-same-sex-marriage.

168   Framing Equality

Since the bill would have to clear both houses of Congress and survive a veto by Lula—to say nothing of having to overcome significant legal challenges—not many people in Brazil are losing sleep over the possibility that the bill might become law. Nonetheless, the bill is a wake-up call for the gay community. At the very least, it points to the need for greater engagement by gay activists with the public about the rights of LGBTQ people, including gay marriage. One of the unintended consequences of the success of the political strategies that made gay marriage possible in Brazil, especially avoiding making marriage demands until the status of stable unions for gay unions was secured, is that gay activists did not spend much time speaking about gay marriage. The time between the legalization of stable unions and gay marriage was less than two years. Not surprisingly, perhaps, support for gay marriage in Brazil (which in 2023 stood at 52 percent) lags behind other large Latin American nations like Argentina and Mexico.[133]

Traditionally, Brazilian gay activists have preferred to operate through the political system and the structures of the PT and other left-wing parties. Engaging with the public either through messaging and/or by mobilizing the gay community and its allies has been, at best, a secondary concern. This political approach worked for getting gay marriage into the books, but it is unlikely to do much to build solid societal support for LGBTQ rights, including gay marriage. Gay rights activists appear fully aware of this unfinished agenda in the struggle to advance the rights of LGBTQ people in Brazil. According to Iotti, "There's a continuing need in Brazil for messaging strategies that demonstrate that LGBTQ+ rights are human rights and not a left-wing agenda. It's a work in progress."[134]

---

[133] See Sneha Gubbala, Jacob Poushter, and Christine Huang, "How People around the World View Same-Sex Marriage," Pew Research Center, November 27, 2023. Available at https://www.pewresearch.org/short-reads/2023/11/27/how-people-around-the-world-view-same-sex-marriage/.
[134] Author's electronic communication with Mr. Iotti (October 7, 2024).

Chapter 5
Comparative Discussion and Takeaways

Social revolutions are rarely easily won. This dictum certainly applies to the marriage equality movement, one of the most controversial and consequential social revolutions of recent times. After all, the movement upended the traditional view of marriage as the exclusive union of one man and one woman that had existed for thousands of years. It also triggered a robust clash between gay rights activists, many of them veterans of previous struggles, such as the fight against HIV/AIDS, and influential religious institutions and interest groups, such as the Roman Catholic Church and the Christian right. All of this said, the so-called war over gay marriage did not make for a common international experience, not even among those nations where the struggle proved victorious. In particular, this book has explored why the culture war over gay marriage varied across countries in two key respects: the severity of the backlash aimed at the gay community and the legacy of the struggle for the expansion of LGBTQ equality.

Framing—broadly understood as the rhetorical arguments that social movements make to build support for their cause—has been my main focus in this book. Capitalizing on the campaign for gay marriage in the United States, Spain, and Brazil, I have argued that the framing of gay marriage generally conforms to one of three approaches: legal, moral, and political. Surely, when encountered in the real world, it is apparent that these framing approaches are not set in stone or stand as independent silos. As seen already, there's considerable fluidity in the arguments and appeals that each approach upholds. In at least two of our cases—Brazil and the United States—there was a marked turn, if not an outright transition, in approaches at the tail end of the campaign. But despite the fluidity apparent in gay marriage framing approaches, one particular approach generally prevails. It sets the tone for the campaign as a whole.

I have also argued that each approach has its justification for opening the institution of marriage to gay and lesbian couples and consequences of its own for how the war over gay marriage unfolds. While the legal framing promotes the purist view of gay marriage as a fundamental civil right, the moral

Framing Equality. Omar G. Encarnación, Oxford University Press. © Oxford University Press (2025).
DOI: 10.1093/9780190880330.003.0006

170 Framing Equality

framing promotes the idealistic notion of gay marriage as an ethical obligation. The political framing is noted by its pragmatism, including mixing legal claims and moral appeals about gay marriage and embracing incremental steps to attaining marriage equality. A key finding of this study is that while any of the three framing approaches noted above can bring the gay marriage campaign to a successful conclusion, the moral framing can do the most to minimize backlash and bolster LGBTQ equality. Of course, it is hardly a given that the moral framing will deliver on these expectations. But the war over gay marriage, like any other culture war, is about a fundamental disagreement over morality. Ultimately, victory in any culture war hinges on whose sense of right and wrong prevails.

My purpose for this concluding chapter is threefold. I first explore the Argentine and Irish gay marriage campaigns. These additional experiences boost my argument about the critical importance of moral arguments in framing gay marriage campaigns. I then offer a broad discussion about the underlying factors shaping gay marriage framing approaches. It highlights the primacy of domestic factors over international trends. In particular, this chapter highlights the political environment that surrounds the gay marriage campaign, especially the connections of the gay rights movement to the political system; the inspiration and lessons that the gay marriage movement derives from other social movements; the "foundational ideals" of the gay rights movement; and the activism of opponents to gay marriage, including their framing strategies. I close with some takeaways about the contributions of this research for future scholarship on gay marriage movements and LGBTQ rights more generally.

Argentina and Ireland

In Argentina, as in Spain, the legalization of gay marriage had a strong political structure behind it. Argentine President Cristina Fernández de Kirchner of the Peronist Party put it all on the line to see Argentina become a gay marriage pioneer in Latin America, including ensuring the successful passage of the gay marriage bill in the Argentine Senate on July 15, 2010. But less apparent is that in Argentina, as in Spain, a gay marriage campaign deeply rooted in moral themes was critical to managing the conservative political backlash and using gay marriage as the platform for expanding LGBTQ equality.[1]

---

[1] For a broader view of Argentina's gay marriage campaign, see Bruno Bimbi, *Matrimonio Igualitario* (Buenos Aires: Editorial Planeta, 2011); Elisabeth Jay Friedman, "Constructing 'The Same Rights with the Same Names: The Impact of Spanish Norm Diffusion on Marriage Equality in Argentina,'" *Latin American Politics and Society* 54, no. 4 (Winter 2012): 29–59; Shawn Schulenberg, "The Construction and Enactment of Same-Sex Marriage in Argentina," *Journal of Human Rights* 11, no. 1 (2012): 106–125; Omar G.

Comparative Discussion and Takeaways **171**

This similarity in the framing of gay marriage in Spain and Argentina is not accidental. "We learned everything from the Spaniards," according to Maria Rachid, president of *Federación Argentina LGBT*, the organization that led the Argentine gay marriage struggle.[2] Its acronym, FALGBT, pays homage to Spain's FELGBT, the organization that spearheaded the Spanish campaign. FELGBT activists and Spanish Socialist Party officials traveled to Buenos Aires to advise local gay activists. Spain also provided financial support. All of this explains why the gay marriage bill enacted by the Argentine Congress was a duplicate of the Spanish gay marriage law.

To be sure, Argentina's gay marriage campaign was not a mirror image of Spain's. For one thing, because the gay marriage bill did not originate with Fernández de Kirchner's administration (in fact, she did not endorse the bill until it had cleared the Chamber of Deputies, the lower house of the Argentine Congress), FALGBT activists pursued a dual-track strategy for legalizing gay marriage by approaching, simultaneously, the courts and the national legislature. Argentina's Supreme Court is believed to have approved gay marriage before the Argentine Congress but withheld announcing a decision to allow the legislators to act first. But the public-facing aspect of the Argentine campaign bore an unmistakable moral framing with broad echoes of the Spanish campaign.

As in Spain, the moral framing of the Argentine campaign emphasized full citizenship for the homosexual community. To that end, the Argentine campaign insisted on a complete moral equivalence between homosexual and heterosexual unions, a stance they borrowed from Spain, including the slogan "The same rights with the same name." Explaining the reasoning behind the slogan, Rachid noted: "We were not talking only about the right to get married—we wanted it to be called the same."[3] As a consequence of this demand, in Argentina, as in Spain, gay marriage arrived with all the rights and responsibilities accorded to heterosexual marriage.

Argentina's gay marriage campaign was also framed as a vehicle to modernize the country rather than as a legal instrument for extending rights and benefits to the gay community. Gay marriage activists stressed that gay marriage was part of a broader social agenda that included expanding rights and opportunities in the realms of gender, sexuality, and healthcare, intended to make Argentina more inclusive, diverse, and progressive. This message

---

Encarnación, "International Influence, Domestic Activism, and Gay Rights in Argentina," *Political Science Quarterly* 128, no. 4 (Winter 2013) 687–716; Jordi Díez, *The Politics of Gay Marriage in Latin America: Argentina, Chile, and Mexico* (New York: Cambridge University Press, 2015); and Omar G. Encarnación, *Out in the Periphery: Latin America's Gay Rights Revolution* (New York: Oxford University Press, 2016).

[2] Author's interview with Ms. Rachid (Buenos Aires, July 20, 2012). Also cited in Encarnación, *Out in the Periphery*, 37.

[3] Irene Caselli, "Campaign Lines: Can Other Campaigns Learn from Argentina's Same-Sex Marriage Campaign?" *Index on Censorship* 47, no. 3 (2018): 42.

172 Framing Equality

was reaffirmed by President Fernández de Kirchner when she signed the gay marriage bill into law. "We have not enacted a law; we have enacted a social construction. And like all good social constructions, this one is transformational, diverse, and pluralistic. And it does not belong to any group in particular: it belongs to those who built it: society."[4]

Finally, the Argentine campaign was framed as an affirmation of universal human rights principles. This emphasis gave the campaign a unique Argentine coloring. Gay marriage activists at FALGBT centered the gay marriage campaign on human rights language and as part of the country's struggle to come to terms with the human rights abuses of the harrowing experience with military rule known around the world as the Dirty War (1976–1983). As reported from Buenos Aires by National Public Radio's Bob Mondello, "The marriage equality debate here has been seen less as a legal matter than as a human rights issue, an argument that resonates in a country that's experienced dictatorships and human rights abuses through the years."[5]

In public relations efforts and congressional testimony, Argentine gay marriage activists argued that advancing the rights of homosexuals was part of the reckoning with the human rights abuses that began in the mid-1980s. At the heart of this reckoning was the prosecution of the military on human rights charges associated with the Dirty War, especially the disappearance of some thirty thousand people, according to human rights activists. Among these victims are an unknown number of homosexuals killed because of their sexual orientation.[6] Since these victims are not identified in official reports, gay activists have taken to referring to them as "the disappeared among the disappeared." Not surprisingly, a recurring theme of the Argentine gay marriage campaign was to compare the discrimination that gays have historically faced in Argentina to the oppression imposed by the country's military dictatorship.

Framing the campaign around moral arguments helped blunt backlash in several mutually supporting ways. For starters, it allowed gay activists to tap into the resources of Argentina's vast universe of human rights organizations. Support from Las Madres de la Plaza de Mayo, the organization of the mothers whose children disappeared during the Dirty War, and in many regards Argentina's moral conscience, lent legitimacy to the gay marriage campaign while at the same time enhancing its cultural resonance. This support also

---

[4] "Argentina: Una Década de Matrimonio Libre, Diverso e Igualitario," France24.com, July 15, 2020. Available at https://www.france24.com/es/20200715-argentina-ley-matrimonio-igualitario-decada.

[5] Bob Mondello, "Gay Marriage Is a Human Rights Issue in Argentina," July 15, 2020. Available at https://www.npr.org/2010/07/15/128545987/gay-marriage-a-human-rights-issue-in-argentina.

[6] See, especially, Pablo Ben and Santiago Joaquim Insausti, "Dictatorial Rule and Sexual Politics in Argentina: The Case of the Frente de Liberación Homosexual, 1967–1976," *Hispanic American Historical Review* 97, no. 2 (May 2017): 295–325.

allowed other human rights organizations to join the gay marriage campaign. It also gave the green light to different civil society sectors to join the struggle, including Argentina's influential trade union movement.[7]

The moral framing also neutralized the Catholic Church's opposition to gay marriage. Buenos Aires Cardinal Archbishop Jorge Bergoglio, the future Pope Francis, criticized the gay marriage bill as "an attack on God's plan." He added: "It is not a mere legislative project but a movement of the father of all lies that seeks to confuse and deceive the children of God."[8] This dark rhetoric backfired with many Catholics who viewed gay marriage through the moral prism adopted by gay activists. As noted by one study of the voting behavior of Catholic legislators in the Argentine Congress on the issue of gay marriage, "Many who self-identified as Catholic actively mobilized to achieve legal change by opposing the hierarchy and official doctrine, thus breaking with Catholicism's seemingly homogenous conception against sexual and reproductive rights. Many of them were influenced by groups of priests mobilized publicly, maintaining that Catholic tradition allowed a favorable stance toward sexual rights, and inscribing religious arguments in favor of rights for same-sex couples."[9]

More importantly, perhaps, the Catholic Church's dark rhetoric gave gay marriage activists an opening to frame their arguments in direct opposition to the Church. According to FALGBT Vice-President Esteban Paulón, "There was a semantic battle, and we clearly won it. The opposite front spoke of perversion, pedophilia, and disease. We spoke of family, life, and love. We ended up with all the nice words. We gave visibility to the stories that we knew were going to create a greater impact."[10] Gay marriage activists and their allies also employed moral claims when rejecting a proposal from conservatives that the issue of gay marriage be left to the voters to decide, as had become the norm across the United States. Responding to this proposal, President Fernández de Kirchner, who had previously criticized Cardinal Bergoglio for using language "reminiscent of the times of the Inquisition," said that "it was unbecoming for a democratic society to put the rights of a vulnerable minority to the whims of the majority." She also noted that civil unions "would stigmatize the gay population as second-class citizens."[11]

---

[7] See, especially, Inés M. Pousadela, "From Embarrassing Subjects to Subjects of Rights: The Argentine LGBT Movement and Equal Marriage and Gender Identity Laws," *Development in Practice* 23, nos. 5–6 (August 2013): 701–720.

[8] Caselli, "Campaign Lines," 42.

[9] Juan Marco Vaggione, "Sexual Rights and Religion: Same-Sex Marriage and Lawmakers' Catholic Identity in Argentina," *University of Miami Law Review* 65, no. 3 (Spring 2011): 953.

[10] Caselli, "Campaign Lines," 42–43.

[11] Encarnación, *Out in the Periphery*, 145.

174 Framing Equality

Framing gay marriage as a moral matter also helped turn gay marriage into a nonpartisan issue, a remarkable accomplishment considering the polarization typical of Argentine politics. Just before the final vote in the Argentine Senate, the major political blocs released their members from voting along partisan-ideological lines; instead, they were allowed to vote according to their conscience. The resulting vote was notable for the number of conservative senators willing to support gay marriage. While casting their vote, many senators remarked that the new law was intended to advance human rights, democracy, and citizenship in Argentina. Senator Norma Morandini of the Civic Front, a coalition of progressive parties, noted: "What defines us is our humanity, and what runs against humanity is intolerance."[12]

As in Spain, the moral framing provided a platform for expanding LGBTQ equality in Argentina. In 2011, the country introduced a gender identity law "hailed internationally as cutting-edge for its underlying model of self-determination. Individuals are allowed to decide about their own body and legal documentation, without either the approval of a judge or a medical diagnosis such as 'gender identity disorder' or 'gender incongruence.'"[13] In 2021, in another breakthrough, Argentina mandated that 1 percent of all public sector jobs be reserved for the transgender community. That policy "mirrors other reparations policies which already exist in Argentina for the victims, and families of victims, of state terrorism during the country's last military dictatorship (1976–1983)."[14] In 2021 Argentina became one the first countries in the world to recognize the designation of "nonbinary" as a third gender in official papers.

Ireland legalized gay marriage in 2015 via a popular referendum, with 62 percent of the vote favoring gay marriage.[15] This was the first national gay marriage referendum in the world. The conventional explanation for why Ireland had to convene a popular vote on gay marriage is that the country needed to change the Irish Constitution and its definition of marriage before gay

---

[12] "Argentina Legalizes Same-Sex Marriages," NPR, July 15, 2010. Available at https://www.npr.org/templates/story/story.php.

[13] Francisco Fernández Romero, "Beyond Identity: Redistributive Transgender Rights in Argentina," *Revista: Harvard Review of Latin America*, November 22, 2023. Available at https://revista.drclas.harvard.edu/beyond-identity-redistributive-transgender-rights-in-argentina.

[14] Ibid.

[15] On Ireland's gay marriage campaign, see, especially, Sonja Tiernan, *The History of Marriage Equality in Ireland: A Social Revolution Begins* (Manchester University Press, 2020); Grainne Healy, Brian Sheehan, and Noel Whelan, eds., *Ireland Says Yes: The Inside Story of How the Vote for Marriage Equality Was Won* (Merrion Press, 2016); and Johan A. Elkink, David M. Farrell, and Jane Suiter, "Understanding the 2015 Marriage Referendum in Ireland: Context, Campaign, and Conservative Ireland," *Irish Political Studies* 32, no. 3 (July 2016): 1–21; and Susan Parker, *The Path to Marriage Equality in Ireland: A Case Study* (The Atlantic Philanthropies, November 2017). Available at https://www.atlanticphilanthropies.org/wp-content/uploads/2018/01/The-Path-to-Marriage-Equality-Ireland.pdf.

marriage could become legal. But, as some have noted, the Irish Constitution "does not make reference to marriage as being between a man and a woman, most likely because in 1937 there was only a traditional view of marriage as that between heterosexual couples." Instead, the decision to hold the vote was made out of an abundance of caution: "In case a marriage equality law was struck down by the Supreme Court and had to go to a referendum anyway."[16]

The Irish introduced a very different way of framing a moral gay marriage campaign. As in Spain and Argentina, the campaign in Ireland privileged universal themes such as citizenship, dignity, and the common good over legal arguments about minority rights, constitutional provisions, and benefits. According to the very comprehensive history of the Yes Campaign published by the *Irish Times*, the campaign stressed the capacity of gay marriage to "enable gay and lesbian people to gain full citizenship" and "the concepts that marriage is a secure foundation for relationships and a social good, and that gay people are entitled to the same foundation for a life together as everybody else."[17] But what truly set the Irish gay marriage campaign apart from other campaigns, including those campaigns infused with moral themes, was the intense focus on extending family values to gay and lesbian couples and their children.

A key message of the Yes Campaign organized by the Gay and Lesbian Equality Network, Marriage Equality, and the Irish Council for Civil Liberties was that Irish society had a moral responsibility to recognize and protect same-sex couples and especially their children. This rhetoric about the protection of children became a central feature of the massive public relations effort that accompanied the Yes Campaign. Remarking on a short video that went viral, the *New York Times* wrote, "Proponents of same-sex marriage in Ireland have promoted the cause as pro-family, and the video attests to how full acceptance of gay marriage can support an entire family. In a sense, it promoted one traditional Catholic value, the importance of family, against a longstanding Catholic prohibition against homosexuality."[18]

The family values messaging of the Yes Campaign stood in striking contrast to the dark and dispiriting messaging of the Irish bishops. In doing so, the messaging of the Yes Campaign pointedly neutralized the messaging of the opposition. The bishops' messaging stressed that "legalizing same-sex

---

[16] Elkink, Farrell, and Suiter, "Understanding the 2015 Marriage Referendum in Ireland," 364.

[17] Grainne Healy, Brian Sheehan, and Noel Whelan, "How the Yes Was Won," *The Irish Times*, November 6, 2015. Available at https://www.irishtimes.com/life-and-style/people/how-the-yes-was-won-the-inside-story-of-the-marriage-referendum-1.2418302.

[18] Hanna Ingber, "For One Irish Couple, Backing Gay Marriage Is a Matter of Family Values," *The New York Times*, May 22, 2015. Available at https://www.nytimes.com/2015/05/23/world/europe/for-one-irish-couple-backing-gay-marriage-is-a-matter-of-family-values.html.

176   Framing Equality

marriage would undermine unions between a man and a woman" and that "marriage has an inherently reproductive purpose."[19] But some bishops went beyond that boilerplate criticism of gay marriage. Most famously, Bishop of Elphin Kevin Doran stated in an interview that "gay parents of children are not necessarily parents," a statement so outlandish and incendiary that he was forced to issue an apology.[20] The emphasis on families and their children by both sides of the gay marriage war made for a very vivid contrast for the average Irish voter. On one side was the gay community, whose families were claiming victimization by discriminatory marriage laws. On the other side was the Catholic Church, with its privileged position within Irish society and well-publicized scandals of priests sexually abusing children, often with the protection of Church leaders. This was a contrast that the Yes Campaign eagerly welcomed.

Moral arguments helped turn the gay marriage referendum into a national debate about the kind of country that the Irish people wanted. Before the vote, Ireland convened a constitutional convention, or an ICC (Irish Constitutional Convention), to vote on whether or not to put the issue of gay marriage to the voters. The ICC was the product of We the Citizens, a government initiative whose principal mission was to put ordinary citizens at the heart of the policy-making process. Comprised of sixty-six citizens selected randomly from the electorate, thirty-three politicians, and one expert serving as chair, for a total of one hundred members, the ICC that authorized the gay marriage referendum was tasked with deliberating on eight specific issues of concern to the nation. By the time deliberations had ended, ICC members had heard from advocacy groups, opponents to gay marriage, grown-up children of same-sex couples, and even a gay man opposed to gay marriage. As reported in the *Washington Post*, marriage equality "generated huge mainstream and social media interest, far more so than for any of the other topics discussed by the ICC."[21]

Taking a page from the Spanish playbook, Irish gay activists leveraged Ireland's dark history of homosexual oppression to give the Yes Campaign a historical grounding in the country's gay rights struggles. That history included criminalizing homosexuality until 1993, the last country in Western Europe to do so, and prosecuting some one thousand gay and bisexual

---

[19] Ibid.

[20] Patsy McGarry, "Bishop of Elphin Expresses Regret over Comments about Gay Parents," *The Irish Times*, March 16, 2015. Available at https://www.irishtimes.com/news/social-affairs/religion-and-beliefs/bishop-of-elphin-expresses-regret-over-comments-about-gay-parents-1.2140902.

[21] David M. Farrell, Clodagh Harris, and Jane Suiter, "The Irish Vote for Gay Marriage Started at a Constitutional Convention," *The Washington Post*, June 5, 2015. Available at https://www.washingtonpost.com/news/monkey-cage/wp/2015/06/05/the-irish-vote-for-marriage-equality-started-at-a-constitutional-convention/.

men in the twentieth century alone.[22] In their testimony to the ICC, Irish gay activists linked marriage equality to a desire among the Irish for a more progressive national identity, one that valued equality and inclusion and that stood at odds with the image of Ireland as a traditional Catholic society. But the most critical testimony heard by the ICC came from the children of gay and lesbian couples, who testified to how they had been personally harmed by the lack of legality of the relationships of their parents.

As reported by Susan Parker in a working paper for The Atlantic Philanthropies, given the limited time allocated to gay marriage activists, "the decision was made to prioritize the testimony of children of gay parents."[23] They chose Clare O'Connell and Conor Prendergast, who "spoke articulately about the real impact on their lives when their parents did not have the right to legally marry." Conor, who at the time was engaged to a woman, noted that his parents, who had been together for thirty-two years, deserved the same recognition of their relationship as he would have. Parker quoted someone who attended the hearing, saying, "People in the Convention needed to see what it is like to be a child in a lesbian or gay household. . . . This is why gay marriage really matters. It was very important to bring the human dimension to the table."

As in Spain and Argentina, the most effective messengers of the morality of gay marriage in Ireland were heterosexual politicians. A prominent figure in the Yes Campaign was Mary Robinson, Ireland's first female president and, in many regards, the nation's moral conscience on issues related to homosexuality. When Robinson announced her support of gay marriage, it was hard to miss the unique role she played in the Irish struggle for equality for gays and lesbians. She became president only a few years after she won the case at the European Court of Human Rights that forced the decriminalization of homosexuality in Ireland, and it was she who, as president, signed the law that decriminalized homosexuality in 1993.[24] Also vital to the Yes Campaign was Mary McAleese, another former Irish president and a devout Catholic. When she announced her support for the marriage equality amendment, "she did so not only as an activist barrister who for forty years had striven to dismantle 'the architecture of homophobia,' but as a parent of twins—one gay and one straight—who would have vastly different legal protections."[25]

---

[22] Jade Wilson, "Criminal Records for Homosexuality to Be Overturned Under New Government Plans," *The Irish Times*, November 19, 2022. Available at https://www.irishtimes.com/crime-law/2022/11/19/gay-men-may-be-pardoned-for-criminal-proceedings-brought-against-them-before-homosexuality-decriminalised-in-ireland/.

[23] Parker, *The Path to Marriage Equality in Ireland: A Case Study*.

[24] Margaret Spillane, "How the Irish Became the World's Leading Gay Activists," *The Nation*, June 15, 2015. Available at https://www.thenation.com/article/archive/how-irish-became-worlds-leading-gay-activists/.

[25] Ibid.

In 2018, as a coda to the gay marriage campaign, the government apologized to some two thousand gay men convicted under Ireland's antigay laws. Minister of Justice Charlie Flanagan acknowledged "the hurt and the harm caused to those who were deterred from being open and honest about their identity with their families and in society."[26] It's hard to envision this act of contrition without the moral framing of the gay marriage campaign.

Tracing the Roots of Different Framing Approaches

The variety of framing approaches adopted by gay marriage activists reveals the agency they brought to their struggles. This agency, however, did not develop in a vacuum. It was shaped by multiple factors found in the domestic environment. This contention underscores the point that for all of the talk about the globalized and transnational nature of the marriage equality movement, the primary influences shaping gay marriage campaigns have been homegrown. Certainly, these factors did not predetermine the framing of the gay marriage campaign. But they created the environment that informed the decision-making process of gay marriage activists. Among the domestic factors influencing the gay marriage campaign, the most apparent is the political environment. It encouraged some framing possibilities while foreclosing others.

The Political Environment

In the United States, the legal framing of the gay marriage campaign cannot be divorced from the Christian right's success in blocking access for gay rights activists to the US Congress and state legislatures across the country. As noted by Jeff Trammell, a former member of the board of directors of the Human Rights Campaign (HRC) and a former advisor on gay issues to former presidential candidate John Kerry, making a legal case out of gay marriage was a way for gay marriage activists to "leapfrog over the political obstacles facing the gay marriage movement put in the way by religious conservatives."[27] Less apparent, but equally important, was the fraught relationship between gay rights activists and the Democratic Party.

For a host of reasons, a political alliance between gay rights organizations and a governing left-wing party of the like that developed in Spain and Brazil never materialized in the United States. For many years, there was

---

[26] Sarah Bardon, "Government to Apologize to Gay Men for Discriminatory Laws," *The Irish Times*, June 19, 2019.
[27] Author's online interview with Mr. Trammell (May 31, 2022).

a hesitancy on the part of gay rights activists to work through the political system to advance their goals. This hesitance was a legacy of the gay liberation movement. Traditionally, American gay rights organizations have placed a premium on political autonomy. They have also relied on mobilization strategies to advance their goals. But just as important, if not more, was the reluctance of Democratic Party leaders to embrace gay marriage. It was not until 2012 that the Democratic platform officially backed the cause. That same year, President Obama, while running for reelection, greenlighted gay marriage. This was not, however, the ringing endorsement that other gay marriage campaigns enjoyed, the kind of endorsement that could make people rethink their assumptions about gay people.

Like most American liberal politicians, Obama was extraordinarily cautious about when and how he spoke about gay marriage. He waited to signal his approval of gay marriage until public opinion was moving decisively in favor of it. And when he talked about gay marriage, he did so modestly as an individual rather than as a leader. When he announced his support for gay marriage, on May 9, 2012, he did so in very personal terms: "For me, personally, it is important for me to go ahead and affirm that—I think same-sex couples should be able to get married."[28] The contrast with his counterpart in Spain, Prime Minister Zapatero, of the Spanish Socialist Workers Party, is striking. Zapatero's forceful defense of gay marriage set the template for how to frame gay marriage around moral themes. During his 2004 inaugural address, Zapatero decried the injustice inflicted upon gay and lesbian couples by their inability to access the institution of marriage. While in office, Zapatero pressed the point that ending the exclusion of gay and lesbian couples from existing marriage laws would boost the dignity of gay people and redeem Spain for its past treatment of the homosexual community.

Indeed, for much of its history, the American gay rights movement has been politically orphaned. Attempts to incorporate gay activists into the Democratic Party date back to the formation of the Stonewall Democrats in San Francisco in the early 1970s.[29] Among the breakthroughs of that period was making Jimmy Carter the first major presidential candidate to oppose discrimination against homosexuals. In 1977, Carter also became the first president to welcome gay activists into the White House. A few years later, in 1980, the Democratic Party became the first major political party in American

---

[28] Katy Steinmetz, "Obama's 20 Year Evolution on LGBT Rights," *Time*, April 10, 2015. Available at https://time.com/3816952/obama-gay-lesbian-transgender-lgbt-rights/.

[29] For a broader view of the relationship between gay activists and the Democratic Party, see John D'Emilio, *The World Turned: Essays in Gay History, Politics and Culture* (Durham, NC: Duke University Press, 2002).

180 Framing Equality

history to embrace gay rights in its platform. This embrace gave rise to hopes among some gay activists of the Democratic Party serving as a vehicle for carrying the gay community to "a paradise of social and economic justice," something that, as noted by historian John D'Emilio, in retrospect, seems "ridiculous."[30] The Defense of Marriage Act, or DOMA, the first salvo in the Christian right's war on gay marriage, was signed into law by a Democratic president, Bill Clinton, in 1996.

According to Trammell, who was active with the Stonewall Democrats, "The Democratic Party was very cautious on the issue of homosexuality, and gay marriage most notably, unsure that the public could be persuaded to embrace the issue." Trammell recalls how the party tore itself apart in the mid-1990s over "Don't Ask, Don't Tell" (DADT), with gay activists and party leaders at each other's throats.[31] Others accused the Democratic Party of co-opting and demobilizing gay activists. In 2009, Andrew Sullivan argued that the HRC was suffering from "battered wife syndrome" for its inability to criticize the Democratic Party for its lack of support for gay marriage.[32] "What HRC has now done is give away any leverage or bargaining power the gay community has with the Obama administration. They are doing what they did with the Clintons: essentially apologize for being a burden and prostrate ourselves to the Democratic Party in the hope that they will be kind to us in the very, very long run."

In Spain, the moral messaging of the gay marriage campaign was entirely in sync with the political agenda of the governing party. Zapatero made gay marriage a centerpiece of "Citizen Socialism," an ambitious policy inspired by the work of the political ethicist Philip Pettit, who served as Zapatero's advisor.[33] Citizen Socialism employed the institutions of the state and the policy-making process to end all forms of discrimination, repression, and domination in Spanish society. Aside from gay marriage, it incorporated expanded access to abortion and divorce, a pathway to citizenship for undocumented immigrants, a stricter divide between church and state, and gender parity at home and in the workplace (a point underscored by Zapatero's cabinet, which was 50 percent female), and near pacifism in foreign policy. This ethical project provided an auspicious policy space for gay marriage to become part of a broader debate about expanding equality and freedom in Spanish society. This debate lent itself well to the argument that advancing

[30] Ibid., 243.

[31] Author's online interview with Mr. Trammell (May 31, 2022).

[32] Andrew Sullivan, "The Battered Wife Syndrome of the Human Rights Campaign," *The Atlantic*, October 10, 2009.

[33] See José Luis Martí and Philip Pettit, *A Political Philosophy in Public Life: Civic Republicanism in Zapatero's Spain* (Princeton: Princeton University Press, 2010).

gay marriage was a moral obligation intended to deepen citizenship rather than a legal matter limited to expanding marriage rights.

The political framing of the Brazilian campaign, especially the pragmatic rhetorical strategy of deferring making demands for gay marriage until after same-sex civil unions were legal nationwide, owes a lot to the close relationship between gay activists and the Workers' Party, or PT. During the 1980s, the Brazilian gay rights movement was incorporated into the PT at a time when most left-wing parties in Western Europe and the Americas were still actively shunning gay activists and their rights agenda. This incorporation was something of a mixed blessing. On the one hand, it afforded gay activists access to the political arena, including a prominent role in drafting a new democratic constitution between 1985 and 1988. Gay activists were also able to begin to push for gay rights through the political system, making Brazil one of the first countries in the world to attempt to legislate gay rights at the federal level. On the other hand, the incorporation of gay activists into the PT also worked to moderate gay rights demands, including putting the brake on demanding gay marriage to conform to the PT's political priorities, which at various junctures included appeasing the evangelical community. Tellingly, gay activists in Brazil did not begin to openly campaign for gay marriage until 2011, the same year that the Federal Supreme Court legalized same-sex civil unions.

Gay Rights Movements and Path Dependence

When thinking about why social movements embrace any particular framing strategy, it is hard to ignore "path dependence," or the idea that "history matters" and that "the past influences the future" in how political actors behave and institutions evolve.[34] In the United States, virtually all contemporary social movements seeking equality have leaned toward a legal framing hoping to re-create the path of the African American civil rights movement and its success in employing constitutional arguments to fight discrimination. As seen already, for organizations such as Freedom to Marry, the US Constitution's Fourteenth Amendment and its call for equality under the law provided the primary justification for the legalization of same-sex marriage.

The trend of gay rights activists copying the civil rights struggle of African Americans goes back to the Homophiles, the cluster of gay rights organizations that emerged after World War II.[35] According to gay rights historian

---

[34] James Mahoney, "Path Dependence in Historical Sociology," *Theory and Society* 29 (2000): 507–548.
[35] See Megan Gambino, "Remembering Gay Rights Activist Frank Kameny (1925–2011)," *Smithsonian Magazine*, October 14, 2011. Available at https://www.smithsonianmag.com/smithsonian-institution/remembering-gay-rights-activist-frank-kameny-1925-2011-105187020/.

182   Framing Equality

Eric Cervini, "Every single element of what we know as Pride and gay rights, especially the pre-Stonewall homophile movement, was borrowed from the Black Freedom Movement."[36] The Homophiles were especially keen to copy litigation strategies. In 1961, Homophile leader Frank Kameny tried unsuccessfully to get the courts to reverse his firing from the US Army Map Survey, arguing that discrimination based on sexual orientation was a violation of the US Constitution. This suit was the first discrimination claim made to the US Supreme Court based on sexual orientation.

Some gay rights organizations formed after the Stonewall uprising in 1969 were also directly inspired by the African American civil rights movement. Created in 1973 to provide pro bono legal aid to the gay community, the Lambda Legal Defense Fund was fashioned after the legal branch of the National Association for the Advancement of Colored People (NAACP). In particular, organizations such as Lambda were inspired by prominent civil rights victories, especially *Brown v. Board of Education*, the 1954 US Supreme Court decision that formally ended state-sanctioned racial segregation in America's public schools.

Curiously, the *Brown* decision also unleashed a massive political backlash. Southern whites rushed to join "Citizens' Councils—organizations pledged to maintain white supremacy by all means short of violence—as southern blacks began filing desegregation petitions with local school boards. These whites reasoned that 'we must make certain that these Negros are not allowed to force their demands on us.'"[37] Gay marriage activists were likely aware of this dark legacy but reckoned that the benefits outweighed the risks. According to Trammell, many in the gay community recalled the *Brown* backlash, noting that in his home state of Florida, the backlash against *Brown* morphed into a gay witch-hunt. Trammell was recalling the Florida Legislative Investigative Committee, better known as the Johns Committee (named after former Florida Governor Charlie Johns). Initially convened to sniff out Communists between the years of 1957 and 1963, the Johns Committee eventually turned its attention to the faculty, staff, and students of Florida's state universities who were homosexual or suspected of being homosexual. Trammell added, "We probably did not think much about the backlash, but were also of the view that you cannot let that deter you."[38]

---

[36] Jo Yurcaba, "Different Fight, Same Goal: How the Black Freedom Movement Inspired Early Gay Activists," NBC News, February 28, 2021. Available at https://www.nbcnews.com/feature/nbc-out/different-fight-same-goal-how-black-freedom-movement-inspired-early-n1259072.

[37] Michael J. Klarman, *From the Closet to the Altar: Courts, Backlash, and the Struggle for Same-Sex Marriage* (New York: Oxford University Press, 2013), 174.

[38] Author's online interview with Mr. Trammell (May 31, 2022).

In Spain and Brazil, gay rights leaders have consciously fashioned their activism after the human rights movement, which explains a lot about the moral themes of the gay marriage campaign in both countries. After the transition to democracy, Spanish and Latin American gay liberation fronts reinvented themselves as human rights organizations. Indeed, in the new democratic regimes inaugurated in Spain, in 1978, and Brazil, in 1988, the gay rights movement became an extension of the human rights community. Some gay rights groups explicitly identified themselves as human rights organizations first and foremost. This human rights reinvention reflected a host of factors, starting with the vibrancy of the human rights movement during the years of the democratic transition. At this pivotal juncture in the reemergence of civil society in Spain and Brazil, no other social movement enjoyed more prestige and sustained domestic or international attention than the human rights movement.

Human rights organizations have continued to influence gay rights activism in Spain and Brazil well past the years of democratic transition. This influence has afforded Spanish and Brazilian gay rights activists with an ample human rights vocabulary and a host of historical justice processes that are mostly absent from gay rights activism in the United States. In Brazil, during the early 1990s, human rights organizations and gay rights activists entered into an extraordinary partnership to fight the HIV/AIDS pandemic. With the support of the human rights community, the gay rights movement successfully employed the argument that access to universal healthcare is a fundamental human right to secure funding to treat all victims of the pandemic. Human rights organizations and gay rights activists came together again in 2011, under the Rousseff administration, with the creation of a truth commission to chronicle the political sins of the military dictatorship, including the oppression of LGBTQ people. Formally known as The National Truth Commission, this body was the first of its kind in the world to document the human rights abuses perpetrated by an authoritarian regime against the LGBTQ community.[39]

In Spain, the gay marriage campaign was broadly influenced by the Association for the Recovery of the Historical Memory. Founded in 2000, this human rights group successfully pressed for a national reckoning with the human rights abuses of the Spanish Civil War and the Franco dictatorship, including the horrid treatment of homosexuals under the old regime. Its most notable achievement was the 2007 Law of Historical Memory. Among other

---

[39] See, Nina Schneider, ed., *The Brazilian Truth Commission: Local, National and Global Perspectives* (Brooklyn, NY: Berghahn Press, 2019).

184 Framing Equality

things, this law declared Francoist institutions illegitimate and offered "moral rehabilitation" for those prosecuted under Franco's homophobic laws. As fate would have it, this reckoning with the past overlapped with the gay marriage campaign.[40] In doing so, the reckoning provided a rare opportunity for gay activists to highlight the victimization of the homosexual community by Franco and to construct a narrative about how gay marriage would act as redemption for past transgressions against homosexuals and other sexual minorities. It also exposed the wide range of societal collaborators with the old regime, especially the Catholic Church, the face of the opposition to gay marriage.

The Ideational Context

As might be expected, ideas have also played a key role in fashioning gay marriage framing approaches. Despite the passage of time and significant upheaval in the contemporary gay rights movement born in the 1970s, such as the trauma of the HIV/AIDS pandemic, the ideas that powered the movement in individual countries have proved to be remarkably resilient—resilient enough to have influenced the gay marriage campaign decades later. This point underscores much of what the "ideational scholarship" tells us about the role of ideas in shaping institutions, organizations, political actors, and public policy. This scholarship stresses that ideas matter to politics and do not exist in a vacuum. Instead, the emergence and impact of ideas hinge on what came before them, including the cumulative effect of previous ideas.

This scholarship also explains changes in the ideational environment, especially why some ideas become rooted in some environments and not others and how ideas evolve.[41] Shedding light on some of these points, Sheri Berman wrote, "Theories that use ideas, norms, or culture to explain political outcomes necessarily entail what the entertainment world calls a backstory: previous events that gave rise to the ideas and then placed them in a position to influence politics. Political scientists must be able to explain the backstory,

[40] See Omar G. Encarnación, *Democracy without Justice in Spain: The Politics of Forgetting* (Philadelphia: University of Pennsylvania Press, 2014).

[41] See, especially, Sheri Berman, "Ideas, Norms, and Culture in Comparative Political Analysis," *Comparative Politics* 33, no. 2 (January 2001): 231–250; Robert C. Liberman, "Ideas, Institutions, and Political Order," *American Political Science Review* 96, no. 4 (December 2002): 697–712; and Marij Swinkels, "How Ideas Matter in Public Policy: A Review of Concepts, Mechanisms, and Methods," *International Review of Public Policy* 2, no. 3 (2020): 281–316.

Comparative Discussion and Takeaways **185**

when some innumerable ideas in circulation achieve prominence in the political realm at particular moments and others do not. Since no true intellectual vacuum ever exists, what is really at issue here is ideational change, how individuals, groups, or societies exchange old ideas for new ones."[42]

A glance at the ideas that have influenced the formation of gay rights activism in Spain, Brazil, and the United States reveals a lot about how the gay marriage campaign came to be framed across these cases. As seen already, gay rights organizations have a long and very significant history of engagement with human rights in Spain and Latin America. In the post-transition era, Spanish and Latin American gay rights organizations reinvented themselves as human rights organizations. In particular, gay activists embraced the views that the free exercise of sexuality is a fundamental human right and that human rights principles supersede domestic laws. An interesting backstory behind this reinvention concerns how earlier ideas and concepts in Spanish and Latin American gay rights organizations, especially gay liberation and revolutionary Marxism, receded into the background and gradually faded away, opening the way for the embrace of human rights.

Before the democratic transition, gay liberation fronts in both Spain and Brazil saw themselves as revolutionary movements invested just as much in changing societal perceptions of homosexuality as in overturning the existing social and economic order. But, as was the case of some left-wing revolutionary leaders, during the transition to democracy, many gay rights activists engaged in a process of political introspection about their past. This process, which entailed abandoning some ideas and embracing new ones, mirrors what Nancy Bermeo has termed "political learning," or the process through which political actors adjust and alter their political behavior in light of past political experience.[43] Following the democratic transition, many gay rights leaders turned their backs on their revolutionary activities and embraced a new political identity more conducive to building democracy. This was especially the case of Latin American gay rights activists who spent the period of authoritarian rule in exile in the 1980s. They returned home from abroad to revive gay rights activism, fully aware that to grow acceptance of homosexuality they needed to moderate their political positions.

By contrast, there's not much of a human rights tradition in the United States to counterbalance the legacy of gay liberation, which remained a key ideological marker for leading American gay rights organizations well into the

[42] Berman, "Ideas, Norms and Culture in Comparative Political Analysis," 233.
[43] Nancy Bermeo, "Democracy and the Lessons of Dictatorship," *Comparative Politics* 24, no. 3 (April 1992): 273–291.

186 Framing Equality

start of the gay marriage campaign. For the most part, human rights rhetoric has been absent from the politics of American social movements, including the gay rights movement. Addressing this point, Holly Pruett of Freedom to Marry noted this in an interview for this book: "Sadly, while the United States positions itself as a defender of human rights in certain parts of the globe, we have never had a strong internal understanding of or commitment to human rights domestically (and certainly contributed to heinous human rights violations in some countries)."[44]

Much of the behavior outlined by Pruett is reflected in the tortured history of human rights in American politics. Although the American delegation to the United Nations was the principal architect of the 1948 Universal Declaration of Human Rights, human rights do not resonate much in American politics and society.[45] In no small way a consequence of the conservative postwar attack on the human rights movement, many Americans regard human rights as something foreign and, more specifically, as a "Soviet-led subversion of American democracy."[46] Over the years, the demonization of human rights by the American right has made it very difficult for social movements to avail themselves of the rhetoric of human rights to advance their causes, including the struggle for civil rights by African Americans. Addressing this point, historian Carol Anderson noted that attacks on human rights as a foreign corruption of American ideals "systematically eliminated human rights as a viable option for the mainstream African American leadership." Consequently, the fight for Black equality was limited "to the narrowly confined traditional arena of political rights."[47]

The persistence of gay liberation ideology in the United States all but precluded framing gay marriage as a moral imperative while actively encouraging a legal framing, which was acceptable to most gay rights activists. At the heart of the liberationist wing of the gay rights movement was an intense hostility toward marriage that complicated making the pursuit of gay marriage a policy priority for the gay community. It also complicated envisioning gay marriage as anything other than a civil right. "Marriage is a contract which smothers both people, denies needs, and places impossible demands on both people. . . . Gay people must stop gauging their self-respect by how well they mimic straight marriages. . . . To accept that their happiness comes through finding a groovy spouse and settling down, showing the world that we're

---

[44] Author's e-mail communication with Ms. Pruett (June 22, 2022).

[45] On this point, see Samuel Moyn, *The Last Utopia: Human Rights in History* (Cambridge: Harvard University Press, 2010).

[46] Carol Anderson, *Eyes off the Prize: The United Nations and the African-American Struggle for Human Rights, 1944–1955* (New York: Cambridge University Press, 2003), 1–7.

[47] Ibid.

Comparative Discussion and Takeaways **187**

just the same as you is avoiding the real issues, and is an expression of self-hatred."[48] These words are taken from a 1970 manifesto from Carl Wittman, an activist with the Gay Liberation Front.

Gay liberation ideology also explains why some American gay activists continued to promote alternatives to gay marriage, such as domestic partnerships, even as the legalization of gay marriage seemed imminent. In 2011, Columbia University Law Professor Katherine Franke argued in the *New York Times*, "While many in our community have worked hard to secure the right of same-sex couples to marry, others of us have been working equally hard to develop alternatives to marriage." She added, "For us, domestic partnerships and civil unions are not a consolation prize made available to lesbian and gay couples because we are barred from legally marrying. Rather, they have offered us an opportunity to order our lives in ways that have given us greater freedom than can be found in the one-size-fits-all rules of marriage."[49]

While the ideological legacy of the gay liberation movement may have precluded a moral framing of the American gay marriage campaign, this legacy did not get in the way of the campaign embracing a robust legal framing. As noted previously, the American gay community had no problem rallying around the idea of gay marriage as a fundamental human right, especially after conservatives began to enact legal roadblocks against gay marriage by passing gay marriage bans. Even those activists who felt that marriage was a rotten institution believed that gays should have the right to access it. Like other aspects of gay rights activism in the United States, embracing the idea of gay rights as civil rights was a key legacy of the African American civil rights movement.

Speaking to NPR on the fiftieth anniversary of the March on Washington, historian George Chauncey explained how the struggle for civil rights by African Americans during the 1960s and beyond influenced the gay rights movement:[50]

"The movement certainly had a profound impact on the lesbian and gay rights movement. Back in the '60s, at the time when the march happened, gays were regarded as mentally ill or people addicted to immoral behavior. And the civil rights

---

[48] Mary Bernstein and Verta Taylor, "Marital Discord: Understanding the Contested Place of Marriage in the Lesbian and Gay Movement," in *The Marrying Kind?: Debating Same-Sex Marriage within the Lesbian and Gay Movement*, eds. Mary Bernstein and Verta Taylor (Minneapolis: University of Minnesota Press, 2013), Introduction.

[49] Katherine M. Franke, "Same-Sex Marriage Is a Mixed Blessing," *The New York Times*, June 23, 2011. Available at https://www.nytimes.com/2011/06/24/opinion/24franke.html.

[50] "How the Civil Rights Movement Launched the Fight for LGBT, Women's Equality," PBS Newshour, September 2, 2013. Available at https://www.pbs.org/newshour/show/civil-rights-launched-the-fight-for-lgbt-women-s-equality#transcript.

188   Framing Equality

movement really pioneered the concept as a powerful political concept of minority rights and made it easier for gays to begin to depict themselves as a minority who deserved the same civil rights that other Americans and other minorities did."

The Opposition's Playbook

Lastly, when thinking about influences in the framing of gay marriage, we need to consider the activism of the opposition to gay marriage. This point echoes the contention by social movement theorists that the framing strategies of any social movement are often a counterreaction and/or a response to the framing strategies of the opposition.[51] Reflecting on this point in light of the experience of the American gay rights movement, Tina Fetner wrote, "The religious right has changed the rhetoric that lesbian and gay activists use to express their claims. It has also influenced the choice of tactics by the lesbian and gay movement, and even the size and shape of organizations within the movement."[52]

Fetner's analysis takes as its point of departure the virulent reaction by the Christian right to the wave of gay rights activism that followed the 1969 Stonewall uprising. She wrote, "From this point on, lesbian and gay activists would never do their work in an antagonistic dialogue with the religious right. Never again would activists be able to focus exclusively on how state legislators would respond to their petitions or how various corporations would include gay-friendly policies in their human resources statements." She concluded, "They (gay rights activists) would also have to consider what impact a counterprotest to their actions might have on their goals. This new worry changed the very nature of lesbian and gay activism."[53]

It is hard not to see how the legalistic framing of the American gay marriage campaign is, in many ways, a direct response to the decades-old playbook by the Christian right to defeat the gay rights movement. For starters, the rights and benefits messaging responded directly to the argument by the Christian right that gays and lesbians wanted "special rights" by pointing out that all the

---

[51] See, especially, David S. Meyer and Suzanne Staggenborg, "Counter Movement Dynamics in Federal Systems: A Comparison of Abortion Politics in Canada and the United States," *Research in Political Sociology* 8 (1998); David S. Meyer and Suzanne Staggenborg, "Movements, Counter Movements and the Structure of Political Opportunity," *American Journal of Sociology* 101 (1996): 1628–1660; and Mayer N. Zald and Bert Useem, "Movement and Counter Movement Interaction: Mobilization, Tactics, and State Involvement," in *Social Movements in an Organized Society*, eds. Mayer N. Zald and John D. McCarthy (New Brunswick, NJ: Transaction, 1987).

[52] Tina Fetner, *How the Religious Right Shaped Lesbian and Gay Activism* (Minneapolis: University of Minnesota Press, 2008), xv.

[53] Ibid., xiv.

Comparative Discussion and Takeaways **189**

marriage equality movement wanted was access to the same rights available to straight couples, nothing less and nothing more. The "special rights" claim, it's worth noting, has a long history in the opposition to gay rights in the United States. Its roots are often traced to Amendment 2, a 1992 ballot initiative approved by Colorado voters that invalidated antigay discrimination ordinances in Aspen, Denver, and Boulder. Before going into effect, it was blocked by the Colorado Supreme Court, and eventually, it was struck down by the US Supreme Court in 1996 with its ruling *Romer v. Evans.*

The campaign for Amendment 2 was framed as an attack on affirmative action and special rights. As noted by a detailed review of the campaign, Amendment 2 emphasized the issue of special rights and the protection of private versus public types of discrimination. The review also added that: "The anti-affirmative action of the 1980s and 1990s stemmed from a general frustration among American workers with what had come to be seen as an increase in government-sanctioned special rights and quota preferences for certain minority groups. . . . By playing on this growing disinclination toward affirmative action and other 'special rights' programs, the proponents of Amendment 2 were able to successfully promote the amendment as a fair and reasonable law and increase the amendment's likelihood of passage."[54]

Further evidence of the impact of the opposition to gay rights on the framing of the gay marriage campaign can be seen in how American gay activists purposely steered clear of claims that gay marriage would entail the transformation of American society by, among other things, expanding notions of citizenship. Such claims were seen as playing directly into the playbook of the Christian right of depicting homosexuals as radicals out to transform society. The weaponization of gay marriage was an early strategy of conservative organizations to fight the gay rights movement that emerged during the 1970s. Groups such as the Moral Majority, which famously waged a "War on Homosexuality," depicted homosexuals as godless pedophiles out to transform the American family. In their telling, gay marriage would be responsible for the coming of genderless children, for discouraging heterosexuals from getting married by diminishing the prestige of marriage, and, by extension, for increasing the number of out-of-wedlock births and abortions.

In subsequent decades, so-called family values organizations, such as the Family Research Council and Concerned Women for America, waged a sustained campaign to demonize and dehumanize gay people. They were guided by the belief that dehumanizing and demonizing gay people would

---

[54] Sharon E. Debbage Alexander, "Romer v. Evans and the Amendment 2 Controversy: The Rhetoric and Reality of Sexual Orientation Discrimination in America," *Texas Journal on Civil Liberties and Civil Rights* 6, no. 1 (December 1, 2001): 281.

190   Framing Equality

make it easier for American society to accept denying gay people their civil rights.[55] Instead of offering religious condemnation, family values organizations focused on spreading "scientific truths" about the supposed dangers that homosexuality posed to homosexuals and society at large. This new framing about the consequences of homosexuality was key to what legal scholar Martha Nussbaum has called "the politics of disgust." These politics depicted the sexual practices of lesbians and especially gay men as "vile and revolting" in an effort by gay rights opponents to argue that such practices worked to "contaminate and defile society, producing decay and degeneration."[56] Nussbaum cited the 1992 documentary *The Gay Agenda* as a prominent example of the politics of disgust. It purports to expose a "hidden agenda" by the homosexual community to recruit and corrupt children and, more broadly, to destroy the moral fabric of America.

Understandably, American gay marriage activists went out of their way to emphasize that gay marriage would not change American society in any meaningful way—other than to grant rights and benefits to the gay community that were already available to heterosexual couples. That sentiment was conveyed in the popular view among American gay marriage activists, especially Freedom to Marry, that gays and lesbians were not out to transform society; they just wanted to join the institution of marriage.[57]

Even the visual representation of gay people in advertising materials was influenced by the Christian right's attempt to depict homosexuals as radical and deviant. As seen already, public relations efforts against gay marriage bans, such as California's Proposition 8, were "de-gayed" for fear that presenting gays and their families openly and candidly might offend the general public's sensibilities. And when gay representation was incorporated into these efforts, it was limited to the least controversial images. As reported by one essay about the "negative representation" of homosexuals in the American media, to counter negative depictions of homosexuals gay activists purposely promoted homosexuals as "typical middle-Americans, working middle-class jobs, raising kids, living the American dream."[58] Such depictions were further assisted by a tendency in the media, especially television, to

---

[55] See, especially, Didi Herman, *The Antigay Agenda: Orthodox Vision and the Christian Right* (Chicago: University of Chicago Press, 1998); Steven P. Brown, *Trumping Religion: The New Christian Right, the Free Speech Clause, and the Courts* (Tuscaloosa and London: University of Alabama Press, 2002); and Michael Cobb, *God Hates Fags: The Rhetorics of Religious Violence* (New York: New York University Press, 2006).

[56] Martha Nussbaum, *From Disgust to Humanity: Sexual Orientation and Constitutional Law* (New York: Oxford University Press, 2010), xiv.

[57] Author's interview with Evan Wolfson, President of Freedom to Marry (New York City, May 17, 2022).

[58] Noah Berlatsky, "What the Gay Community Lost While It Was Winning Gay Marriage," *The Atlantic*, November 15, 2013. Available at https://www.theatlantic.com/national/archive/2013/11/what-the-gay-community-lost-while-it-was-winning-gay-marriage/281525/.

Comparative Discussion and Takeaways **191**

show gay couples "who looked and acted as much like traditional heterosexual couples as possible."[59] An unintended consequence of this effort against negative representation was to repress and potentially marginalize gay people who did not conform to the image of the ordinary American.

Finally, the Christian right's success in putting morality at the center of its attack on gay marriage left little room for gay activists to bring morality into discussions of homosexual unions. Addressing this point, legal scholar Carlos Ball wrote that during the 1980s, with the rise of the Moral Majority, "conservative activists successfully gained political traction by arguing that governmental policies in matters such as gay rights and abortion no longer reflected the moral views of a majority of Americans. By the 1990s, conservatives had so successfully set the moral terms of the policy debates over LGBTQ rights that morality and values became closely associated with opposition to those rights." Ball added that "in response to this political reality, LGBT rights supporters generally eschewed consideration of morality in framing their arguments and instead relied on seemingly more neutral values such as equality and liberty."[60] As seen already, gay activists did not challenge the Christian right's claim that homosexual relationships were immoral and a threat to society, leaving this claim to linger in the public's consciousness.

There is nothing remotely similar in Spain and Brazil (and arguably in any other mature democracy) to the sustained campaign in the United States by the Christian right to politicize gay marriage and to demonize and dehumanize homosexuals that unfolded right before the gay marriage campaign. But in their way, the opposition to gay marriage also shaped the activism of gay marriage advocates in Spain and Brazil. The Spanish Catholic Church's framing of gay marriage as "family-phobic" provided an opening for gay marriage activists to seize the higher moral ground when making the case for gay marriage. In the eyes of Spanish gay activists, the Church's complicity with the human rights abuses of the Franco regime, which included separating children from their mothers for ideological reasons, disqualified the Church from making a credible case that gay marriage posed a threat to the family.

A different dynamic played out in Brazil, suggesting that the connection between Catholicism and gay marriage in Catholic nations is not monolithic. As seen previously, in contrast to Spain, the Catholic Church boldly criticized the military dictatorship because of its human rights abuses. In the democratic era, the Brazilian Catholic Church partnered with the gay

---

[59] Ibid. This comment draws upon Leigh Moscowitz, *The Battle over Marriage: Gay Rights Activism through the Media* (University of Illinois Press, 2013).

[60] Carlos A. Ball, "The Proper Role of Morality in State Policies on Sexual Orientation and Intimate Relationships," *New York University Review of Law & Social Change* 34 (2010): 87.

192 Framing Equality

community in the battle against HIV/AIDS and antigay violence. Very cleverly, in embracing the language of human rights, Brazilian gay activists were capitalizing on the Church's history of upholding human rights. These activists were also banking on this history serving to discourage Catholic officials from joining the evangelical churches in orchestrating a backlash against the gay community. A significant lesson in all of this is that gay marriage found a hospitable environment in some Catholic countries, not despite Catholicism but because of it.

Gay Marriage Takeaways

The most important lesson we can take from this study is something that generally should go without saying but that in this case bears repeating: the critical importance of comparative political analysis. This type of analysis is often thought to entail sacrificing national peculiarities to tell a larger story that can lead to generalizable propositions. In her much-cited review of the scholarship on "historical institutionalism in comparative politics," Kathleen Thelen wrote that while the "comparative method" often leads to "the loss of a comprehensive history of each country," the payoff is "a set of general propositions."[61] But even if this tradeoff is unavoidable, the payoff is not limited to generalizable propositions. It can also include fresh insights about the politics of any country that can only come into view when the country is placed in a comparative perspective. This appears to be the case with gay marriage wars.

For starters, it is only with the benefit of a comparative perspective that the richness of gay marriage politics around the globe can be fully appreciated. Because of the dearth of comparative research on gay marriage politics, it is commonplace to think of the marriage equality campaign as a struggle for the right of gay and lesbian couples to marry. Although accurate, this impression also misses a lot. Across our cases, the marriage equality campaign diverged significantly. While in the United States gay activists fought for the expansion of marriage, their counterparts in Spain fought for the transformation of citizenship. In Brazil, activists focused on affirming universal human rights principles. These differences entailed emphasizing rights and benefits in the United States versus dignity and respect in Spain and Brazil. Moreover, a comparative perspective allows the most beneficial angle for successfully challenging prevailing notions about the gay marriage politics of any country.

---

[61] Kathleen Thelen, "Historical Institutionalism in Comparative Politics," *American Review of Political Science* 2 (1999): 372.

The conventional wisdom about the gay marriage backlash in the United States emphasizes the organizational capacity of the Christian right to orchestrate a massive moral panic around the issue of gay marriage. No one can question the veracity of this wisdom. But when placed in a comparative perspective, a more complex picture of the religious opposition to gay marriage emerges. The United States is not the only country where the gay marriage movement had to confront powerful religious institutions with deep connections to the political system. In Spain, gay marriage activists had to contend with the Spanish Episcopal Conference, one of the most powerful Catholic establishments in all of Christendom, to say nothing of the Vatican's global effort to defeat gay marriage, which began in Spain.

In Brazil, an influential evangelical movement that takes its inspiration directly from the United States is the main threat to gay rights, including gay marriage. As seen already, some of the same groups active in the American culture wars over homosexuality, abortion, and guns have, in recent years, set up shop in Brazil, sensing that the Brazil of today is a more receptive environment for their activism than the United States. Such expectations are encouraged by the fact that polls show Brazilians to be vastly more religious than Americans and, hence, more receptive to homophobic messages.[62] Unsurprisingly, the Christian right's playbook to defeat the marriage equality movement in the United States is broadly reflected in Brazil. Yet, as seen in this study, Brazil's gay marriage backlash pales in comparison to that of the United States.

The foregoing highlights the need for a more comparative approach to studying gay rights politics in the United States. A dearth of comparative analysis hinders our understanding of how different things might have been for the American gay marriage campaign. It also leads to misconceptions and even distortions about the campaign. A case in point is the claim by Sasha Issenberg, the author of a history of the American marriage equality movement, that "the battle for gay marriage was easily won."[63] Many (maybe most) American gay rights activists and scholars would strongly disagree with that statement. But, in any case, Issenberg seems unaware of how much more difficult the gay marriage struggle was in the United States relative to peer democracies. By the time the United States legalized gay marriage nationwide in 2015, the country had fallen behind some twenty other democracies in

---

[62] "Global Attitudes and Trends: Religiosity," Pew Research Center, September 17, 2008. Available at https://www.pewresearch.org/global/2008/09/17/chapter-2-religiosity/.

[63] Sasha Issenberg, "Why the Battle for Gay Marriage was Easily Won," *The Washington Post*, June 4, 2021. Available at https://www.washingtonpost.com/outlook/why-the-battle-for-gay-marriage-was-won-so-easily/2021/06/03/b63d3d62-c47e-11eb-93f5-ee9558eecf4b_story.html.

194 Framing Equality

allowing same-sex couples to marry. And no other democracy saw fit to enact a law as odious as DOMA. This gratuitous law banned something—gay marriage—that at the time when it was passed (in 1996) did not exist anywhere in the United States and, indeed, the entire world.

This book also reveals more precise takeaways about the politics of gay marriage that might be useful in guiding future scholarship about gay marriage politics and gay rights politics in general. The first one speaks directly to what makes for a successful gay marriage campaign. While success hinges on well-organized activists, a point that underscores the traditional emphasis that scholars have placed on organizational resources to the viability of any social movement, an effective messaging strategy is just as important, if not more. It is telling that of the three gay marriage campaigns examined in this study, the one with the smallest and least organizationally resourceful gay rights movement—Spain's—was the most successful at keeping backlash at bay and expanding LGBTQ equality. It was also the first one to achieve the goal of legalizing gay marriage. By contrast, the campaign that struggled the most and that faced the fiercest political backlash—that of the United States—had the backing of the world's largest and most resourceful gay rights movement. It also took the longest to legalize gay marriage.

But what Spanish gay marriage activists lacked in organizational resources, they more than made up in messaging skills. They understood that to win hearts and minds, they needed to do more than inform the public about the discrimination affecting gay and lesbian couples. They needed to inspire the public and make it care about the lives and travails of gay and lesbian couples, a task accomplished by linking gay marriage to moral concepts such as dignity, citizenship, and historical justice. By contrast, gay marriage activists in the United States were less skilled at messaging. Indeed, for the most part, the messaging skills of American gay activists left a lot to be desired. For years, they stuck to a message—rights and benefits—that was failing at increasing public support for gay marriage. Moreover, they rarely challenged entrenched biases against gay people or affirmed the morality of same-sex relationships.

The second takeaway concerns the emerging understanding of backlash politics and, specifically, what shapes the outcomes of any backlash against gay marriage. These outcomes are not determined entirely by the "backlashers." The target of any backlash also has a say in the matter. Because so much of our thinking about backlash politics is biased toward the actions of those orchestrating the backlash, it is easy to overlook the skills and capacities of the target of the backlash to fight back. While gay marriage activists are not in complete control of the fate of their struggle, they do have considerable discretion over how they speak about their desire for gay marriage. It is within their capacity to craft messages that bring the public to their side and provide a compelling counter-narrative to the messages from the opposition.

Like no other marriage equality movement examined in this book, the Spanish movement was aware of the power of rhetoric to advance social change. It is telling that from the moment Spanish gay marriage activists made gay marriage their top priority, they intuitively knew that a rights-based discourse would not be enough to bring the general public to their side and to undermine the attacks coming from the opposition. They were cognizant of the need to humanize same-sex couples and to make gay marriage mean more than rights and benefits. Gay activists in the United States eventually arrived at this same realization. But they did so many years into the gay marriage campaign and after conducting extensive polling to see how the American public would respond to different messaging strategies.

A third and final takeaway deals with gay marriage wars and their eventual resolution. How the war is won is just as important as winning itself. Whether it is won on legal, moral, or political arguments matters to the severity of the backlash. It also bears on the continuing struggle for LGBTQ equality. Winning with moral arguments does the most to minimize backlash and advance equality. Perhaps this should not be that surprising since moral arguments about gay marriage aim to humanize same-sex couples while calling out the opposition on its prejudices and misconceptions. A moral win, however, is also the hardest one to achieve. To be sure, there is no one-size-fits-all approach for framing a gay marriage campaign around moral arguments. In Spain, the campaign emphasized redressing historical injustices against the gay community and expanding citizenship for LGBTQ people. In Ireland, it stressed extending traditional Irish family values to gay and lesbian couples. In Argentina, it affirmed universal human rights principles.

But a common denominator in the framing of all of these campaigns was asking the public to do more than acquiesce to changing the laws that for centuries kept the institution of marriage the exclusive province of heterosexual people. It also emphasized transforming the culture by demanding that gay and lesbian couples be accorded dignity and respect.

Index

Against Equality, 98

Agrupación Homosexual para la Igualdad Sexual, 53

AIDS Coalition to Unleash Power (ACT-UP), 96

AIDS moral panic, 37

Alito, Samuel, 125

Alter, Karen, 43

American Civil Liberties Union (ACLU), 123

Anderson, Carol, 186

Argentina
Catholic Church, 29, 173
Civic Front, 174
comparisons to Spain and Ireland, 29, 90, 170
congressional debate on gay marriage law, 171
"Dirty War," 30, 172
FALGBT, 171–172
gay liberation politics, 134
gay marriage campaign, 170–174
history of gay rights movement, 134
influence on Brazil's gay marriage campaign, 147, 151
Las Madres de la Plaza de Mayo, 172
military prosecutions, 172
moral framing of gay marriage, 170–174
non-binary rights, 174
repression of homosexuals, 172
Spanish gay marriage campaign, 171
transgender community, 171

Arthur, John, 90

Asociación Pro Derechos Humanos de España (APDHE), 61

Associação Brasileira de Gays, Lésbicas, Bissexuais, Travestis e Transexuais (ABGLT), 137

Association for the Recovery of the Historical Memory (ARMH), 68

Attey, Phil, 28

Australia, 26

Aznar, José María, 66, 71

Backlash
against Baehr decision, 25
against Brown decision, 182
backlash politics, 43
Christian right, 193
comparative politics of backlash, 43–44
definition, 43
gay marriage, 44
gay rights, 44
outcomes, 43–44

Baehr v. Lewin, 25, 99, 101

Baker, Jack, 102

Ball, Carlos A., 108–109

Ball, Molly, 111

Balz, Dan, 116

Belgium, 4, 22, 62

Berenice Dias, Maria, 148

Bergoglio, Jorge, 173 (see Pope Francis)

Berman, Sheri, 184

Bermeo, Nancy, 185

Bernardes, Gustavo, 130, 140, 149

Beyond Marriage, 98

Biden, Joe, 89

Bimbi, Bruno, 147, 151, 153, 167

Birch, Elizabeth, 95, 100

Bloomberg, Michael, 113

Bolsonaro, Jair, 129, 131, 158–159, 167

Bostock v. Clayton County, Georgia, 124

Brazilian Catholic Church
AIDS activism, 165
comparisons to Spanish Catholic Church, 132
criticism of inequality in Brazil, 163
criticism of military dictatorship, 163
defense of LGBTQ rights, 192
Liberation Theology, 164
receptivity to human rights, 16, 151, 163–164
support for same-sex civil unions, 167
Vatican, 164
war on marriage, 132

Brazilian Civil Code, 147

Brazilian Constitution (1988), 23, 146–147, 150, 152, 154, 162
Brazilian National AIDS Program (PNDA), 136
Brazilian National Conference of Bishops (see Brazilian Catholic Church)
Brazilian National Truth Commission, 149
Brown v. Board of Education, 91, 182
Bryant, Anita, 35–36, 115 (see also Save Our Children)
Buckley, William F. Jr., 37
Bush, George W., 34, 95, 117

Calvo, Kerman, 59–62
Canada, 87
Carabanchel prison (Madrid), 69
Carrera, Joan, 84
Carter, Jimmy, 179–180
Castresana, Carlos, 85
Center for Sociological Investigations (CIS), 63, 80
Chauncey, George, 40, 112, 187
Chile, 3, 26, 160
Christian right
  animosity towards homosexuals, 127
  backlash politics, 115
  Christian victimization, 123
  depictions of homosexuals, 189, 191
  fight against gay marriage, 125, 193
  framing of gay marriage, 92, 189, 193
  gay marriage moral panic, 34
  opposition to gay rights, 15
  politicization of religion, 39, 191
  shaping gay marriage framing, 188
  Stonewall Uprising, 188
  Republican Party, 124
  weaponization of gay marriage, 39, 189
Citizen socialism, 70–71, 180
citizenship, 51, 66, 46
Civic Republicanism, 71
Clinton, Bill, 180
Cohen, Stanley, 32
Colaço, Rita, 138
Colectivo de Gais de Madrid (COGAM), 60–61, 64
Colombia, 3, 9, 23, 163
Constitutional Tribunal (Spain), 11, 50, 63, 79

Coordinadora Gay y Lesbiana de Cataluña (CGL), 60
culture war, 1, 5

Daughters of Bilitis, 93
Davidson Hunter, James, 1, 39
Davis, Kim, 123
Defense of Marriage Act (DOMA)
  and American exceptionalism, 34
  as backlash, 15
  Bill Clinton, 33
  Christian right, 180
  contents, 10–11
  foreign comparisons, 11, 34, 193
  legacy, 33
  repeal, 124
  Respect for Marriage Act, 124
D'Emilio, John, 90, 180
Democratic backsliding, 10
Democratic Party, 37, 178–180
Dobbs v. Jackson Women's Health Organization, 124
Dodge, David, 106
domestic partnerships, 13, 98, 111, 187
Don't Ask, Don't Tell (DADT), 180

Ebrard, Marcelo, 31
Eisenhower's Executive Order 10450 (1953), 102
El Mundo, 59, 77, 152
El País, 49, 58, 67, 69, 74
Empire State Pride Agenda, 106
Equal Rights Amendment (ERA), 40
Eskridge, William, Jr., 24, 96
Ettelbrick, Paula, 97
European Court of Human Rights, 177

Faderman, Lilian, 122
Falwell, Jerry, 36, 39
Family Research Council (FRC), 34–35, 120, 189
Federación Argentina LGBT (FALGBT), 147, 171–172
Federación Española LGBT (FELGBT), 63–64, 69, 73, 85, 171
Federal Marriage Amendment (FMA), 117–118
Federal Supreme Court (Brazil), 11, 130, 131, 146–150, 181
Feldblum, Chai R., 45–46, 108, 116

198　Index

Fernández de Kirchner, Cristina, 170
Fernández, Miquel A., 67
Florida, 35, 103, 182
de Fluvià, Armand 53
Foley, Daniel, 100
Folha de S. Paulo, 135
Framing
　counter-framing, 42, 44, 48
　definition, 5–7
　gay marriage, 7–9
　resonance, 6, 42, 52
　resource mobilization, 41
France, 3, 4, 11, 26, 38, 50, 53, 61
Francis, Charles, 109
Franco, Francisco, 13, 51, 53, 55–56, 68, 191
Frank, Gillian, 40
Franke, Katherine, 187
Freedom to Marry
　founding, 103
　informational approach, 103
　legal framing of gay marriage, 103
　love and commitment, 113
　media campaigns, 127
　rights and benefits, 103, 114, 126
　US Constitution, 181
Frente de Liberación Homosexual (FLH), 134

Gallagher, Maggie, 109, 120
García Lorca, Federico, 54
Gay and Lesbian Equality Network
　(Ireland), 175
"gay" civil war (United States), 112
Gay liberation, 53, 93, 105, 134, 179, 187
Gay Liberation Front (GLF), 53, 93, 187
Gay Liberation Front of Catalonia, 53
Gay marriage referenda
　affront to democracy, 173
　Argentina, 173
　as an expression of popular will, 119
　George W. Bush's re-election, 117
　Ireland, 174–175
　United States, 104, 118
　U.S. 2004 elections, 116
gay reparations, 87
gay violence (Brazil), 136, 139, 145, 150, 152
Generelo, Jesús, 65, 67, 72, 80, 83, 74
Germany, 3, 11, 50, 87
Gimeno, Beatriz, 64
González, Felipe, 62

Goodridge v. Department of Public Health,
　117, 25
Great Britain, 11, 38, 87
Green, James, 134, 137, 150
Grupo Gay da Bahia, 133, 138, 150

Herdt, Gilbert, 33, 34
HIV/AIDS
　Bolsonaro, 156
　Brazil, 132, 136, 165, 183
　Brazilian Catholic Church, 165
　Christian right, 35–36
　gay marriage activism, 96
　Influence on marriage attitudes among
　　gays, 96, 97
　legal demands for marriage, 96
　moral panic, 37
　National AIDS Program (Brazil), 165, 183
　Spain, 61–62, 77
　United States, 95, 96, 101, 104, 119
　World Bank, 136
Homo-affection, 148
Homophiles, 182
Huard, Geoffroy, 53
Huckabee, Mike, 2
Human Rights Campaign (HRC), 94, 95,
　100, 101, 125, 127, 178, 180

Inglehart, Ronald, 39
Inquisition, 13, 173
International Lesbian and Gay Association
　(ILGA), 137
Iotti, Paulo, 147, 152, 154
Ireland
　apology to the gay community, 178
　Catholic Church, 176
　comparisons to Spain and Argentina, 175
　decriminalization of homosexuality, 177
　family values, 175
　gay marriage referendum, 174–175
　Irish Constitutional Convention, 176
　moral argument in gay marriage
　　campaign, 175
　oppression of homosexuality, 176
　Yes campaign, 175
Irish Constitutional Convention (ICC), 176
Irish Council for Civil Liberties, 175

Jeffress, Robert, 2
Johns Committee, 182

Index

Kahramanoglu, Kürsad, 85
Kaiser, Charles, 94
Kameny, Frank, 102, 182
Kennedy, Anthony, 114
Kerry, John, 178
King Juan Carlos, 58
King, Martin Luther, Jr., 3
Klarman, Michael J., 24, 25, 100, 116
Kramer, Larry, 96

La Movida, 82
Lambda Legal, 94, 97, 101, 182
LaRouche, Lyndon, 37
La Vanguardia, 57, 62
Law of Historical Memory (Spain), 68
Law of Social Menaces and Rehabilitation
   (1970), 57, 60
Law of Stable Couples (Catalonia), 62
Law of Vagabonds and Thugs (1954), 13, 56
Lawrence v. Texas, 103
Liberation Theology
   Brazilian Catholic Church, 132
   connection to LGBTQ rights, 164
   definition, 163
   historical roots, 163
   legacy in Brazil and Latin America, 163
   Medellin Conference, 163
   theology of the body, 164
Log Cabin Republicans, 117
Lundrigan, Paul, 31

MacRae, Edward, 133
Malafaia, Silas, 142
March for Jesus, 144
March on Washington for Lesbian and Gay
   Rights (1987), 187
Marxism, 4, 60, 136, 185
Mascarenhas, João Antonio, 135
Mattachine Society, 93
Mattachine Society of Washington, DC, 102,
   109
McAleese, Mary, 177
McConnell, Michael, 102
Medellin Conference (see Liberation
   Theology)
Mello, Amy, 104, 106, 110, 162
Mexico, 3, 9, 27, 31, 168
Mexico City, 31, 86, 146
Miret, Enrique, 84
modernization theory, 12

Moral Majority, 36, 141, 189, 191
Moral panic
   American history, 34
   American exceptionalism, 34
   Christian right, 34
   DOMA, 33
   definition, 32, 33
   HIV/AIDS, 37
   role of the media, 37
   social conservatives, 37
Mott, Luiz, 133, 135, 138
Movimento Homossexual Brasileiro (MHB),
   134
*Movimiento Español de Liberación
   Homosexual* (MELH), 53

National Association for the Advancement
   of Colored People (NAACP), 182
National Campaign to Protect Marriage, 34
National Catholicism, 13, 154, 78, 83
National Council of Justice (Brazil), 130,
   153, 154
National Organization for Marriage (NOM)
   critique of marriage equality, 109
   demise, 120
   framing of opposition to gay marriage, 122
   Gathering Storm (advertisement), 121
   gay marriage messaging, 113
   history, 121
   organization, 121
   strategies and tactics, 120–121
   support for, 121
National Public Radio (NPR), 187
Netherlands, 2, 4, 13, 22, 49, 63, 86

Obama, Barack, 2, 110, 113, 115, 123, 179,
   180
Obergefell v. Hodges, 10, 90–91, 109, 114,
   123–125
O'Connell, Clare, 177
ONE magazine, 93
Opus Dei, 77
Out/Look magazine, 97

Pact of Forgetting (Spain), 30, 68
Paulón, Esteban, 173
People's Party (Spain), 70
Petit, Jordi, 59
Pettit, Philip, 71, 180
political learning, 185

200 Index

Pope Benedict, 2, 79
Pope Francis, 28, 165, 173
post-materialism, 12, 19
Prendergast, Conor, 177
Proposition 8
  budget, 110
  impact on gay marriage messaging, 110
  legacy, 122
  opposition to, 190
  origins, 110
  purpose, 110, 115
  response by gay activists, 122
  tactics, 121
Pruett, Holly, 104, 186
Puerto Rico, 30

Queers for Economic Justice, 98

Rauch, Jonathan, 99, 105
Rayside, David, 12
Reis, Toni, 137, 146
Religion Freedom Restoration Acts
  (RFRAS), 123
Republican Party (Brazil), 144
Republican Party (United States), 39, 124,
  144
resource mobilization, 41
Respect for Marriage Act (2022), 124
Robinson, Mary, 177
Rosenberg, Gerald N., 24
Rousseff, Dilma, 130, 139, 140, 145, 149, 155,
  183
Ruiz, Antoni, 69

same-sex civil unions
  alternative to gay marriage, 2, 187
  and "stable unions" in Brazil, 16
  comparisons to gay marriage in Spain, 47,
    64, 107
  second class citizenship, 174
  support from Pope Francis, 28
Sammon, Patrick, 117
Sánchez, Pedro, 88
Save Our Children (see also Anita Bryant)
  Anita Bryant, 35
  children's protection, 35
  history, 35
  impact, 36
  legacy, 36, 115
  moral panic, 115

Proposition 8
Schacter, Jane, 24
Schlafly, Phyllis, 40
Schwartz, Jorge, 158
Sheldon, Louis P., 143
Silva, Emilo, 68
da Silva, Luiz Inácio "Lula", 139, 140,
  142–143, 145
Silvério Trevisan, João, 138, 140
Somos, 133, 134
South Africa, 11
South Korea, 38
Spanish Catholic Church (see also Spanish
  Episcopal Conference)
  campaign against gay marriage, 15
  complicity with the Franco regime, 15, 51,
    55, 191
  framing of gay marriage, 15
  mobilization against gay marriage, 77
  opposition to gay marriage, 75–77
  oppression of homosexuals, 55
  relations with the Vatican, 55
Spanish Civil Code, 72, 73, 74
Spanish Civil War, 15, 53, 79, 183
Spanish Constitution (1978), 50, 57, 63, 84
Spanish Episcopal Conference, 40, 52, 73,
  76, 193
Spanish Holocaust, 30, 55
Spanish Workers' Socialist Party (PSOE), 62,
  64, 70, 71, 73
Stoddard, Tom, 97
Stonewall Riots, 101, 182
Sullivan, Andrew, 96, 180
Supreme Court of California, 110

Thelen, Kathleen, 192
Thomas, Clarence, 125
Trammell, Jeff, 117, 178, 180, 182, 183
Transgender rights, 127, 131, 159, 163, 174
Triângulo Rosa, 135
Trump, Donald, J., 36, 125
Tufvesson, Carlos, 140

United States v. Windsor, 34
Universal Church of the Kingdom of God
  (Brazil), 144
Universal Declaration of Human Rights
  (1948), 47, 162
Uruguay, 3, 130

Index

U.S. Civil Rights Movement, 3, 92, 102, 107, 182, 187
US Constitution, 91, 101, 102, 117, 124, 181
US Supreme Court, 91, 109, 112, 125, 182

Valiente, Celia, 64
Vatican, 40, 50, 55, 78
Venezuela, 67
Vox, 87

Wittman, Carl, 187

Wolfson, Evan, 86, 101–103, 108, 113, 126, 127, 190
Workers' Party (PT), 132, 134–135, 138–139
World Meeting of Families, 78
Wyllys, Jean, 150–152

Yes Campaign (Ireland), 175, 177

Zapatero, José Luis Rodríguez, 50–51, 70–75, 77, 79, 84, 179, 180
Zerolo, Pedro, 67, 69, 70, 86, 151
Zürn, Michael, 43